Also by Michael Adams

Sex in the Snow
The Surprising Revolution in Canadian Social Values

Better Happy Than Rich?
Canadians, Money and the Meaning of Life

American Backlash
The Untold Story of Social Change in the United States

Unlikely Utopia
The Surprising Triumph of Canadian Pluralism

Fire and Ice
The United States, Canada and the Myth of Converging Values

Stayin' *Alive*

Stayin' Alive

HOW CANADIAN BABY BOOMERS WILL
WORK, PLAY, AND FIND MEANING
IN THE SECOND HALF OF THEIR ADULT LIVES

MICHAEL ADAMS
WITH AMY LANGSTAFF

VIKING
CANADA

VIKING CANADA

Published by the Penguin Group

Penguin Group (Canada), 90 Eglinton Avenue East, Suite 700, Toronto, Ontario, Canada M4P 2Y3 (a division of Pearson Canada Inc.)

Penguin Group (USA) Inc., 375 Hudson Street, New York, New York 10014, U.S.A.
Penguin Books Ltd, 80 Strand, London WC2R 0RL, England
Penguin Ireland, 25 St Stephen's Green, Dublin 2, Ireland (a division of Penguin Books Ltd)
Penguin Group (Australia), 250 Camberwell Road, Camberwell, Victoria 3124, Australia
(a division of Pearson Australia Group Pty Ltd)
Penguin Books India Pvt Ltd, 11 Community Centre, Panchsheel Park, New Delhi – 110 017, India
Penguin Group (NZ), 67 Apollo Drive, Rosedale, North Shore 0745, Auckland, New Zealand
(a division of Pearson New Zealand Ltd)
Penguin Books (South Africa) (Pty) Ltd, 24 Sturdee Avenue, Rosebank,
Johannesburg 2196, South Africa

Penguin Books Ltd, Registered Offices: 80 Strand, London WC2R 0RL, England

First published 2010

1 2 3 4 5 6 7 8 9 10 (RRD)

Copyright © Michael Adams, 2010

Manufactured in the U.S.A.

LIBRARY AND ARCHIVES CANADA CATALOGUING IN PUBLICATION

Adams, Michael, 1946 Sept. 29-
Stayin' alive : how Canadian baby boomers will work, play, and find meaning in the second half
of their adult lives / Michael Adams.

Includes index.
ISBN 978-0-670-06369-7

1. Baby boom generation—Canada. I. Title. II. Title: Staying alive.

HQ1059.4.A43 2010   305.244   C2010-905412-1

Visit the Penguin Group (Canada) website at **www.penguin.ca**

Special and corporate bulk purchase rates available; please see
www.penguin.ca/corporatesales or call 1-800-810-3104, ext. 2477 or 2474

For my parents and my kids

Contents

Introduction

"*The Seven Ages of Man*"

All the world's a stage,
And all the men and women merely players:
They have their exits and their entrances....

... At first the infant,
Mewling and puking in the nurse's arms....

... Last scene of all,
That ends this strange eventful history,
Is second childishness and mere oblivion,
Sans teeth, sans eyes, sans taste, sans everything.

—Shakespeare, *As You Like It*

I was born on September 29, 1946, one of Canada's first postwar babies. Unbeknownst to me or my parents, I instantly became a member (some would say an early warning sign) of what would eventually be called the Baby Boom generation. The term "baby boom" had been used prior to this era in reference to surges in fertility. But the animal known as the Baby Boomer—with its extensive cultural baggage, including sexual liberation, idealism, marijuana, feminism, narcissism, the Beatles, environmentalism, and so on—has existed for only about five decades.

If this first paragraph has struck fear into your heart, take comfort: I promise you this book is not my autobiography. But I do identify—with a mixture of pride and self-deprecation—as a Baby Boomer, and I believe that in many ways my experience has been typical of my cohort. Most of this book is dedicated to the discussion of Baby Boomer values and attitudes as expressed in Environics' survey research over the past two decades. But where personal anecdotes illustrate more general points I will offer them; would the reader expect anything else from a member of this notoriously self-absorbed generation?

My parents were married in July 1945, just after my dad returned from five years of service in the Royal Canadian Navy in the Atlantic theatre. After Germany surrendered in May, my dad had volunteered to fight in the Pacific. But with the Japanese surrender, he was free to remain home in Walkerton, Ontario. Dad observed that had the war in Europe not ended when it did, he wouldn't have returned to Walkerton in the spring of 1945, and he might not have met my mother (who was dating his air force brother at the time; Walkerton was and is a small town)—or if he had met her, it might not have been in time to win her heart and make her his wife instead of his sister-in-law.

As for the trajectory that put my mom in my dad's path, she was a newly minted registered nurse, just back in Walkerton after three years' training at Toronto's St. Michael's Hospital. A devout Catholic, my mother told her doctor (and he told God) that I would be born on September 29 because that was the feast of St. Michael the Archangel. Today, Canadians tend to trust Caesarean sections to ensure their babies are born without incident and under the right stars; one in five hospital births in 2002 occurred by Caesarean, compared to one in twenty in 1968. In Walkerton in the mid-1940s, the preferred technology for promoting a healthy birth was prayer—and I arrived through the traditional channels, right on time.[1]

Over 340,000 of us were born in Canada in 1946 as other couples joined my mom and dad in postwar wedded bliss. I and my Boomer brother, Doug, were among millions of others born throughout the late 1940s and 1950s and into the early 1960s. The boom died out during the mid-60s with a sharp decline in the birth rate beginning in 1964. Researchers use various cut-offs to mark the end of the Baby Boom; we at Environics use 1965—a somewhat arbitrary choice, but you have to stop somewhere (as even the hyper-fertile generation that produced us finally admitted).

This book is a portrait of the over 8.8 million people born in Canada during those years, and those who immigrated as children during the same period.[2] It argues that we were and are different from our parents' generation—and that these differences will persist until we die. (Indeed, Boomer values will assert themselves even from beyond the grave, as the death-related rituals discussed in Chapter Eight attest.)

Why study Boomers? It's a fair question. A great deal of ink has already been spilled in analyzing, celebrating, criticizing, and teasing the Baby Boomers. Much of the writing about this generation has been nostalgic, recalling our youth in dreamy, sometimes self-mythologizing tones—the music we loved, the suburban tract homes that soothed or stifled us, our activism, our convictions, our innovations, and our rebellions, both public and private.

For all the trees that have given their lives to the analysis of Baby Boomers, however, two vital aspects of this generation remain surprisingly little discussed. The first is its diversity. To hear some commentators describe these 9.1 million Canadians—not to mention their even more numerous American counterparts—one might think they had all shaken hands (or perhaps shared a hug or more in the mud at Woodstock) over some official generational values consensus. Our social values data show again and again that no such consensus exists: sharp variations occur across the Boomer generation on a huge range of questions, from social norms, religion, and gender roles to money, consumption, and global issues.

When we look at Baby Boomer social values from 35,000 feet, four distinct segments (or social values "tribes") are evident; all are Boomers, but each group has its own way of belonging to this generation. This diversity makes a lot of sense, given that this is a cohort whose members have enjoyed unprecedented freedom to express themselves and live out their values. Notably, the largest of the four values tribes—the Disengaged Darwinists, who make up 48 percent of the cohort—is the one that least resembles the Boomer stereotype of the aging hippie. Although Boomers did usher in a tidal wave of socio-cultural change— and aging hippies are not altogether irrelevant to that process— those who want to understand how Boomers think and how they will continue to shape Canadian society would be well advised to park their stereotypes and pay attention to what Boomers themselves have told us about their values over the past two decades.

A second major gap in many discussions of Baby Boomers is the influence they still exert—culturally, professionally, socially, and politically—and will continue to exert for many years to come. Often when people talk about the changes Boomers have wrought in Canada, they focus on the past: the 1960s and 70s, the Trudeau years, feminism, the maturation of Canada as a recovering colony, and the emergence of the Québécois as a confident national minority. When pundits talk about emerging trends, they sometimes assume the Boomers have had their day, and they look instead to young people for signs about the future. (At present, this long-standing tendency to see youth as the main drivers of social change is even stronger because young people tend to be experts in the new communications technologies whose implications we're all groping to figure out.)

But Baby Boomers remain the most populous generation in this country, and they're still making waves: their late life is going to be at least as revolutionary as their youth was—maybe even more so. After all, everyone expects young people to push the boundaries of their society, challenge conventions, defy norms. But Boomers may be the first generation whose health, energy, resources, and self-image will enable them to be rebellious change-makers even in old age. To the extent that anyone talks about the changes the cohort will bring about in the future, the focus tends to be on the strain this stampede of old folks will place on our pension and health care systems. These are valid questions, but they're purely demographic; Baby Boomers' psychographics—their values—are every bit as interesting and significant as their sheer numbers. Indeed, for those who want to understand where this country is headed—for marketers, human resources professionals, policymakers, NGOs, and curious citizens—Boomer psychographics are required reading.

People's values, what we think is good and bad, and what we

therefore aspire to for ourselves and for our society, crystallize early in life and are largely fixed by the time we're teenagers. The context in which Boomers grew up—the milieu in which our values took shape—was very different from the one that shaped our parents' values.

The world in which Baby Boomers' parents (we call them "the Elders") came of age was defined by economic hardship, traditional religious belief and practice, patriarchal family values, and communitarian sensibilities that were both comforting and at times stultifying. And, of course, Elders' values were heavily influenced by war: the traumatic cultural memory of World War I, which their parents would have impressed upon them, and then the harrowing war against fascism, which they experienced directly. When the Elders were young, *Snow White and the Seven Dwarfs* and *The Wizard of Oz* were middle-American cinematic milestones. They grew up at a time when relatively benign quips from Mae West (who uttered such famous chestnuts as "Why don't you come up and see me some time" and "When I'm good I'm very good, but when I'm bad I'm better") were considered scandalous. In Canada, divorces were extremely difficult to obtain, and the social and religious pressures against the dissolution of marriages were such that until World War II, Canada had one of the lowest divorce rates in the Western world. Homosexuality was not only unspeakable but punishable by up to fourteen years in prison. Canada remained profoundly deferential to Great Britain: a royal visit to this country by George VI in 1939 was greeted with shuddering excitement, the monarch's first steps off the ship covered breathlessly on CBC Radio ("His foot is *on Canadian soil!*") and described as "the culmination of weeks of planning and hoping and waiting."

Boomers, by contrast, grew up in a time of postwar prosperity, technological progress, a much more visual culture, post-colonial movements, and a peace we called the Cold War: a battle between Soviet communism and Western democracy, led by the United States—with Canada, the younger sibling, standing proudly at Uncle Sam's side.

Canadian Boomers had a famously easy go of it early in life: their lives revolved around television, consumption, rock 'n' roll, and fun. Early Boomers north of the border were even spared the major trauma that beset our American cousins: Vietnam. (We might have been troubled by the images we saw on television, but we knew we'd never receive a draft card in the mail. This is one fact that helps explain the significant divergence in values between Canadian and American Baby Boomers that I described in my 2003 book, *Fire and Ice.*) Culturally, *The Wizard of Oz* gave way to the likes of *Psycho, Cool Hand Luke,* and *Easy Rider* in the 1960s and *One Flew Over the Cuckoo's Nest, The Godfather,* and *Annie Hall* in the 1970s. Band leaders such as Tommy Dorsey on the radio were replaced by new music and much else on television: Motown, the Beatles, and, of course, Elvis shaking his hips on *The Ed Sullivan Show*. The 1960s did feature a royal visit: Elizabeth II came to Expo 67 in Montreal. But this time, Canada was throwing a party and the Queen was invited—a contrast to 1939, when the visiting royals were the party.

The economic security Boomers experienced as the natural state of the world was hard-won by previous generations. To furnish their children with televisions and TV dinners in the 1950s, the Elders paid their dues in the 1920s and 30s. While the 1920s were celebrated as the "Roaring Twenties," not everyone spent those years foxtrotting on Jay Gatsby's lawn. This was a period of economic growth, but for most North Americans life was not a champagne-sodden affair. My grandparents owned, operated, and worked grindingly long hours in the general store of the hamlet of Chepstow, just outside Walkerton in Bruce County. Indeed, although the latter half of the twentieth century is seen as the time when women began to enter the labour force in earnest (at least after the anomalous Rosie-the-Riveter phase during World War II), plenty of women like my grandmother were hard at work, especially in rural Canada, long before a self-conscious feminism took hold. It would have been inconceivable for my grandmother not to help with the family business; my mother and her younger brother, Jack, were also pressed into service as soon as they were old enough to stock shelves and make home deliveries, which was well before the age of ten. And if the 1920s were not all roses, the 1930s were almost impossible. Nearly everyone relied on the essential pillars to get by: family, church, and hard work. Their values were religious, communitarian, and necessarily frugal. Fun was a family gathering or a church social (potluck, of course: "Ladies, please bring lunch," the bulletins would say). Eating at a restaurant or in the dining room of a local hotel was an exotic experience, unthinkable to many.

With frugality, the courage of their (often religious) convictions, a willingness to defer gratification, and the grit to fight and win a war with terrifying stakes, the Elders triumphed over the adversity of their early lives, earning the name "The Great Generation." For better or worse, most members of this cohort would never take their material security for granted in the way their Boomer children would. But even if it didn't change the Elders' mindsets, their material security did improve. In the late 1940s and 1950s, the standard of living rose throughout North America. More people were able to afford those Fords and Chevys, and more households were able to purchase appliances that radically changed millions of women's lives at a time when women were solely responsible for domestic labour.

I think it's fair to say that in the 1950s the Canadian dream was virtually indistinguishable from the American dream of material progress and soft hedonism: a house in the suburbs, a smart set of wheels, a martini before dinner after a hard day's work. On both sides of the border, more people than ever before were enjoying these middle-class luxuries. In their family sedans and in front of their television sets and sitting around their hi-fis, Boomer children bonded with their parents. Together, they occupied a world that the parents called a dream and the kids called ordinary life. What the Elders experienced in the 1950s as a long-awaited reward after years of sacrifice and toil, the first wave of Boomers experienced as normal, even boring. This disjunction accounts for the many novels and movies by Baby Boomers satirizing and deriding family life in the 1950s and 60s. It also accounts for the baffled irritation with which these cultural products were received by many members of the Elder generation. ("You think a suburban bungalow is no fun, try eating gruel in your teens and fighting Hitler in your twenties, you ingrate!")

Experiences shape values, and values motivate behaviour. It's little wonder that Baby Boomers' goals and aspirations have, on the whole, differed sharply from those of their parents. But not all Boomers have pursued the same path. Some of us were motivated to replicate our parents' values and lifestyles. These Boomers emerge strongly in our social values data, and they're more numerous than their cultural footprint might suggest. But significant numbers deliberately struck out on other paths in life, and it's these Boomers (labelled "rebellious" and "counter-cultural" when they were young) who tend to loom largest in the imaginations of both their fans and their critics in discussions of socio-cultural change over the last half-century. These two strains of Boomers have always coexisted uneasily—not only in Canada as a whole but also within individual families. If I do a good job of describing our data—which in turn describe the various creatures in the Baby Boomer menagerie—you'll smile to see the values cleavages you undoubtedly observe in your own family and social circles.

Just as it's a mistake to assume that all Boomers are rebellious hedonists, it's folly to imagine that all Elders are or were tradition-oriented stoics. As I described them in *Sex in the Snow*, the Elders were characterized by a much greater homogeneity of values than were their children.[3] The majority of the Elder generation were either Rational Traditionalists or Extroverted Traditionalists. To describe them in their most stereotyped form, the former tribe consists of husbands slaving away at the office or factory and expecting a hot dinner from their wives when they got home. The latter consists of wives organizing the family and preparing jellied salads for socials in the church basement. The third, smaller, tribe of Elders were the Cosmopolitan Modernists (often more affluent and with better access to education), whose relatively open-minded values and iconoclastic thinking about gender, ethnicity, nationalism, and hierarchy set the stage for some of the social revolutions the Boomers would usher into the mainstream.

While some Elders scorned the rebellious pretensions Baby Boomers began to exhibit in their teens and twenties, others thought the kids might have a few good points and cheered them on. Some Boomers were fortunate enough to be aided and abetted by their parents even as they embarked on very different lives. My parents were small-town Ontarians who, though denied their own aspirations toward higher education, fell in love with the possibilities it offered and were thrilled when I went to university with the help of a bursary and some student loans. A belief in the primacy of education was the Elders' own social and economic revolution: less splashy than free love, but even more transformative. Statistics Canada data on post-secondary education enrolment from 1951 to 1970 speak volumes about the change that happened in Canada during this period. (The early Boomers didn't begin to enter post-secondary institutions until the 1960s, but the postwar surge in educational aspirations set the stage for this generation's educational attainment.) From 1951 to 1955 university enrolment in Canada grew by 14.5 percent. In the next five years it grew by 56.4 percent; in the five years after that, by a staggering 79.6 percent. From 1965 to 1970, my cohort, enrolment grew by another 51.6 percent.[4] Those two decades represent an astonishing surge in the numbers of young Canadians who were seeking degrees and professional careers, a surge driven by both cultural change and the demographic tsunami that was and is my generation.

My parents, who pursued work-specific training (nursing school for my mother, an apprenticeship in carpentry for my father), were typical of their generation: as of 2007, only a third (34 percent) of Canadians over the age of 65 had post-secondary certification, and an even larger proportion (45 percent) didn't even hold a high-school diploma. In pursuing a degree in the social sciences, I was more typical of my own generation: among those aged 45 to 64 in 2007, a slight majority (55 percent) held post-secondary certification—either university degrees or college diplomas—while only 18 percent were without a high-school diploma.[5]

Boomers were the watershed generation in educational attainment; they look much more like their children than like their parents. When the Boomers were growing up, Canada was becoming increasingly urban, and so were its jobs: fewer people worked in farming and resource sectors, and "indoor work" in cities and towns beckoned many of the young. William Bruneau, a professor emeritus at the University of British Columbia whose research centres on the history of universities in Canada, argues that urbanization alone would have been enough to lead young Canadians to universities in droves. Added to urbanization, however, were the affluence of the postwar period, the increased interest in the arts and "cultural production" (of which Montreal's Expo 67 was perhaps the most flamboyant celebration), and a nascent student movement that argued for equity in post-secondary education.[6] Suddenly university was the place to be if you were going places; it was no longer an extravagance for a few Upper Canada elites, but a right for everyone with the smarts and the ambition to go.

The fact that Baby Boomers had unprecedented levels of education is one reason why they've exerted such a powerful socio-cultural influence—and yet another reason why it's vital to understand not only the demographics but also the psychographics of this cohort. When people pursue education, they're exposed to a broader range of ideas, they gain the tools to look at their society more critically, and they become, on average, more mobile and more affluent. Partly because they were born at the right time and partly because they seized educational opportunities with zeal, Baby Boomers had the confidence to develop their own ideas about how to live and how to shape their society and the resources to manifest these beliefs in their daily life. They still do, and many will for decades to come.

Like millions of other North Americans, my parents saw that society was changing around them—and very quickly. They did whatever they could to make sure my brother and I had every chance to succeed, and they agreed with the consensus of their generation: education was the key. They could see that the economy had shifted from agriculture to industry, from country to city, from physical manpower to a knowledge economy where it was the high-level professional service workers who would achieve successful middle-class lives. My parents and their generation saw a future in which the boys would become doctors and lawyers and the girls would become teachers and social workers. And for the exceptional girls who wanted to pursue medicine or law, the doors were by now ajar, if not always wide open.

I am fortunate that my parents, although traditional in many ways, did their best to equip their kids for the future instead of the past. This preparation went beyond the encouragement of formal schooling. My adventuresome mother took every opportunity she could to expose me and my brother to new ideas and experiences. Soon after I got my driver's licence at the age of sixteen, my mom proposed a road trip: we would hit the open highway (me at the wheel) and visit our cousins in Michigan. It was 1963; the future itself was rolling off the assembly lines in Detroit every fall, and a road trip seemed the perfect pilgrimage. I liked our cousins well enough, but I was especially looking forward to seeing the antique cars on display at Henry Ford's museum in Dearborn.

Once we arrived at the museum, however, I found a more wide-ranging testament to twentieth-century innovations than the latest car models. Also on exhibit were technologies that had transformed household life: washing machines, refrigerators, electric ovens, vacuum cleaners. In later years it occurred to me that while the cars were the toys for the boys, the household appliances embodied a revolution of sorts for the girls. Although cars were the great romantic symbols of North American freedom (my mom would never have convinced me to visit a museum of laundry machines), new household appliances surely had an equally powerful liberating effect. It's hard to imagine the drudgery of managing a household at a time when laundry alone could occupy several full days of work every week. With domestic work made vastly less time-consuming by labour-saving devices, the idea of women earning a living outside the home began to seem plausible to more families who weren't absolutely compelled to have a second income. That was how it worked in my family. Dad's contracting work was the main revenue stream, and Mom worked as a nurse to "top up" the family coffers. (She actually worked nights—the graveyard shift, midnight to 8:00 A.M.—so that she could be home during the day to tend to me and my brother when we were too young for school. God knows how she did it; I guess she's now catching up on her sleep in the afterlife.)

In the case of household appliances, as in many others, technological change, social change, and economic change unfolded together. The Boomers found themselves in a world where faith in progress, in technology, in education, and in America coexisted uneasily with fear of nuclear war, of communism, of environmental destruction, and of social upheaval. My generation's reactions to these unusual conditions—conditions that were at once comfortable (hi-fi sets and Easy-Bake Ovens), exciting (the space race and fast cars), and deeply frightening (the nuclear threat and silent springs)—would profoundly affect the remainder of the twentieth century in Canada.

That was then. Today, there are millions of us still around. With decent life expectancies, substantial resources, and an abiding (if sometimes less than charming) sense that Boomers know best, my generation will leave our mark on the twenty-first century as well. To paraphrase the plague sufferer in the old Monty Python sketch, we're not dead yet.

one

What's Your Tribe?

"The times they are a-changin'."

—Bob Dylan

Baby Boomers are indulgent parents. Baby Boomers are in denial of death. Baby Boomers are spendthrifts. Baby Boomers are tree-huggers. Baby Boomers are nostalgic. Baby Boomers love to travel. Baby Boomers are self-satisfied. Baby Boomers are hopelessly self-centred narcissists. Baby Boomers are sellouts.

More often than not, Baby Boomers are treated as a single, monolithic social bloc. In purely material or demographic matters, this approach can work reasonably well. For instance, Canadian Boomers really will rely more heavily on the health care system in the years to come; if they didn't, it would mean some miracle—either a fast-working plague or a fountain of youth—had intervened to eliminate their dotage. More likely, we'll all get a little sicker, a little weaker, a little more brittle, and we'll lean on the system at least a little bit more (in some cases a lot more, and in some enviable cases not at all). Although values strongly influence how people conceive of their health (see Chapter Three), nearly everyone relies on mainstream medicine; therefore, people in the health care system are somewhat justified in seeing aging Boomers as a single phenomenon, as just one big tidal wave.

In anything less elemental than flesh and bone, however, Baby Boomers are far from homogeneous. Their values shape their choices in every area of their lives and vary widely. To design a product "for Baby Boomers" is to design a product that Stockwell Day, Maude Barlow, Eugene Levy, and Michaëlle Jean would all be equally excited about; if you can do it, congratulations—you're a zillionaire. If you don't think you can make such a universally appealing widget, you'll need to understand the diversity within this generation.

The first secret you should understand about Boomers is that their largest social values segment is the one that's most invisible and conforms least to the Boomer stereotype. Many other important features of this generation are often obscured by false assumptions. Other than individual conversations over lunch, our social values surveys are the best tool I've encountered for uncovering the sometimes hidden, sometimes hidden-in-plain-sight variations across this huge cohort.

Environics' social values surveys measure values and attitudes by taking a couple of unique approaches. First, we ask questions that are unusual and sometimes quite oblique—questions that would almost never appear in the kind of day-to-day polling that appears in the newspaper. Those kinds of surveys ask people whether they think the economy is doing well or badly, whether the government is doing a good or a bad job, and whether a given policy should be changed or left alone. Such questions certainly have their uses, but they don't gather the kind of cultural information the social values method seeks out.

Environics' surveys ask questions that cut deeper into the way people see the world, as well as their own lives. For instance, one polling question that was in the news a great deal a couple of years ago was whether Canadians found the idea of same-sex marriage acceptable or appalling. One reason why the debate was so heated was that a person's response to that one question is often the tip of a huge iceberg of values; if you disagree with your neighbour on same-sex marriage, it's safe to assume that you'll disagree on some other things as well, such as the role of the father in the family.

What the Environics social values method aims to do is reveal the more hidden aspects of people's values. Instead of asking whether people favour or oppose same-sex marriage, we try to understand Canadians' perspectives on the issue by probing their thinking about gender and family more broadly. Is it okay for men and women to wear each other's clothing or to do the jobs traditionally associated with the opposite sex? Is it okay for people—including heterosexuals—to sometimes feel more feminine and sometimes feel more masculine: Is there room for flexibility in how people experience and express their gender? In a heterosexual marriage, are both partners' responsibilities the same, or do household chores "naturally" fall more to women? Is it inappropriate or embarrassing for a man to earn less money than his wife does? Questions like these reveal values and attitudes that are connected to people's thinking about same-sex marriage; the correlations can be demonstrated by analyzing the responses to different questions together.

Once we've asked the questions, our data wizards perform statistical analyses that find connections and correlations across various concepts (for more information on the analysis, please see Appendix A). For instance, some of the questions I ask above are related to the value *Flexibility of Gender Identity*; some are related to *Equality of the Sexes;* and all relate to the value most strongly associated with same-sex marriage, *Flexible Definition of the Family* (which also measures people's view of common-law unions and other nontraditional family arrangements).

In the Introduction, I discussed some of the broad social

factors that shaped Baby Boomers' values and made those values distinct from those of the previous generation. This chapter is devoted to the differences among the Boomers themselves, who can be categorized into four main groups we call "values tribes." We establish our tribes by finding people who have similar values profiles and grouping them together. In every tribe, some people are "perfect" examples: they espouse nearly every value and attitude that's characteristic of their tribe. Other tribe members fulfill fewer of the criteria for membership. A values tribe is a little like a political party: you might not agree with your party's position on every issue, but you survey the available options and pick the one that fits you best. The difference is that you choose your own political party; in our social values method it's the job of data analysts to slot you into a tribe based on your answers to hundreds of questions.

In 1997 I introduced the Environics values tribes to the public in my book *Sex in the Snow*. I described how the values of Baby Boomers and their children (Generations X and Y) were reshaping Canada. At that time, Environics identified three tribes among the Boomers' parents (the Elders), four tribes of Boomers, and five tribes of Gen Xers. Over time, as Canadians' values evolve, the tribes themselves change a bit. We have to revisit our analysis regularly to ensure that the correlations and mental postures that originally gave rise to the tribes still apply. And indeed, we've found that our four Boomer tribes remain robust thirteen years later. Their attitudes and values are evolving modestly over time, but the four tribes remain distinct, and each maintains some core defining characteristics.[1]

If widespread social and economic conditions—wars, a Depression, boom times, an altered media landscape—made Baby Boomers' values unlike those of their parents, variations across society created the differences within these generations. When considered in the abstract or from a historical distance, generations within a given society have a lot in common: they're subject to broadly the same social, political, and economic conditions; they have access to the same technologies; they endure major events like wars, pandemics, natural disasters, or national triumphs together. But up close, as anyone can tell from walking down the street, people's lives vary hugely. Simply being roughly the same age as someone else—even being the same age and the same sex and living in the same town—is no guarantee that you'll share any tastes, sensibilities, values, or attitudes. Just look at the variations within families—your own, for instance.

Demography is not destiny. The circumstances of our individual lives—our families, our education, our successes and failures, our genetic makeup, and the accidents that can propel us forward or knock us backward—shape our understanding of the world at least as much as the historical moment in which we live. This is why within the Boomer generation we find four distinct mental postures belonging to four distinct values tribes. We find the Disengaged Darwinists, a traditional group of Boomers who are frustrated at what they see as the abandonment of the values that made their society great—like male heroism, female nurturance, and the "common sense" of their parents and grandparents. We find the Connected Enthusiasts, a sociable segment of Boomers who revel in the changes they see around them; for this open, exploratory group, the more diversity—of ethnicity, of experiences, of ideas, of everything—the better. We find the Anxious Communitarians, a group for whom social status is deeply meaningful: having a tidy home and a nice car is as important as having a good reputation as a responsible, caring person. For these Boomers, the loss of social status is a terrifying fate. Finally, we find the Autonomous Rebels, an outspoken segment that's small in number but large in influence. These Boomers' skepticism of authority and wariness of received wisdom made them bridle in their youth and have led them to push for change in many areas, from their own family lives to the workplace and national politics. In order to understand how this huge cohort in Canadian society will behave—and affect others—in the years to come, it's essential to understand the four personalities that populate the Baby Boomer landscape.[2]

DISENGAGED DARWINISTS

Disengaged Darwinists are the silent plurality of the Baby Boom cohort. Although this is the largest of the four tribes, representing nearly half of all Boomers (48 percent), its members couldn't be more different from the politicized, Beatles-loving, tie-dyed idealist stereotype. Far from plotting flower-power rebellion, Disengaged Darwinists were prepared to embrace the values of the generation that came before them—and have been mightily dismayed to see the world change during the course of their lives. Just striving to be as strong as Dad or as loving and long-suffering as Mom was good enough for them.

In their youth, the Disengaged Darwinists were left cold by the movements toward sexual liberation, gender equality, multiculturalism, and individualistic quests for personal fulfillment. For this tribe, the status quo made a lot of sense: men were men (on top, naturally), women were women, children knew their place, and good parents weren't afraid to spank them. Divorce was a scandal, and gays ("confirmed bachelors" in the case of men, "good friends" in the case of female couples) at least had the decency to stay in the closet. The Disengaged Darwinists skew male (58 percent), so a critic might say they accepted the status quo because they benefited from it. It's easier to believe Dad should be king of the castle when you're the heir to the throne. But 42 percent of Disengaged Darwinists are women, and many of these women (who number about 1.8 million) also believe society was better off a couple of generations ago, when social roles were clear and "celebrating diversity" meant sharing that joke once again about the Englishman, the Scotsman, and the Irishman walking into a bar.

Despite their large numbers, the Disengaged Darwinists have looked on as their more rebellious peers have taken up most of the cultural oxygen from the 1960s to the present. All that is new seems to be created for someone else; everything that is satirized, from *All in the Family* to *The Simpsons*, seems aimed at them; all that is old and revered seems to be disappearing: heroism, loyalty, patriotism, deference to authority, and respect for the rules, along with the necessary punishments for transgressing them. The whole culture seems to have gone soft.

It's notable that although they have relatively traditional values, members of this tribe are concentrated at the younger end of the Baby Boom generation. They have lower levels of education than other Boomers, but through hard work (particularly in skilled trades, manufacturing, and mid-level office jobs) they've established themselves firmly in the middle class. Nevertheless, each recession takes its toll, and finding another job becomes increasingly difficult as the culture puts greater value on paper qualifications. Those years of loyal service to your employer aren't worth very much in a dog-eat-dog world—with ever more dogs entering the fray from Latin America and Asia to join the European dogs who've been here for three generations or more. If Disengaged Darwinists were characters in a movie, they'd be the younger brother who stayed home to take over Dad's business while the older brothers and sisters (particularly the Autonomous Rebels and Connected Enthusiasts) went off to university and became liberal, materialistic, professional, hedonistic, pretentious, dissolute, gay, or all of the above.

In Canada, the cultural gap between the Disengaged Darwinists and the increasingly mainstream social values of their age peers didn't lead to an all-out culture war, unlike in the United States, where squabbles about religion, government, guns, abortion, and homosexuality have come to define the political landscape over the past forty years. Although the Disengaged Darwinists have certainly been dissatisfied with many of the changes of the last few decades, they've shown their dissent more often through private grumbling than through public revolt of the kind angry conservatives have carried out south of the border. This is in part because Canadian Disengaged Darwinists' orientations toward religion, collective bargaining, and government are very different from their American counterparts'.

The relatively low profile that Disengaged Darwinists have kept amid the socio-cultural evolution of the last half-century can also be partly explained by the fact that these Canadians are, well, disengaged. The culture war in the States was fuelled to a great extent by the disgust Christians felt at the growing liberalism of the American mainstream during the 1960s and 70s. The Disengaged Darwinists in Canada may be unimpressed by the broad movements of social change—toward gender equality, Quebec nationalism, multiculturalism, gay rights, and so on—but this group's relative traditionalism is not underpinned by religion; indeed, this tribe is second only to the Autonomous Rebels in its rejection of formal religion. Labour unions and the state play much larger roles in the lives of Canada's disengaged than in the lives of their American peers (through medicare; public, private, and company pensions; employment insurance; and the like). Because they value these collective and public entitlements, Canadian Disengaged Darwinists feel less motivated than their American counterparts to mount a backlash at the institutions that grant them. It's not moralism or a hatred of government but an aversion to change and complexity that drives this segment's traditionalism. Disengaged Darwinists tend to believe that their own attitudes are just "common sense," but they don't assume that God agrees with them.

When I studied the Disengaged Darwinists in the late 1990s, the segment's frustration and sense of exclusion were strongly apparent in their values. These Canadians were not only more traditional in their values than most of their age peers, but they also scored high on values like *Fatalism*, suggesting that they felt they had little control over their own lives, and low on values associated with social connectedness like *Primacy of the Family* and *Community Involvement.*

People with traditional values don't always feel cut off; many Canadians and even more Americans, particularly the religious, hold deeply traditional values while also expressing a strong sense of engagement and belonging. They are fulfilled and happy. Not so the Disengaged Darwinists. The combination of their distaste for change and their lack of strong social attachments has left them feeling a little unmoored. In the absence of religion or a country with a heroic national mission, many feel lost. Even professional hockey seems to dish out one betrayal and disappointment after another.

And it's not just popular culture and an increasingly diverse and complex society that troubles the Disengaged Darwinists. These Canadians worry a great deal about their finances; they're matched only by the spendthrift (but more affluent) Connected Enthusiasts on the value *Financial Concern Regarding the Future.* At the close of 2008 Disengaged Darwinists were about average in their sense of being personally threatened by the economic downturn, but they're the least likely of the four Boomer tribes to be satisfied with their current financial situation, and the most likely to say that they believe it will get worse in the future. This feeling of financial angst only compounds the Disengaged Darwinists' sense of exclusion and disempowerment. In an increasingly competitive world, they feel more and more like the underdogs, dispossessed in a country they see as rightfully theirs but now overrun by people unlike them—whether it's young girls who wear too few clothes or immigrant women who wear too many.

Disengaged Darwinists don't see themselves as constitutionally negative. They believe their take on the world is only rational. They score high on the value *Hyper-Rationality*, for instance, stating that they aren't easily swayed by emotion or ill-conceived idealism or both but make decisions according to logic, pure and simple. Only a fool would pay too much for a meal or a socket wrench, or believe the nonsense that comes out of the mouths of politicians in Ottawa. In the Disengaged Darwinists' estimation, they see the world as it really is: full of half-baked ideas and people trying to get their hands into your pocket. They relish stories about the excesses of Canada's human-rights commissions because these tales confirm their assumption that those in power are mostly politically correct eggheads who are out of touch with the real world. They love the urban legends about people who successfully sued chain restaurants for millions after spilling hot coffee on themselves, or of a thief who sued a homeowner after falling down the stairs while trying to steal the stereo. They see ample evidence that common sense is in short supply on this planet, and they sometimes feel as if they're the only ones with their heads on straight. Their greatest fear is to realize that they've been naive about something. To this segment, most people will take advantage of you if you let them—from government to big business, to phony refugee claimants and supposedly needy people looking for a handout. It's little wonder that Disengaged Darwinists score above average on *Cynicism*, with nearly seven in ten (68 percent) agreeing, "It doesn't matter what our political, economic, or business leaders propose—I absolutely do not believe them."

In 1994 Paul Newman starred in a movie called *Nobody's Fool* about a curmudgeon who has little use for anything in the world—except for his pickup and the local bar. Jessica Tandy, his vivacious and religious landlady, asks him, "Doesn't it ever bother you that you haven't done more with the life God gave you?" Newman replies, "Not often." And then, with a twinkle in his eye, he admits, "Now and then." Disengaged Darwinists have made some significant achievements in their lives. Despite modest levels of education, they've worked hard and attained solidly middle-class material status: a nice house in a suburb or mid-sized city; an SUV for him; a reliable Honda for her; a February escape to Florida or Las Vegas from time to time. And they're the most likely of all the tribes to be in still-intact first marriages, an achievement in itself. But their wariness of people who are different from them—and their lack of interest in a range of experiences that fulfill others, from exotic travel to consumption to religion—has left them feeling dissatisfied. They also sometimes regret that they, unlike their forebears, never had the chance to fight in and survive a great war for a great cause; proving your sound character used to be incredibly hard in some ways, but there was a simplicity about it that no longer seems to be available. These Canadians have especially deep respect for the men and women who serve in the military and are immensely proud of our fallen heroes in Afghanistan. They do their part by slapping "Support our troops" bumper stickers on the SUV and voting for politicians who understand and respect military-style duty and strength.

As they reach late middle age and gain some perspective on the first half of their lives, Disengaged Darwinists appear to be opening up at least a little bit to the changes happening around them. They remain distrustful of social diversity and in many ways continue to feel cut off from society (their scores on *Anomie* remain high, as does their sense of *Fatalism*—the feeling that they can do little to change the course of their lives). But their attitudes toward new technology are changing, and they're expressing a greater desire to leave a mark on the world. If they can convince themselves to get out of the La-Z-Boy or the four-by-four and interact with the world, Disengaged Darwinists may yet change their status as the silent plurality of the Baby Boom generation.

Several years ago, I spotted a story in the newspaper about a retired Canadian who felt he was being mistreated by his insurance company; they had sent him a bill to which he objected. After trying in vain to persuade them of their unfairness, he decided to pay them. One penny at a time, at the slowest rate possible. If they were going to kick him around, he was going to give them the biggest administrative headache he could. He told one of the reporters covering the story that this was a warning to any heavy-handed business that dealt with the public: "You have to watch out for us old guys," he said. "We have a lot of time on our hands—and we're pissed."

Whether the Disengaged Darwinists will assume the "Angry Old Man" identity more forcefully in the years to come, ranting on talk radio and extolling the past to their kids, or whether they will find new ways of relating to a changing world is the next big question. These Canadians like the idea of doing the right thing—but sometimes wonder if the right thing died along with John Wayne.

ANXIOUS COMMUNITARIANS

The Anxious Communitarians, representing 12 percent of Boomers and about 1.1 million Canadians in all, are the worriers of their generation. If the stereotypical Boomer is a self-indulgent narcissist who does what he wants and lets the chips fall where they may, the Anxious Communitarians are the opposite: they are the concerned, conciliatory glue that tries to hold the group together. When the Baby Boomers were young and the Autonomous Rebel stormed from the dinner table after a blow-up with Dad over accepting nuclear arms on Canadian soil, the Anxious Communitarian quietly helped Mom clear the table and do the dishes. (Six in ten, or 61 percent, of Anxious Communitarians are women, and they were likely to see domestic chores as their lot; this wasn't a group of staunch feminists.)

Anxious Communitarians have spent their lives in the service of others, trying to make them happy: parents, children, siblings, and even God. In Freudian terms, these people have overdeveloped superegos: like their mothers, they're motivated by conscience, guilt, and a sense of duty. (Although this tribe scores only about average on formal religious participation, it scores higher than any other Boomer segment on belief in most religious phenomena, from God and miracles to heaven and hell. You never know; better to be good, just in case. Besides, since these Boomers have often felt they weren't in control of their own lives, the idea of supernatural forces that no one can fathom makes perfect sense to them.)

Not surprisingly, Anxious Communitarians score higher than any other group in their cohort on the value *Flexibility of Personality*: they report that they find themselves always trying to adapt to the demands and expectations of the social groups they belong to—being the dutiful son or daughter, the affectionate parent, the reliable spouse, the cheerful employee. (Disengaged Darwinists have the lowest score on that value. Their attitude is "This is me. Take it or leave it," in contrast to the Anxious Communitarians, who are the most insecure and other-directed of all the Boomer tribes. On this dimension, the Anxious Communitarians are pure Edith Bunker: they will do whatever it takes to make others happy—no matter how unreasonable and cantankerous those others may be.)

In the television series *Six Feet Under*, the character of the mother, Ruth Fisher, is a long-suffering widow (and would probably prove to be an Anxious Communitarian if we could get her to fill out our survey) who feels abandoned as she watches her adult children lead increasingly independent lives. After a while, Ruth is befriended by a fearless Woman-Who-Runs-with-the-Wolves type who tries to shake Ruth out of her needy depression and get her to start living her way. In one scene, the friend fancies a silk scarf in a department store and stuffs it in her purse. Ruth is scandalized, but the rebellious friend replies nonchalantly, "Fortunately, women our age are invisible—so we can get away with murder."

Those words would stop the Anxious Communitarians in their tracks. Invisibility, far from being a passport to fun and recklessness, is this tribe's greatest fear. Anxious Communitarians wouldn't dream of shoplifting; their belief in rules and upstanding living is powerful and lifelong. Still, many can't imagine what they *would* do if they were unmoored from their social roles. Their positions as spouses, parents, and community members structure not only daily life but also their sense of self. To be cut off from the demands and expectations of others would be an unbearable form of exile for these Canadians, who find satisfaction as well as security in their relationships.

Baby Boomers are the first generation for which divorce hasn't been a powerful taboo. When they came into the world, the divorce rate in Canada was 180 per 100,000 married couples (the rate was the same in 1951 and 1961); in other words, divorce was almost unheard of. By the time the first members of the Boomer generation hit their forties (in 1986), the rate was 1220 per 100,000 married couples. Since the late 1980s divorce in Canada has actually declined modestly (it was down to 1080 per 100,000 married couples in 2003), but we don't need Statistics Canada to tell us that it remains common.[3] When the Boomers were children, many of their parents saw even infidelity and serious abuse as insufficient cause to end a holy matrimonial union. Today, "growing apart" is considered a good enough reason to call it quits. Many Boomers decided somewhere along the line that the upheaval of divorce, however painful, was preferable to a future spent with a spouse who'd seemed like a good idea years ago, but was no longer an agreeable companion. But while Boomers as a generation have been responsible for a wave of divorces, their responses to these ruptures have been diverse. Some have climbed to the rooftop decks of their new downtown condos and shouted, "Free at last!" Others have looked around their deteriorating homes and realized, "She really *did* do a lot of work around here." Still others have wondered how they would ever regain their sense of a balanced identity. The Anxious Communitarians fall decidedly into this last category.

We asked Baby Boomers who are single, divorced, widowed, or separated, "How important is it for you to find a new partner?" Among the Disengaged Darwinists, Connected Enthusiasts, and Autonomous Rebels, between five and six in ten replied that it was "very" or "somewhat unimportant." Among the Anxious Communitarians, however, a strong majority (72 percent) felt it was important to find a new partner (37 percent said it was very important); just 26 percent said that finding a new partner was *not* an urgent priority. Anxious Communitarians were three times as likely as Autonomous Rebels or Connected Enthusiasts to say remarriage was very important. Anxious Communitarians are the most likely of the Boomer tribes to feel the need for someone to take care of and someone to depend on. Without this symbiosis, their lives feel empty.

For Anxious Communitarians, becoming single again is neither a relief nor an opportunity to rediscover themselves after years of couplehood and family responsibilities. In this regard, they're different from their Autonomous Rebel peers, who, after divorce, find themselves finally free from the jerk they married for all the wrong reasons in their desperate twenties. For the Anxious Communitarians, by contrast, whose identities are so powerfully entwined with relationships, being alone is just plain lonely, not to mention scary. The Anxious Communitarians are slightly above average in their financial worries (these Boomers have low incomes but are accustomed to living within their means) but are powerfully worried about their physical safety—and growing more afraid over time. In 2008 six in ten Anxious Communitarians (60 percent) agreed at least somewhat with the statement "I am afraid to walk alone at night in my neighbour-hood." The next most fearful tribe, the Connected Enthusiasts, were about half as likely (32 percent) to agree with that statement, while Disengaged Darwinists (30 percent) and Autonomous Rebels (21 percent) scored even lower. Given that Anxious Com-munitarians have lower incomes, they may have limited choice in the homes or apartments they can afford; as a result, they may live in neighbourhoods that suffer more crime on average than those of the generally more affluent Autonomous Rebels. But the Anxious Communitarians' fear of violence is one part of a timorous outlook; their sense of unease probably isn't based purely on a rational assessment of their risk of being victims of crime. For instance, 71 percent of Anxious Communitarians agree that "I feel that violence is all around us and that we must constantly be on the lookout"; the other tribes score substantially lower on this item too, with Autonomous Rebels least likely (33 percent) to agree. Television ads for security systems that feature a woman at home alone and an intruder preparing to break in the back door evoke the worst and most frequent nightmare of the Anxious Communitarians. "When will those politicians finally get tough on crime?" they lament over coffee at Tim's.

"I feel that violence is all around us and that we must constantly be on the lookout."

	Anxious Communitarians	Connected Enthusiasts	Disengaged Darwinists	Autonomous Rebels
Rarely/Never	29	42	46	67
Occasionally/Often	71	58	54	33

Although the Anxious Communitarians are not as staunchly traditional in their values as the Disengaged Darwinists—and likely not as angry about the social changes that have taken place over their lifetimes—these Boomers do feel some nostalgia for what they see as the simplicity of the past. Our data suggest that they remain attached, for instance, to old-fashioned ideas of status and respectability. I suspect that these people love the yuletide movies *It's a Wonderful Life* and *White Christmas*, which extol a simple set of enduring small-town values. A well-kept yard, a freshly painted fence, and a tidy personal appearance are, to these Canadians, signs of a sound mind and a good character (as evidenced by their high scores on values like *Concern for Appearance* and *Need for Status Recognition*). It's a good bet that Anxious Communitarian mothers repeat to their children the advice so often given since the internal combustion engine was invented: put on clean underwear in case you're in a car accident.

It's little wonder the Anxious Communitarians long for a simpler time. These Canadians have played by the rules throughout their lives, doing their best to fulfill their duties and please others. But these efforts haven't yielded the rewards once promised by parents, schools, churches, advertising, and magazines. This tribe is the poorest of the four, with about half (51 percent) reporting household incomes of less than $50,000 annually. That high-school diploma wasn't the ticket to a comfortable middle-class life they'd hoped it would be. Their marriages are largely intact—six in ten are either still in their first marriage (50 percent) or remarried (11 percent)—which is a comfort, but not all these unions are total bliss. Anxious Communitarians are more likely (17 percent) than any other tribe (7 to 8 percent) to say that they anticipate retirement will place stress on their relationships (as opposed to enriching them by giving them more time with their spouses).

Of the four tribes, the Anxious Communitarians score highest on the value *Cynicism*, saying they no longer believe the claims that society's leaders make about anything. Asked to agree or disagree with the statement "It doesn't matter what our political, economic, or business leaders propose, I absolutely do not believe them," three-quarters (75 percent) of Anxious Communitarians agree, compared to about two-thirds (68 percent) of Disengaged Darwinists and smaller proportions of Connected Enthusiasts (59 percent) and Autonomous Rebels (54 percent). Not surprisingly in light of this deep suspicion of society's leaders, Anxious Communitarians are the group most likely to say they will not vote. (Still, their expectations about government involvement in society are going up over time. As these Canadians approach retirement they hope that someone will give them a hand and that the Canada Pension Plan won't go bust before they do.)

While most Boomers have become less intimidated by technology—and more excited by its possibilities—over the past several years, Anxious Communitarians are the one group that remains markedly above average in fearing technology. As far as they're concerned, computers, the Internet, the iPhone, blogs, and Twitter aren't for them—and will bring them little more than stress. Indeed, about half of Anxious Communitarians (49 percent, twelve points higher than the Boomer average) believe that "new technologies are causing more problems than they are solving." The telephone (most often the prehistoric land line) is how they communicate with loved ones. Overall, the Anxious Communitarians feel disoriented, disappointed, and overwhelmed by the profusion of technologies.

The Anxious Communitarians are running out of steam; they aren't sure they can put up with another thirty years of self-sacrifice, particularly if their health begins to deteriorate. For all their sociability, they're more likely than any other Boomer tribe to say that in retirement, "I would like to spend more time on my own solitary pursuits."

Perhaps retirement will be the time when Anxious Communitarians finally get a little bit selfish, seizing control of the television once in a while ("TSN and Spike aren't the only channels, darling") or jumping in the car to visit a friend or relative to catch up on life and gossip about the family. More likely, they won't know where to begin to assert themselves. They will take on grandparental responsibilities, grumpy ailing spouses, and duties toward elderly parents (with women doing double duty, visiting their own as well as their husbands' parents: "You're so good at that, dear"). They will cater to others' needs graciously until their own bodies finally give out. If, as the Anxious Communitarians believe, there is indeed a heaven, they will look down from that cloudy perch onto their own funerals (traditional religious ones for 57 percent of them, if they have their way). It will be nice to hear the eulogists call them "saints," but most satisfying of all to the Anxious Communitarians will be that for once they're not the ones tasked with feeding the assembled guests and cleaning up afterwards.

CONNECTED ENTHUSIASTS

The Connected Enthusiasts are the live wires of their generation. If the Autonomous Rebels carried the placards and bull-
horns at the student protests of their youth, the Connected
Enthusiasts brought the music (and in some cases, the pot).
Rather than protest, they preferred to party; they believed in
the cause but weren't going to waste the moment by getting too
angry. Fun and bonding with others were their definitions of
social progress. Their revolutions were the sexual and feminist
revolutions, not the one envisioned by Karl Marx. The passionate, emotional Connected Enthusiasts are probably the
members of their generation who were told most often by their
parents, "Wait till you're older. You'll settle down and see the
world the way we do." This defiant streak must have seemed
especially unsustainable in the eyes of the Elders because the
majority of this saucy tribe (58 percent) is female.

But like the Autonomous Rebels, the Connected Enthusiasts haven't become their parents. They've maintained their
ebullient outlook on life, as well as the egalitarian idealism of
their youth. While the Disengaged Darwinists feel alienated
from the social change their generation helped propel, the Connected Enthusiasts revel in it. Indeed, members of this tribe,
which represents about 21 percent of Boomers, feel lucky
because they see themselves as having been born at the right
time—into a society that's willing to let people be themselves

and enjoy soft hedonistic pleasures within a meaningful social context of friends and family. Whereas household appliances liberated their mothers, the women of this tribe celebrated the birth control pill in their youth and the information technologies that let them connect with kindred spirits around the world today.

It's not that Connected Enthusiasts are in favour of reckless indulgence; they score low on the value *Pursuit of Happiness to the Detriment of Duty* and high on *Primacy of the Family*, and some of their top priorities for retirement include caring for aging parents and sick spouses as necessary. Also, some might be surprised to learn that the fun-loving Connected Enthusiasts are considerably more religious than the average Canadian— and by far the most religious of the four Boomer tribes. These Boomers don't fit the stereotype of the "if it feels good, do it" social liberal. But they are energized by change and difference, approaching new experiences and people different from themselves with good-natured curiosity. ("Where do you come from? How interesting! I'd love to go there someday!") These are the Boomers who signed up for Facebook to keep in touch with their adult children—and then found themselves using it more than their kids do.

Some in this tribe are part of the small army of North American women who, despite happy marriages to men and minimal anxiety about their sexuality, will nevertheless admit to having a slight crush on the cheerful Ellen DeGeneres, delighting in the comedian's playful, upbeat attitude and impressive sneaker collection.

In *Sex in the Snow*, I referred to the Connected Enthusiasts as the Peter Pans of their generation. They were highly social, highly emotional, tapped into youth culture, and always up for a shopping whirlwind—especially to buy a surprise gift for a friend or family member. Although they clearly didn't shy away from responsibility—their families meant everything to them, and they took pride in their work—there was something determinedly carefree about this group of Baby Boomers.

Over the past decade, without losing any of their vitality or enthusiasm, the Connected Enthusiasts have shown signs of growing maturity. Although they still enjoy giving their credit cards a workout, these Canadians have become more restrained and focused in their consumption. They are less likely than they were ten years ago to be seduced by the latest trends or the splashiest ads. Today, Connected Enthusiasts tend to invest their disposable dollars strategically in areas of special interest or enthusiasm, such as serious hobbies, favourite sports, carefully planned travel, or gifts for parents, friends, or the kids. Experiences count more and more for Connected Enthusiasts, so they see the "best ever" birthday, anniversary, bat mitzvah, Christmas, or just plain party (whatever the excuse) as entirely worthy of spending money on.

This more careful approach to consumption is consistent with the Connected Enthusiasts' general evolution toward a more careful, contemplative mindset. As they reach late adulthood, these Canadians say they're reflecting more often on the meaning of their lives. They also find themselves thinking about loved ones who've died, and considering their own eventual deaths. It's not that this happy-go-lucky tribe has become maudlin with age—quite the opposite. Connected Enthusiasts remain open and sociable, creative and optimistic. But a growing emphasis on the quest for meaning suggests that these Canadians are thinking harder about their priorities, putting away childish things in order to ensure that the second half of their adult lives delivers all the relationships and experiences they want to squeeze out of their time on earth.

You'll meet Connected Enthusiasts at the Y or helping out in religious communities because their attachments to these mainstream organizations allow them to enjoy the company of other energetic, open, and curious people. The Connected Enthusiasts are natural volunteers and natural leaders. They like people, and therefore people like them. They get things done and make doing so fun.

Although it might seem surprising that Connected Enthusiasts would express religious inclinations simultaneously with such flexible, pleasure-seeking values related to social life and even sexuality, it's important to bear in mind that not all religious

communities are the same, and not all of their members march in
lockstep. The Connected Enthusiasts are deeply thoughtful, as
their high scores on *Awareness of Mortality* attest, and also exceptionally sociable and empathic. Religion is one significant way—
often the primary way—in which people seek meaning and
connect with one another. If in contemporary discourse religiosity has become synonymous with rigid intolerance, this is because
of the media strategies of a highly motivated subset of the religious. Those like the Connected Enthusiasts who see religious
belonging as a means of contributing to their communities and
reflecting on the great human questions are unlikely to buy ad
space to announce this practice; they simply do it. As for which
religious groups the Connected Enthusiasts belong to, they have
the second-lowest concentration of Catholics but enough to have
a Catholic plurality (37 percent). Three in ten are Protestant (30
percent), with higher than average concentrations in the Anglican,
Lutheran, and Pentecostal churches (United Church membership is about average in this segment). Although 14 percent of
Connected Enthusiasts claim no religion, just 1 percent identify
explicitly as atheists. As for non-Christian religions, the Connected Enthusiasts have an above-average concentration of
Muslims; adherents of Islam make up just 5 percent of this tribe,
but this is a few points higher than the 2 percent of the Boomer
cohort Muslims make up overall. (If you're looking for a face-to-
face encounter with a Muslim Connected Enthusiast, I'd give two

to one odds that the Ismaili community that has served a community pancake breakfast at the Calgary Stampede for the past thirteen years contains more than a few.)

Connected Enthusiasts thrive on difference and exchange. They score exceptionally high on the value *Social Learning*, agreeing at much higher rates than other Boomers, for instance, that "I learn a great deal from meeting people who are different from me." Seven in ten Connected Enthusiasts agree strongly with this statement, compared to about four in ten Autonomous Rebels and Anxious Communitarians, and two in ten Disengaged Darwinists.

"I learn a great deal from meeting people who are different from me."

	Connected Enthusiasts	Anxious Communitarians	Autonomous Rebels	Disengaged Darwinists
Strongly agree	70	40	38	19

Characteristically, the Connected Enthusiasts aren't waiting for life to come to them; they are, as always, ready to take the future by storm. Of the four Boomer tribes, Connected Enthusiasts score lowest on the value *Fatalism*, reasoning that you build your own destiny in life—and you make your own fun. Connected Enthusiasts are the most likely of all Boomers to express enthusiasm about working in some capacity after their so-called retirement, probably because for them work is not work. They're also the most likely to say they plan to take classes, exercise, and explore their spirituality. They know their books, adult education, and adventures will cost money; this may be why they're the most likely of the four tribes to say they plan to leave no significant material legacy to their children. Ideally, they'll spend their last dime on their dying day.

	Connected Enthusiasts	Anxious Communitarians	Autonomous Rebels	Disengaged Darwinists
"I will have spent my whole life working and I would like to avoid working in retirement."	16	30	38	40
"I would be happy to do some work to keep myself active and mentally sharp."	81	69	60	57

Knowing the priority this tribe places on family, however, it's safe to assume they won't leave their next of kin entirely in the lurch. I suspect many Connected Enthusiasts will set aside a small parcel of money to keep the bar open at their memorial celebration or will have thoughtfully made an arrangement with the Simple Alternative. (These Boomers are the most likely to say they just want a party—no ceremony—when they die.) The Connected Enthusiasts appreciate the line E.M. Forster adapted from the Book of Job: "Naked I came into this world, naked I shall go out of it. And a very good thing too, for it reminds me that I am naked under my shirt, whatever its colour."

Naked they may be under their shirts, but the Connected Enthusiasts should be able to fund a fair amount of fun between now and the end of the line: this is the second-most affluent of the four Boomer tribes (after the Autonomous Rebels)—and, significantly, a relatively high proportion of Connected Enthusiasts have made good by going into business for themselves. These Canadians are the most likely of all Boomers to have pursued community college diplomas. They are as likely as Disengaged Darwinists (19 percent in each tribe) to have chosen a career in a skilled trade. But while the Disengaged Darwinists are more likely to have gone into a big manufacturing or resource company—and in many cases now find themselves a bit down on their economic luck as the Great Recession buffets their industries—the adaptable Connected Enthusiasts have struck out on their own, perhaps running their own small carpentry or electrical companies. Not all of these Boomers are happy craftspeople; some are happy desk jockeys. About a third of this tribe (35 percent) describe themselves as professionals, and they are the second most likely (after the Autonomous Rebels) to hold graduate degrees. Connected Enthusiasts do fret about their finances, but they're in solid shape overall—both in terms of household income and household assets.

Despite the Connected Enthusiasts' general optimism, a cloud of worry hangs over this tribe: they think the planet is about to commit suicide (or, more accurately, be the victim of homicide, the culprit being humankind). This tribe does its best to shop ethically and live sustainably, but they think that ecological calamity is coming fast—and their anxiety about total collapse has doubled since 1992. Connected Enthusiasts feel guilty and frustrated: guilty about the suffering they may be leaving to their children (and to those in less affluent parts of the globe), frustrated at their own powerlessness. This is a group that's used to adapting with pluck and aplomb to whatever comes, dismissing petty stresses by saying, "It's not the end of the world." At a time when that comforting adage might no longer apply, the Connected Enthusiasts are feeling an uncharacteristic degree of panic. Whether this sense of doom will keep them from pursuing some of their retirement travel plans—or whether the purchase of carbon offsets will ease their conscience long enough to permit that bucket-list trip to Machu Picchu—remains to be seen.

AUTONOMOUS REBELS

In later life, the Autonomous Rebels are more rebellious than ever. As these Baby Boomers have aged, they've maintained many of their youthful, egalitarian ideals while growing in confidence and financial security. The result is that they're even more unwilling to take orders now than when they were young. They also try not to give too many orders; they dislike hierarchy and say that young people should be treated as the equals of their elders. But because these Baby Boomers tend to occupy positions of authority at work—this tribe has more high-earning professionals than any other—giving orders is probably hard for some Autonomous Rebels to avoid.

The Autonomous Rebels have been the standard-bearers of the Baby Boom generation, despite representing only about a fifth (19 percent) of the cohort. Whereas the Disengaged Darwinists are the silent plurality of the generation, the Autonomous Rebels are the outspoken minority. The rebelliousness of this tribe stems from their constitutional inability to swallow the illogic of social conventions. In their youth they questioned religion, patriarchy, and secular institutional authority. Everything was political and they refused to shut up and go with the flow.

Youth today tend to steer clear of authority structures they don't like, which is one reason why older people call them "disengaged." In fact, the idealistic members of Generations X and Y would rather start their own NGO than spend forty years working their way up through the ranks of some political party, government agency, or large corporation, making incremental bureaucratic change along the way. By contrast, the Autonomous Rebels in their youth generally plotted to reform the authority structures that frustrated them: they joined national political parties or pursued careers of activist public service in government or education.

The Autonomous Rebels asked why people of different races couldn't marry; why state-sanctioned marriage was more valuable to society than private commitment between partners; why young people could vote before they could order a drink. They began asking these questions in their teens and never stopped.

The Autonomous Rebels have a great deal in common with Connected Enthusiasts in terms of the principles they would espouse in public: both groups are comfortable with ethno-cultural diversity, passionate about gender equality, generally supportive of gay rights, concerned about the environment, and serious about ethical consumption. They love the idea of Canada being a microcosm of the world and are determined to die with their boots on, trekking around the rest of the planet; some will spend several months a year in other parts of the world during their semi-retirement. But the two tribes come to these mental postures by very different routes: the Connected Enthusiasts through an intuitive, empathic process, and the Autonomous Rebels through internal debate that they experience as purely rational.

The Autonomous Rebels are second only to the Disengaged Darwinists on the value *Hyper-Rationality*. Both tribes dislike the idea of being swayed by emotion or intuition; this isn't to say that they don't have their share of knee-jerk reactions, but they see themselves as operating with a certain tough-minded rationality. Although the Autonomous Rebels and Disengaged Darwinists disagree about many things, they both take pride in meeting the world with a healthy skepticism (not to be confused with the Anxious Communitarians' *Cynicism*: their automatic dismissal of nearly all leaders and promises for the future, predicated on a sense of disillusionment and vulnerability). The Disengaged Darwinists are proud that they don't fall for the mumbo-jumbo of political correctness. The Autonomous Rebels are proud that they don't blindly follow old-fashioned traditions or conventions dreamt up long ago to serve someone else's interests.

The Autonomous Rebels' loner streak, combined with their insistence on rationality, may have caused them to appear a little aloof over time. A quarter of Autonomous Rebels live alone; the proportions of solo dwellers in the other tribes are in the mid- to high teens. And at 26 percent, the Autonomous Rebels are also the most likely of the four tribes to be divorced. Most Autonomous Rebels, however, are married (either in first or second unions), but even so are committed to their independence—and tend to have found spouses who understand this imperative. The relationship dynamics of the Autonomous Rebels are the polar opposite of the Anxious Communitarians'.

Whereas the Autonomous Rebels believe that independent travel, socializing, and intellectual exploration are essential to one's sanity and therefore to a sustainable marriage, the Anxious Communitarians see so much solo activity as downright eccentric. Being married means that you sleep together, eat together, watch television together, visit your children together. Maybe you do it all in silence, but both parties must be present and accounted for. Autonomous Rebels imagine such an existence and begin to clutch at their throats and gasp for air. Those who have divorced have found their freedom in solitude; those who remain married either maintain a respectful distance with a partner who "gets it" or are added to the ranks of the divorced before the game is up.

Autonomous Rebels have always bristled at institutional constraints and ritual conventions. But as they age, they become even more impatient with these things. Responsibility? Sure—if it's personally meaningful and a bit of fun. But if it's drudgery, to hell with it; their time on earth is running out, and they're the least likely of all Boomers to believe that anything comes next.

Like wine, our Boomer tribes are becoming more themselves over time: some have become more acidic; others have grown more balanced and supple. Having become acquainted with the four tribes, we're now prepared to see how Disengaged Darwinists, Anxious Communitarians, Connected Enthusiasts, and Autonomous Rebels plan to face the many facets of life in the years to come: health, work, family, fun, money—and, of course, the last hurrah.

two

The Unclear Family: Kids, Parents, Grandparents, Spouses ... and Even Romance

"Friends are God's apology for relations."
—Hugh Kingsmill

Someone recently asked actress Joan Collins, age seventy-five at the time, whether she was worried about the age difference between her and her forty-two-year-old husband. Collins shrugged: "If he dies, he dies." Born in 1933, Collins isn't a Baby Boomer, but she certainly qualifies as an early adopter of some Baby Boomer thinking about marriage and sexuality. She has been divorced several times, continues to be openly and proudly sexual in her seventies, and would apparently score off the charts on the Environics value *Flexibility of Age Identity*. She feels young enough to not just keep pace with but actually run laps around a spouse three decades her junior. (It's difficult to imagine where Collins would fit in the tribe schema; she has the joie de vivre of a Connected Enthusiast, the obvious remarriage inclination of an Anxious Communitarian, the independent streak of an Autonomous Rebel, and perhaps even some of the traditional gender ideals of a Disengaged Darwinist. All this and she's not even a Boomer—let alone Canadian!)

Still, while Collins may have a little of every Boomer tribe in her larger-than-life persona, the realities of marriage and family life for most Canadian Boomers are considerably more sedate— and even a little old-fashioned. Divorce rates did grow in Canada as the Boomers reached maturity, in part with the introduction of no-fault divorce in the Divorce Act of 1968, legislation engineered under the cool and Catholic Justice Minister Pierre Trudeau. But divorces in Canada peaked in the 80s and have been falling ever since. The old saw that half of all marriages end in divorce is false; the statistic is imported (guess the source country!) and is now outdated both in Canada and the United States. In fact, the risk of a Canadian couple divorcing by their thirtieth wedding anniversary was 38 percent in 2005.[1]

As York University sociologist Anne-Marie Ambert points out, this average figure includes second and third marriages, which tend to be less stable than first marriages—so those getting married for the first time have an even lower divorce risk. Substantial regional variations also exist: only 17 percent of Newfoundland marriages end in divorce, while in Quebec the figure is 50 percent (the same proportion that voted for divorce from Canada in the 1995 referendum).

Divorce is only part of the story of changes in family models and expectations over the past half-century. Along with declines in divorce we're seeing declines in formal marriage and growth in cohabitation. The marriage rate in Canada reached a high of 10.6 per 1000 population in 1941; by 2001 it was less than half that: 5.0. Ambert cautions against the assumption that cohabitation is the sole explanation for this decline, but it's true that rates of cohabitation have increased in Canada, with particularly strong growth during the 1990s: more Canadians are getting together (and in some cases splitting up) without making their amorous feelings known to church or state, other than on their tax returns. Overall, about one in six Canadian couples (16 percent) is "living in sin," as my granny would have said. Cohabitation is especially common after divorce, suggesting that among Boomers who find a companion after the dissolution of their first marriage, many take a "been there, done that" view of formal vows.[2]

While the Baby Boom generation has done a lot to reshape society's expectations about marriage, cohabitation, divorce, and remarriage, most Canadian Boomers (68 percent) are either married or living with a partner—and many of those who aren't say they'd like to be. A strong majority of Boomers report that one of their main priorities for retirement is to spend time with their spouses—and, if necessary, take care of them. This isn't a matter of having nothing else to do: when asked about the ideal retirement for those with long-term partners, majorities of Baby Boomers—across demographic groups and social values tribes—say that it's a time for couples to reconnect and grow closer. While the Boomer tribes differ on many dimensions, both in their values and in their self-reported behaviours, remarkably little variation occurs among the tribes on questions about late-life romance. Nine in ten Boomers believe that retirement will be an opportunity for spousal quality time (as opposed to a lengthy period beset with bickering, protracted silences while watching television, and dyspeptic discontent). Attention, young people: if you're hoping for a dinner reservation in the next thirty years or so, you might want to make it now before the local bistros are overrun with retired lovebirds holding hands and eating oysters by candlelight, talking about how hard it must be to be young these days (like you).

Boomers differ moderately from their parents' generation in their ideas about how their marriages or romantic partnerships should operate during retirement. (Although nine in ten say they hope to spend more time with their spouse, we asked some priority-setting questions to get additional detail about the lifestyles Boomers anticipate in the years to come.) When asked to choose the one person they'd like to spend more time with in retirement, 46 percent of Baby Boomers say their spouse; children and grandchildren come in a distant second (19 percent). By contrast, 37 percent of Elders choose their spouse, with children and grandchildren (24 percent) making a better showing than among Boomers. To some extent, we can chalk up these differences to different life stages. Elders are more likely to already have grandchildren and know just how charming those little jaspers can be, while for many Boomers grandkids remain an aspiration. And most Elders have already experienced (as opposed to just dreamt about) retirement; perhaps they've concluded that getting reacquainted with the lump on the other side of the bed isn't exactly *Casablanca* (more like *From Here to Eternity*).

What might be most surprising about the Boomers' and Elders' responses is how similar they are, given that Baby Boomers are the generation reputed to have laid waste to the nuclear family with their loosey-goosey common-law arrangements and their penchant for divorce. Our data suggest that Baby Boomers are deeply committed to their current partners[3] and are hopeful that retirement will make their relationships even more meaningful.

Although men and women are equally likely to agree that in theory retirement is a great time for spouses to reconnect, when they're asked to state their priorities for whom to spend time with—spouses, kids, friends, and so on—a marked gender split emerges; some Boomer men may be in for a surprise when they do get around to slowing down their work schedules. Most Boomer men (54 percent) say that spending time with their spouse is their top social priority for retirement, but just 38 percent of women say the same. Women are nearly twice as likely as men (25 percent versus 14 percent) to name children and grandchildren as their main social focus in retirement. Women are also slightly more likely to say they plan to focus on friends and community networks when work slows down.

I generally insist that our social values data can reveal the very depths of Canadians' souls. But in matters as personal as marriage, even the crystal ball of our values research begins to get a little foggy. When Baby Boomers tell us they want to spend more time with their spouses in retirement, are they merely giving the socially acceptable answer? Are they hoping against hope that when life slows down a little their unsatisfying relationships will magically begin to recover their early enchantments? Or do Canadian Baby Boomers just plain like their spouses and genuinely long to see more of that slightly worn but still rather lovable face? Are plans to cozy up to the old ball and chain simply a sign of resignation—a coming to terms with mortality, a recognition that while romance may be a distant memory, the two of you share at least half a lifetime of memories, good and bad, and that on the final third of the trip you're better off together than alone, whether in sickness or in health? There are probably as many stories as there are Boomers (and the kids, as always, have their own version of events and household dynamics). But whatever the emotional intricacies of their relationships, Baby Boomers are remarkably uniform in what they tell us they hope for: more time with their spouses, and a stronger emotional connection as a result. Nearly all Baby Boomers who currently have a romantic partner say they want to walk into the years ahead with that very person, sharing travel and family rites of passage, the marriages of children, the arrival of grandchildren, birthdays, anniversaries, the deaths of parents, and the funerals of friends. This Boomer aspiration is no surprise to the makers of Viagra, to judge by their ads.

For Tolstoy, all happy families were alike and all unhappy families were unhappy in their own way. Among Canadian Baby Boomers, all married couples are alike and all single Boomers are single in their own way. (Or at least, each tribe is single in its own way.) For some Baby Boomers who've been widowed or divorced, life goes on, sometimes quite pleasantly. After the pain of the marital rupture or the bereavement of spousal loss is past, half of Baby Boomers (51 percent) report that it doesn't matter much to them whether they find another partner or not.

They've had a kid or two, sometimes three, and known the delights and travails of a sacred union … and they're not eager to return to that particular hearth. They may also sense that finding a sympathetic partner is a crapshoot, and the downside of guessing wrong at this stage of life is too great.

Other divorced and widowed Boomers feel vulnerable, incomplete, or just plain lonely on their own; these ones are in a big hurry to partner up again. Among formerly married Boomers, 48 percent say it's at least somewhat important to them to find a new mate; one in five (20 percent) says it's very important. Many of these Boomers would agree with the rueful joke comedian Louis C.K. makes: "I'm in my forties and I'm divorced. That doesn't mean I'm single; it means I'm *alone.*"

For Boomers who are hoping to meet a partner, the possible venues for connection are diverse: high-school and post-secondary reunions and alumni association activities, religious communities, volunteer jobs, book clubs, group travel packages, and, of course, work. And unlike in the past, there's no stigma attached to seeking out a mate in later life after one's duty to procreate has been fulfilled and one's co-parent has left the picture. Canine-loving Boomers may hold their heads high as they stride over to the park with a charming retriever, hoping to snare a silver-haired fox to bring back to their dens.

A significant gender gap appears when we examine the urgency single Boomers feel about reconnecting with a mate.

The reader may wish to pause for a moment and consider which sex, left to itself, would more eagerly desire the return of the other. Have you got your hypothesis ready? As it turns out, Boomer women are relatively contented on their own; men are markedly more likely to feel an urgent need to pair off once more. Among women, a modest majority say it's not especially important to them to find a new mate. A third of Boomer women (34 percent) describe a new relationship as "very unimportant" in the grand scheme of their lives; that's more than twice the proportion (15 percent) who say it's "very important." Some of my unattached female friends have told me that they wouldn't mind having someone in their life—but the bar is high and the time for compromise is past. "He'd better be very healthy, very nice, and preferably have a few bucks" is the consensus. If being alone is plenty of fun, pairing up again makes sense only if the partner brings some real assets to the table.

Meanwhile, over in the La-Z-Boy, things are looking a bit more desperate. Fifty-eight percent of divorced, separated, or widowed men say it's at least somewhat important to them to find a new partner, and a quarter (26 percent—eleven points higher than on the women's side) say it's very important. The fact that divorced and widowed men are more interested than women are in seeking partners echoes the finding that married men are more interested in spending time with their wives in retirement than vice versa. Some Boomer men who hope to spend blissful time at home after demanding careers may end up, like Odysseus returning from his twenty years at sea, being recognized only by the family dog. It's sad to think of these men coming home for good after work and realizing that at some point people stopped missing them. Finding meaning at home after retirement is a major challenge for many people of both sexes; this is one reason why many Boomers are increasingly opting not to retire at all. Home alone or exchanging clichés and tired jokes with the guys at the bar, golf club, or Tim Hortons every day is a "Freedom 55" scenario that sounds more like purgatory than nirvana.

Subsample: Baby Boomers who are divorced, widowed, or separated

"How important is it to you to find a new partner?"

	Men	Women
Very Important	26	15
Somewhat Important	32	26
Total	58	41

The fact that our survey finds women less eager than men to pair off again fits with behavioural data from Statistics Canada: on average, 70 percent of men remarry compared to 58 percent of women. This also fits with the anecdotal data I've gathered among my own friends. The boys tend to be fairly happily attached to wife or partner number one, two, or three. Almost all the girls who have divorced number one are determined not to make the same mistake again. Many consider their friends, kids, books, and cats better company than the grumpy heaps of resentment who used to share their beds. And many find little reason to believe that Masculine Heap 2.0 would be a vast improvement on the original version. With trips to the museum and lunch with the ladies, a good dinner out once in a while with friends of either gender or both, and an occasional trip, flying solo through the future looks rather pleasant for most of them.

As for those divorced and widowed Boomer men who are so eager to find a new mate, are they really seeking wives, or are they seeking mothers: women who will minister to their quotidian needs—cooking, laundry, and even nursing as the need arises? Notably, it's the tribes with the most traditional visions of gender roles who are most intent on seeking new mates when they end up alone in late middle age. Although married Boomers across tribes give similar answers when we ask them about their current marriages, when Boomers are out on their own, their divergent worldviews assert themselves—and strongly colour their attitudes toward partnering up again.

The Connected Enthusiasts could scarcely care less if they entered into another long-term relationship: they're having so much fun working, shopping, travelling, and pursuing their interests that they hardly notice the house is empty when they get home. Just one in ten (10 percent) says it's very important to them to find a new mate—half the Boomer average (19 percent). These happy-go-lucky Boomers aren't slamming the door on a new union, however: they're also below average in saying a new relationship is very unimportant to them. The Connected Enthusiasts are simply doing what all the self-help books suggest: living life to the fullest, doing things they enjoy, and letting the chips fall where they may. If they run into someone charming at the art gallery, at the synagogue, or at that new Moroccan restaurant they'd been meaning to try with friends, great. If not ... well, that's great too. The Connected Enthusiasts' boundless energy and positive outlook make them at once self-sufficient and presumably appealing to others; living single or pairing off—it's a win-win for these Boomers.

The Autonomous Rebels, like the Connected Enthusiasts, aren't rushing into a new relationship. But they're not quite as indifferent to a new union, perhaps because this tribe skews more male: 49 percent of Autonomous Rebels say a new relationship is at least somewhat important, compared to just 37 percent of Connected Enthusiasts. The Autonomous Rebels seem a little like a character Jack Nicholson might play in a romantic comedy: successful, protective of his autonomy, a little rigid, and pretending that he never wonders if his life might be improved by some fun and emotional connection. The Autonomous Rebels are sexually liberal, scoring high on values like *Sexual Permissiveness* and *Flexible Definition of the Family*, and they say that retirement is a time for couples to deepen their relationships and grow closer. But they're also the most likely of the four tribes to be divorced and the most likely to live alone, and they're not especially interested in finding a new relationship. In short, the Autonomous Rebels like romance in theory but not in practice. Perhaps some of these people who are used to success and getting what they want have become too self-centred to make the empathic effort to really connect with someone over the long term.

The Anxious Communitarians who find themselves in the (to their minds) catastrophic condition of being divorced, separated, or widowed are desperate to become reattached. Seven in ten members of this tribe (72 percent) say pairing off again is at least somewhat important to them, and 37 percent say it's very important—nearly twice the Boomer average of 19 percent. This finding is all the more remarkable since Anxious Communitarians skew strongly female, and as we've seen, women tend to be less eager to remarry than men are. It seems that in their outlook on couplehood in mid-life, the Anxious Communitarians' values are more salient than their gender. Members of this tribe need to find mates who are equally interested in a full-court-press relationship; Autonomous Rebels need not apply.

Three strains of values probably feed into the Anxious Communitarians' intense desire to pair up again. First, their general sense of vulnerability and anxiety is likely compounded by loneliness. Since the Anxious Communitarians feel (and indeed are) financially vulnerable, the prospect of a solitary and impoverished retirement is probably deeply unsettling: having someone to lean on emotionally—not to mention split costs with—would certainly have its appeal.

Second, this tribe is more preoccupied than any other with appearances and propriety. Although there's nothing altogether unseemly about being single in your fifties or sixties, certain forms of social approval still accrue to those whose marriages resemble a margarine commercial: robust, silver-haired couples guffawing as they take long walks and attend local theatre performances with friends. Indeed, since the Anxious Communitarians are the most preoccupied of the four tribes with status-seeking, they may wish to be seen as "winning" or "succeeding" in the game of later life. For some women in this segment, courtship is a *Sex and the City* redux where a desirable (healthy!) husband is the ultimate status symbol.

Finally, Anxious Communitarians believe that they're defined to a great extent by their social roles—in particular, by their family. A sense of family responsibility is the central focus in their lives, and they feel a little lost when there's no one around to make demands of them. The needs and wants of children, parents, and spouses have offered the Anxious Communitarians an almost inexhaustible set of cues by which to live. But now that their kids are older—maybe out of the house—and their parents are in some cases deceased, many of the old cues have vanished. Having a partner in the little tasks of daily life— someone to cook for, someone to remind about their pills—has never been a more important part of the Anxious Communitarians' sense of self.

The Disengaged Darwinists are similar to the Anxious Communitarians in their desire to have a partner to share the work of daily life. And like the Anxious Communitarians, but unlike the other two tribes, they see convention itself as a compelling reason for being married: a one-person household seems inherently a little off-balance to these traditional-minded Canadians. Being married is what real heterosexual men and women do. For these reasons, the Disengaged Darwinists are more likely than the Autonomous Rebels or Connected Enthusiasts to say that finding a new mate is at least somewhat important to them. But the Disengaged Darwinists stand out from all the other tribes in one way: four in ten Disengaged Darwinists (39 percent) say pairing up is very *unimportant*, a markedly higher proportion than Anxious Communitarians (20 percent), Autonomous Rebels (26 percent), or Connected Enthusiasts (27 percent). Although Connected Enthusiasts and Autonomous Rebels are unlikely to express a strong compulsion to find new mates, they don't reject the idea with any particular force. Both tribes' answers are concentrated in the lukewarm "somewhat" zone—either "somewhat important" or "somewhat unimportant"—suggesting a certain que sera sera ambivalence about the whole thing.

For the Disengaged Darwinists, many aspects of life—from television to politics to the way the NHL is run—are disappointing. It seems that marriage has been no exception for a certain segment of this tribe: a good number of Disengaged Darwinists feel burned by their nuptial journey and, instead of chalking it up to incompatibility, bad timing, or life lessons, have vowed never to re-enter the trap of a union with another human being. Always wary of being made fools of, the Disengaged Darwinists aren't going to be taken for a ride a second time.

It's worth noting that the two tribes who are clearly less interested in pursuing relationships—the Connected Enthusiasts and Autonomous Rebels—are not only the most autonomous of the four tribes but are also the most committed to gender equality and flexibility of gender roles. For instance, 56 percent of Connected Enthusiasts and 46 percent of Autonomous Rebels agree strongly with the statement "It is perfectly normal for even the most feminine woman to demonstrate what are thought of as masculine qualities." By contrast, less than a quarter of Anxious Communitarians (22 percent) and Disengaged Darwinists

(24 percent) feel the same way. (When Boomers are asked about masculine men displaying feminine characteristics, the numbers are roughly the same.)

The Connected Enthusiasts are also the most likely to acknowledge a sense that their own gender identity is somewhat fluid: 46 percent say that they sometimes feel more feminine, and at other times, more masculine. At the other end of the spectrum, just 30 percent of Disengaged Darwinists feel their gender ebbs and flows. The Anxious Communitarians and Disengaged Darwinists, therefore, may be eager to reconnect with a member of the opposite sex[4] because they're more likely to have built their lives around a model of gender complementarity. For Disengaged Darwinists and Anxious Communitarians, a gendered division of labour around the house is to be expected: men taking out the garbage, mowing the lawn, and shovelling the snow, and women doing the cleaning and cooking (but never "manning" the grill, of course). Having lived a life with defined male and female roles and tasks—even personality traits ("She's good with people" and "He's more decisive; I'd worry about choosing wrong!")—it may be more difficult for Disengaged Darwinists and Anxious Communitarians of either sex to see themselves as fully autonomous and not as one half of a broken social unit.

For those Boomers who do find themselves alone and decide to throw themselves back into the wilds of the dating world, a proliferation of explicit manuals on the mating rituals of later life will presumably be available soon—because times have changed, and preparation (emotional, physical, and depilatory) might be required. A couple of years ago, a raft of books came out on the growing sexualization of young girls. Ariel Levy's *Female Chauvinist Pigs* (2005) described the rise of "raunch culture" in the United States: the mainstreaming of pornography and its poses. Levy questioned the general assumption that in a "post-feminist" world, flashing frat boys is feminist empowerment and that *Girls Gone Wild* is the equivalent of a consciousness-raising session. In 2007, Laura Sessions Stepp published a book that was concerned less with feminism and more with old-fashioned restraint. In *Unhooked: How Young Women Pursue Sex, Delay Love and Lose at Both*, Stepp decried "hook-up culture": the atmosphere of ubiquitous casual sex that reportedly reigns among adolescents. (As in "We're not together or anything, we just hook up once in a while.") If we believe what we read, sex is becoming a matter of jaded routine for many young people—and the age at which suggestive clothing and talk are acceptable seems to be getting younger and younger.

Amid all this discussion about the growing sexualization of the young, it's easy to forget that the old are facing their own pressures in this regard. It used to be that people could focus on their desirability to potential mates mostly in their twenties or perhaps in their thirties (for the as-yet-unclaimed among the flock). After that, you were either married, relegated to "spinsterhood," or a "confirmed bachelor" (the latter two categories meaning you were either truly celibate or discreetly gay). Today, with our changing expectations about longevity, health, and above all marriage (if you get divorced, you may find yourself playing the field again in your fifties, sixties, or even seventies), many Canadians find that there's no longer any room for the time-honoured tradition of letting oneself go.

Where wisdom once replaced beauty, older people are now expected to remain viably sexual until they're no longer viably sentient. In the summer of 2009 the online magazine *Nerve.com* published a list of the "Top 21 Sexiest Elderly" (with elderly being defined as sixty-five and over). The editors introduced this comely group by saying they were "celebrating the bounty of well-developed fruit." Said bounty included actors Julie Christie ("knockout"), Patrick Stewart ("hair is irrelevant"), and Sidney Poitier ("classy, erudite") and authors Toni Morrison ("soul-penetrating") and Gloria Steinem ("graceful")—all still looking great. Helen Mirren, whose astonishingly pert and reportedly unreconstructed shape caused a stir when her beach-holiday photos circulated online, failed to make the cut. This was not because she wasn't hot enough but because she wasn't old enough; at sixty-three, Mirren is barely out of puberty.

Like Helen Mirren, Canadian Baby Boomers haven't yet reached the "elderly" threshold. But to judge by their answers to a question about their sex lives, they've certainly reached the sexy threshold. (Or, at least, whoever they're sleeping with has reached it.) Nearly three-quarters (73 percent) of Canadian Boomers say they're at least somewhat satisfied with their sex lives. Among those who are married, satisfaction rises to 80 percent. The single (65 percent) and widowed (71 percent) are slightly less satisfied, but it's the divorced (52 percent) who are the most dismayed with the new normal in the bedroom.

In matters sexual, as in matters romantic, remarkably few tribal differences exist: satisfaction hovers between 72 and 75 percent across the four tribes. Disengaged Darwinists are the most likely to express extreme disappointment with their sex lives—but still only about one in ten take this position. Our questionnaire didn't get specific on the quantity or quality of Boomers' sexual encounters.

The Boomer tribes undoubtedly have had distinct reactions toward the liberal sexual culture their generation is both blamed for and credited with ushering in. The Anxious Communitarians probably spend more time gasping and being horrified at the seismic shifts in our cultural expectations about sexuality than do the Autonomous Rebels. The Disengaged Darwinists are unlikely to be leafing through the Kama Sutra, whereas many Connected Enthusiasts probably have that ancient volume on their retirement reading list. One can only speculate so much about questions as deeply personal (not to mention irrational) as those of sexuality. Nevertheless, as a social scientist and the author of a book called *Sex in the Snow*, I'm compelled to speculate on some issues and activities usually left to novelists and pornographers. I do so because the Boomers are the generation that began to reject religious sexual taboos and embrace gender equality, two socio-cultural revolutions that had immense implications for sexuality in our culture.

Boomers were the first generation to be blessed with the pill during their adolescence and young adulthood. Not only was fear of eternal damnation for premarital sex alleviated, but fear of pregnancy was often eliminated as well; Boomers were the lucky ones who got to experience sex with much diminished levels of terror. Safe, legal abortions were not what anyone was dreaming of when they undressed with their new favourite person, but those, too, were available to my generation thanks to the liberalization of Canadian laws through the Criminal Law Amendment Act in 1968–69.

And voila: unlike their mothers, Boomer women didn't produce a baby boom. A moderate echo boom took place in the late 1980s, but nothing on the scale of the continent-wide postwar festival of fertility. From a peak of 3.9 children per woman in 1959, the height of the boom, birth rates plummeted to below replacement levels (that is, less than two children per couple) by 1972. At that point some of the earliest Boomers, born in the late 1940s, would have been having children, but the latest Boomers, born in the early 1960s, would have been children themselves. The birth rate in 2007 was 1.66 children per woman and there has been a moderate upward trend in recent years, but our society has yet to regain the level of generational replacement (2.1), which last occurred in 1971.[5] (Diminishing fertility was, in turn, a large part of the impetus for Canada opening its doors ever wider to newcomers. Following the introduction of a less racist and more meritocratic immigration policy in 1967, the world began coming to Canada as never before, leading to our uniquely diverse society, governed by a nebulous but broadly successful policy framework known as multiculturalism.)

The shift from the official version of sex as intimate relations between a married man and his wife for the purpose of creating children was momentous. A wider range of sexual activities oriented toward sheer pleasure became acceptable to the mainstream, and the reign of the "missionary position" as the model of "normal" sex was over. Couples enhanced their sex lives with the help of Alex Comfort's groundbreaking 1972 volume *The Joy of Sex*, which promised an "unanxious account of the full repertoire of human heterosexuality." Even those without partners were able to become a little more "unanxious." Whereas "being improper with yourself" had once been the gravest of taboos (and was reputed to make you go blind!), by 1977

Woody Allen could defend it in *Annie Hall*: "Don't knock masturbation—it's sex with someone I love."

During the Boomer era homosexuals also were gradually able to come out of the closet. Gay liberation extended the sexual revolution to include new sexual orientations and identities, most commonly lesbian, gay, bisexual, and transgendered, the shorthand for which is now "LGBT." (When I was young, we would probably have assumed these letters stood for some kind of sandwich.) We've come a long way from the simplistic M and F at the beginning of institutional questionnaires.

Literature in the 1960s abundantly reflected this new openness about sex. Boys evolved from sharing dog-eared copies of the banned D.H. Lawrence novel *Lady Chatterley's Lover* (whose juiciest passages were generally marked with folded corners) to accessing titillating novels with ease. A generation of macho American writers were speaking our language: Henry Miller (*Tropic of Cancer* and *Tropic of Capricorn*), Philip Roth (*Portnoy's Complaint*), John Updike (*Couples*), Norman Mailer (*An American Dream*). As Katie Roiphe put it in an essay in *The New York Times*, these books created a distinct sense that something profound was shifting in North American culture: "There was a feeling that their authors were reporting from a new frontier of sexual behavior: adultery, anal sex, oral sex, threesomes—all of it had the thrill of the new, or at least of the newly discussed."[6] It seemed that everyone was talking about sex in the 1960s and 70s, and as they grew up many Boomers were doing it with much more gay abandon than was condoned or even possible just a couple of decades earlier.

It has been quite a ride from the classic face-to-face position to our current multisexual mosaic. And, of course, if this multisexuality describes the sexually liberated leading-edge Boomer tribes, it applies even more so to their children. Boomers' kids were much more likely than their parents were at the same age to belong to—or at least know—families with divorced, common-law, gay, or single parents. Blended families, step-parents, step-siblings, half-siblings born twenty years apart: all of these are part of the socio-cultural condition for my kids in a way that would have been unthinkable when I was young.

This increasingly complex reality was emerging at a time when schools were taking more seriously their responsibility to prepare young people for the rigours of adolescence. And while the schools were rolling out their official sex-ed curricula, the pornography industry was emerging from its hiding place under the mattress and going mainstream. During the past year, no less a matriarch than Martha Stewart has engaged in (fully clothed) pole dancing on her television show in the name of exercise. And no less a porn star than Jenna Jameson recently appeared on *Oprah* to show off her twins (that's not a metaphor: Ms. Jameson is the mother of two boys) and meditate on sex, professionalism, and female empowerment.

The upshot of all this mainstream sex talk is that by the time many Baby Boomer parents got around to explaining the facts of life to their kids, as their parents had awkwardly tried to do for them, the kids already knew more than the parents themselves knew or could even imagine. I recall sitting next to my adolescent son at the breakfast table and noticing that he had a textbook open beside his cereal bowl, presumably in preparation for an imminent test. "So, Will, looks like you're now studying exotic fruit" was my guess. "That's a uterus, Dad."

"Of course it is," I muttered as I retreated to bury my red face back in *The Globe and Mail.*

As Canadian Boomers embark on the rest of their adulthood (some in their mid-sixties, others closing in on their first half-century), we find most committed to their spouses and satisfied with their relationships, and many looking forward to the possibility—however distant—of grandchildren. Social scientist Roderic Beaujot has written that the reproductive imperative of the family in the mid-twentieth century shifted from child quantity to child quality. On the farm, you needed as many kids as you could have to help share the work. With urbanization and suburbanization, people had fewer children but invested in them more heavily—especially to educate them and prepare them for a more bureaucratic, knowledge-driven economy. Leading-edge Boomers have made the next step in this progression by investing in the "quality" of their children, and enjoying that quality through relationships that feel like friendships as well as familial relations.

Of course Baby Boomers didn't invent the idea of loving or bonding deeply with one's children. But this generation's attitude toward parenting has been informed by an altered sensibility—one that focuses not just on the duty of procreation (with love and discipline as necessary ingredients of the process) but on children as sources of meaning and inspiration for the mutual exploration of identity, inheritance, and legacy. Baby Boomers are often painted as narcissistic, and the charge isn't always baseless. But it might be more accurate to say that Baby Boomers simply think and talk more than their parents or grandparents did about how their relationships inform their own identities. This doesn't mean that "it's all about me," but it might mean that "when I talk to you I learn things about me" or "being your parent makes me a different person—and I want to tell you about it." Self-absorption is not absent from this equation, but it's not the only ingredient.

The Connected Enthusiasts in particular are delighting in their families as sites of emotional connection and deep exchange. In the absence of live-in family members, the Connected Enthusiasts make families out of long-time friends: supporting and bonding deeply with the buddies who've stood by through thick and thin. If they are materially comfortable, they are also probably expanding the boundaries of their family: for instance, "adopting" kids abroad by paying for schooling or essentials. The Autonomous Rebels are either flying solo, pursuing personal projects and making rational arguments about why they're better off alone, or living at a companionable distance with a romantic partner who's also a respected peer. The Disengaged Darwinists are showing devotion in their own way by sticking around, sharing the work, and perhaps even sounding an affirming "That's right!" when their beloved shoots an irritated objection at the evening news. The Anxious Communitarians are grateful to have family in their lives, to help protect, appreciate, and define them. Those who find themselves alone likely feel at loose ends and are probably a worry to their adult kids. These folks would be the ideal market for an online dating site for older people—if only they weren't so afraid of their computers.

three

Body, Mind, and Spirit: Beyond Stayin' Alive

*"The trouble with always trying to preserve the health of the
body is that it is so difficult to do without destroying the health
of the mind."*

—G.K. Chesterton, "The Health of the Mind"

There's an ancient myth about a prophetess—the Cumaean
Sybil—who asks the god Apollo to grant her eternal life. In the
canny way of gods who demonstrate the folly of mortals by
giving us exactly what we want, Apollo grants the Sybil her wish
of eternal life. But he withholds the additional gift she leaves
unspoken: eternal youth. The Sybil lives on and on, becoming

increasingly decrepit, shrinking and decaying until the towns-people hoist her aloft in a cage in the town square to be scorned by passersby. After a thousand years, the Sybil has wasted away completely; only her pitiful voice remains. When some local boys tauntingly ask her what she wants, the answer is obvious: "I want to die." As those with frustrated and increasingly inca-pacitated parents, friends, or spouses have experienced first-hand, living longer is great; dying longer is not so good.

During the first half of the last century, a range of factors, from nutrition and vaccination to public health initiatives, sub-stantially increased life expectancy among Canadians. A baby boy born in 1956 could expect to live to nearly sixty-seven if he proved average, and a baby girl could look forward to nearly seventy-three years of life. Life expectancy for these lucky babies was nearly a decade longer than their parents' and almost 50 percent longer than that of someone born at the turn of the last century. As for the turn of *this* century, an article published in *The Lancet* in the fall of 2009 projected that babies born in affluent societies in the early 2000s are likely to live past the age of a hundred. Scientists' best estimate for the lifespan of a healthy Canadian baby is 104 years, three years short of the anticipated lifespan of a Japanese baby.[1]

Today's kids are lucky, but Baby Boomers were the watershed generation, the first to benefit from the wide range of health and accident-prevention advances that had emerged over the early part of the twentieth century. More than their parents, Boomers wore seat belts, were vaccinated against deadly diseases, and knew that smoking was bad for you (doctors' endorsements of cigarette brands petered out during the 1950s). The sheer affluence of the period in which they grew up also insulated Boomers from some of the dangers their parents and grandparents faced. Not only did Boomers have better nutrition and safer environments to live in, but they were also less likely to be subjected to dangerous work: as of 1961 (when the first Boomers were in their mid-teens), about 40 percent of boys aged fourteen to nineteen were gainfully employed, and all of those under sixteen were required by law to be in school. (This means that some of those in the fourteen to sixteen group who were "gainfully employed" were delivering newspapers or pouring coffee after school at the local doughnut shop.) Forty years earlier, the number of gainfully employed male teens was closer to seven in ten (68 percent), and many of these were working in physically taxing jobs (such as farming, forestry, manufacturing, and even mining) full-time.[2]

Canadian Boomers got lucky in a lot of ways—but their good health may be the greatest gift bestowed on them by the work of their forebears. And Baby Boomers, recognizing that the sheer quantity of their lives will be unprecedented, have poured tremendous energy and resources into ensuring that their quality of life is high from beginning to end. The holy grail for this generation is the opposite of the Sybil's fate: it's something George Merriam, a professor of medicine at the University of Washington in Seattle, calls "the rectangularization of morbidity" (this is a fancy name for feeling great and having fun until the minute you sputter to a stop).

Merriam says that as most people age today, they move along a downward-sloping curve of health. When they're young, they're at the "fun" level: they feel great, they have lots of energy, and everything works as it should. After a while, they slide down to the "functional" level: they're fifty and they can't do everything they used to, but they feel okay. Then their health status slides down to "frail": they're seventy-eight, often sick, and fearful of falls and injury. The final stop is "failure" (death), where the previously downward-sloping curve drops off and hits bottom. Merriam says that the goal of anti-aging science is not to help us live forever, but to keep us at the "fun" level of health and vitality until we die. Instead of a downward-sloping curve, your life graph would look like a rectangle: a high, straight line (fun living) until your instantaneous death. My own fantasy ending is to plough into a mountain in a plane, with only enough warning to spit out a choice expletive before impact.

Although most of us wouldn't express it with those exact words, this rectangularization of morbidity idea sounds pretty good. Pete Townshend (born 1945) spoke for many of his fellow Boomers when he wrote at age twenty in The Who's hit song

"My Generation," "I hope I die before I get old." Of course, Baby Boomers aren't the first generation to want to be hale throughout their lives. Nobody aspires to infirmity. What really differentiates Baby Boomers—especially those belonging to the values tribes that have defined the generation in the North American cultural imagination—is the extent to which they believe it's within their power to determine their own health and vitality. Boomers' hubris has been to challenge biological fatalism toward their own bodies and minds.

Just as economic and technological change have radically altered the way Canadians relate to other people, they've also changed the way Canadians—and people in many other affluent societies—relate to themselves: the way we see our own bodies and brains is much different from how most of our parents saw theirs. New scientific knowledge has illuminated mind–body connections and generally broadened our understanding of what constitutes health, from nutrition and exercise to stress and social connections. Disagreeing sharply with G.K. Chesterton, quoted above, a friend recently told me, "I exercise for my mind, not for my body." Changes in our attitudes toward health—physical, mental, emotional—have also been driven by shifts in our social values: the rise of personal autonomy and decline of deference to authority have meant that we feel more responsible for our own health; our doctors, if we've chosen them well, are our partners and coaches, not divine oracles who give orders and dispense pills. We have agency; our fate isn't in the hands of the gods (Greek or otherwise) or their earthly surrogates. The increasing acceptance of mind–body physiological connections and the growth of autonomous social values have made many Baby Boomers see almost everything in their lives as a choice with implications for their health.

If you're looking for a marker of how much our assumptions about healthy living have changed in the last fifty years, take in a few episodes of the television series *Mad Men*. The show depicts the lives of Manhattan advertising executives (and their truly desperate housewives) in the early 60s. Praised as much for its art direction as for its plot and characters, *Mad Men* painstakingly recreates the lifestyles of middle-class profession-als and families of the era. For an early-twenty-first-century viewer, these "normal" suburban lives, banal at the time, appear positively reckless. On display are the myriad small choices we've since become convinced are either immediately dangerous (like drunk driving and the eschewing, or absence, of seat belts) or cumulatively disastrous (like constant smoking, ubiquitous hard liquor, and daily red meat—not to mention plenty of unpro-tected sex within and beyond the secretarial pool). Our under-standing of what constitutes a reasonably healthful lifestyle has changed so profoundly over the past several decades that we can laugh out loud to see—and, in many cases, remember—the habits that seemed natural just a generation ago.

Again, Baby Boomers didn't invent the notion of healthy living. But they've been crucial to the cultural shift that has expanded the mainstream conception of "health" to include a huge range of factors, from stress and accident prevention to social life and pollution. The Boomers' parents, the Elders, take their health seriously: they report making efforts to eat well and exercise regularly. (And this isn't just a case of the Elders scrambling to get healthy now that old age is truly at hand; they were making these efforts back in 1992, when they were the same age the Boomers are today. Between their *Mad Men* days and the early 90s most must have become convinced of the error of their ways.) Indeed, Elders are more likely than Boomers to say that they make efforts to exercise and eat a balanced diet—a finding that runs counter to the stereotype of Boomers as health-obsessed. Despite their (self-reported) efforts in daily life, however, Elders' survey responses suggest that they are ultimately more fatalistic about their health than the Boomers are. Pre-Boomers tend to see health as the absence of illness, and doctors as their best defence against poor health. Boomers are more likely to see health as a lifelong quest for balance and vitality, and doctors as one set of consultants. For autonomous Boomer tribes, acupuncturists, naturopaths, yoga instructors, and even personal trainers are also valuable counsellors in certain kinds of emergencies.

It's not that Baby Boomers have gone completely granola in

their approach to their health. Most remain deeply respectful of and grateful for the expertise that doctors offer in fighting serious illness, stopping the bleeding, and replacing body parts that have worn out. When given the choice between two statements about modern clinical medicine, a majority of Boomers agree with "I feel fortunate to live in an age of modern scientific medicine," and fewer than one in five agree that "sometimes I think we would be better off depending less on modern medicine and more on natural approaches such as acupuncture and healing with herbs." Boomers are more likely than their parents to consider natural medicine and non-Western approaches to healing viable options, but they don't see them as displacing mainstream clinical medicine.

What differentiates Baby Boomers isn't any lack of trust in doctors, but rather their understanding of where their own choices and behaviours fit into their health; for Boomers, doctors have an invaluable supporting role to play, but the patient is the central decision maker. (Indeed, leading-edge Boomers see one of their main jobs as preventing themselves from being labelled "patients.") Boomers are less likely than Elders to agree that doctors always know more about what's best for patients than the patients themselves do. Boomers are more likely to reject the statement "As far as my health is concerned, there's not much I can do except deal with illness as it comes." And Boomers are more likely than Elders to say that when they do become sick, their first thought is to get well on their own (as opposed to consulting a doctor). Boomers don't imagine that they control everything about their health: genes, luck, pandemics, fate, cancer, and oddball accidents can ambush anyone. But on average they're more likely than their parents to see themselves as Mission Control in a lifelong project of feeling good and, of course, staying alive.

At any conference centre or resort, you'll find plenty of Boomers hitting the exercise facilities instead of bellying up to the bar—taking off 300 calories instead of adding the same number with a drink and a few handfuls of pretzels. In the morning, watch them glance past the bacon and eggs on the menu and order granola with fresh fruit and yogourt. Not all are making these efforts, but the more autonomous tribes certainly are, and it's part of a general shift from a worldview defined by fatalism to one defined by (at least *imagined*) mastery.

Indeed, if my Boomer friends are falling apart, it's often because they've been overzealous in "taking charge" of their health through too-aggressive exercise. Some have ground down their knees running on city pavement; some of the erstwhile jocks haven't been sufficiently careful with their old high-school and university sports injuries and are paying the price for that bygone glory when they throw their bodies into macho combat forty or fifty years later. It turns out that sixty might be the new forty in our minds and lifestyles, but our joints have other ideas.

"Ever heard of Tai Chi?" our knees moan as we lace up our hockey skates, runners, tennis shoes, or cleats.

In health, as in most things, not all Boomers think alike. There are major differences among the Boomer tribes in their ideas about health. Some are convinced that their health is very much in their own hands. Others run against the grain of their generation, expressing doubt that their own choices are *really* that important in determining how healthy they are. The tribes that tend to be more confident about their own ability to influence their physical well-being are also, not coincidentally, those that are more confident about their efficacy in life in general.

The Disengaged Darwinists are the Boomer tribe that has most resolutely stood apart from the changes that have emerged over the past several decades. This tribe's outlook tends to be more characteristic of Elders than Boomers, and the Disengaged Darwinists' thinking about health is no exception. The other three Boomer tribes vary widely in their ideas and choices about their health, but all three are markedly different from the generation that preceded them. The Anxious Communitarians are still powerfully deferential to their doctors, but believe in a host of nontraditional remedies and are convinced that positive thinking can improve their health. The Connected Enthusiasts are the most holistic in their thinking: they leap at every opportunity to enhance their well-being—be it a vitamin supplement or a hike up Kilimanjaro. The tough-minded Autonomous

Rebels are wary of many of the new health trends they see others embracing—you're not likely to spot one of these Boomers in your Pilates class—but they're profoundly contemporary in the way they relate to the traditional authorities of the medical profession: doctors. (Their attitude toward taking advice from their doctors might be summed up as "Respect the expert—but get three opinions and Google like hell.") In some way, every tribe holds beliefs about good health that would have seemed eccentric in their parents' day. Every tribe, that is, except the Disengaged Darwinists.

While the members of other tribes might shake their heads at the folly of the *Mad Men* characters' lifestyles, the Disengaged Darwinists are more apt to observe their dated way of life with respectful nostalgia, or even envy. It's satisfying to watch those men throwing back a mid-afternoon Scotch at the office, then coming home to a martini or two before tucking into a plate of beef Wellington or meatballs cooked by a "real" wife. The Disengaged Darwinists are the least likely to wring their hands about all the alcohol and cholesterol these manly men were ingesting—in fact, they're more likely to approve of their red-blooded approach to life. Disengaged Darwinists tend to see contemporary society as emasculated and infantilized: a seatbelted, low-fat, low-salt, omega-3-enhanced bubble where smoking is (absurdly, in their view) seen as a graver social offence than cross-dressing. What kind of a society, they ask, contains men who sip Pinot Noir and eat salade Niçoise, then drive home on a bicycle or a Vespa and still claim to be hetero-sexual? The Disengaged Darwinists prefer Don Draper any day—no matter how high his blood pressure.

In the last half-century, it seems that many Baby Boomers have become increasingly convinced that health is a spectrum and that there's always something they can be doing to move toward greater wellness and vitality. "I might feel fine today," many of us think, "but maybe if I did a little stretching or ate some more leafy greens, I'd feel even better tomorrow!" In 2009 *The Globe and Mail* ran short profiles of several Baby Boomers who'd decided in their forties, as they began to feel the effects of aging, that they needed to be more deliberate about promoting their own good health. One transformation was prompted by a heart attack, but the others were inspired simply by the refusal to drift helplessly into immobility, obesity, or incapacity. One woman went from being an inactive and overweight forty-year-old to Ms. Bikini America at forty-nine. One became a long-distance runner and qualified for the Boston Marathon, the sport's most discriminating event. A former boxing champion got back into competitive shape for a Masters bout as he turned fifty—and won. With the exception of the heart-attack victim, none of these Boomers were "sick"; they just recognized that if they took more control of their lifestyles, they could feel and look better at fifty—and even at sixty—than they had at forty.[3] (With sixty the new forty and forty the new twenty, by the end of the century we may all end up back in the womb, eating granola and sipping smoothies.)

The Disengaged Darwinists are not in this camp. They tend to take a cut-and-dried view of health and illness. If you're not sick (suffering from anything from a cold to cancer), then you're healthy. What's the point of wasting your time thinking about multivitamins and exotic exercise regimens? Something is going to get you in the end; what and when are out of your hands.

Because they're disinclined to think about health holistically, Disengaged Darwinists are generally the least likely to report making efforts to pursue healthful lifestyles. They are the most likely to say they don't really pay attention to the nutritional value of food they eat—just the taste. They are the least likely to say they take any kind of supplement, such as calcium or vitamins. Of the four Boomer tribes, the fewest Disengaged Darwinists report exercising regularly, and they're by far the least likely to say that being physically active will be an important part of their lives in retirement. Not surprisingly, given their reported lifestyles, when we ask the Boomers about their height and weight, we find that the Disengaged Darwinists are the most likely to be overweight or obese.

"It is very important to me to exercise on a regular basis when I retire."

	Disengaged Darwinists	Autonomous Rebels	Anxious Communitarians	Connected Enthusiasts
Very important	33	55	60	63

The healthful or unhealthful behaviours that constitute "lifestyle" tend to be factors within a person's own control—as opposed to clinical interventions that doctors or pharmacists offer. The Disengaged Darwinists' relative inattention to the health implications of their lifestyles goes hand in hand with a generally weak sense of autonomy and personal empowerment. Just as members of this tribe feel there's not much they can do to affect the course of their lives in general, they also tend to feel there's not much they can do to bolster their health. Life seems like a crapshoot to this tribe. They're sure that if they gave up steak for the sake of their hearts, they'd be dead within a year from some obscure cancer—and on their deathbed they'd wish they had eaten that New York striploin, rare, while they still could. They take a certain satisfaction in watching people such as stogie-chomping, Scotch-drinking, nocturnal George Burns live to a ripe old age: they see it as a perfect rebuke to all the meddlesome "experts" who try to tell everyone how to live. A hundred-year-old George Burns is proof, from the Disengaged Darwinists' perspective, that life is pretty much random. You never know when or why you're going to drop dead, so you might as well do what you want—whether it's eating fried chicken or cracking another beer in front of the hockey game.

To encourage a Disengaged Darwinist to explore "alternative therapies" for what ails him or her is to provoke a skeptical snort. This tribe is the least likely to see treatments like acupuncture as worthwhile; in this regard these Boomers resemble the Elders, who express considerable wariness about anything other than mainstream clinical medicine. But the Disengaged Darwinists are even more doubtful than the Elders about connections between mind and body. The Disengaged Darwinists are more likely than any other Boomer segment *and* any Elder segment to believe that the connection between physical and mental health is often overstated. In short, the Disengaged Darwinists have a mechanistic rather than an organic understanding of their health: if it ain't broke, don't fix it—and if it is broke, take it to a doctor so he can give you some pills, cut it out, or put you out of your misery, as he deems appropriate.

Although the Disengaged Darwinists are fatalistic about their health, they exhibit equanimity about life, death, sickness, and health. It's the Anxious Communitarians who stand out as the Boomer group most likely to feel both powerless and fearful about their health. The Anxious Communitarians are the most likely to say that illness is something they "greatly fear." Powerfully concerned with family and friends, and predominantly

(61 percent) female, the Anxious Communitarians worry about illness partly on their own behalf and partly because they wonder (with good reason) how others would get on without them. If they were incapacitated—or worse—by a devastating illness, who would organize family dinners? Who would head up the fortieth high-school reunion? Who would make sure that the cousins got their birthday cards, or that the right wedding gifts were chosen? They don't even want to think about the social errors and omissions that would pile up if they were out of commission. But they do think about it. They can't help themselves.

"Illness is something I greatly fear."

	Anxious Communitarians	Connected Enthusiasts	Disengaged Darwinists	Autonomous Rebels
Agree	47	38	34	33

When these fatalistic Boomers consider what might cause this illness they so greatly fear, they cite something nebulous that they can't control: almost nine in ten agree with the statement "The biggest threat to my health is from environmental pollution." Although large proportions of Canadians see environmental pollution as a serious health issue, it's the more fatalistic groups (not necessarily the most ecologically conscious ones) that tend to see pollution as the key determinant of their physical well-being. Environmental activists are blind to this anxious psychographic segment who, on the surface, may seem unlikely to be sympathetic to their cause. The federal Conservatives, however, have these Boomers in their sights. In his statements about "emissions," Stephen Harper often shifts the emphasis from climate change (a delicate matter for his supporters in the oil patch and gas industry, as well as for the climate-change skeptics in his camp) to pollution. Curbing emissions to improve air quality sounds like a red herring to many environmentalists, for whom climate change and a shift to renewable energy are the real issues, but to Anxious Communitarians the prime minister's ideas sound like just what the doctor ordered.

The Anxious Communitarians' worried and disempowered outlook is consistent with their overall sense that life is beyond their control and they can only brace themselves for whatever the universe may throw at them. For instance, four in ten Anxious Communitarians (42 percent) agree with the statement "As far as my health is concerned, there's not much I can do except deal with sickness when it comes." You can see them shrugging sadly and making resigned statements like "Mom had arthritis too. All I ask is a little sympathy, and help opening the occasional jar." By contrast, the Autonomous Rebels, who like to believe they can control just about everything, reject the idea completely: just 13 percent agree with the statement about sickness and health. "I fought to shake off my parents' religion," they say to themselves, "so maybe by sheer force of will I can neutralize their genes!"

Although the Anxious Communitarians' outlook tends to be marked by worry—hence the tribe's name—it's more than a generalized fearfulness that causes this tribe's health-related stress. As Canadian society has evolved over the past several decades, the choices available to individuals have grown immensely. In the consumer marketplace, we have more options than ever before: selecting jeans used to be a matter of finding your size; now there's cut, wash, colour, and brand to consider. Dinner out used to mean a steak or a lobster. Now we can choose cuisines from around the world—and whether we want them delivered to our front door. The newspaper used to show up on the doorstep, and if you read it you knew what was happening in the world—or at least you knew as much as your neighbour did. Now the Internet gives us more information than we can ever hope to take in. We've gone from scarcity to glut in a generation.

As Barry Schwartz writes in his book *The Paradox of Choice*, some amount of choice gives us a sense of autonomy and satisfaction. Your ice cream cone tastes a little better when you know you've chosen that strawberry scoop over the chocolate and vanilla. But at some point, choice becomes overwhelming and causes us to feel disempowered: we don't have the time or mental energy to make considered decisions about all the options we face in a day, and we end up guessing or regretting our selections, which causes us stress. Coffee used to come in small, medium, or large: you couldn't choose wrong. Now it comes in a bewildering array of forms, with and without caffeine, accompanied by milk that might be skim, 2%, whole, or soy. In the end, you might find the one that tastes great but learn that it was harvested by abused workers in the worst plantation on earth. (Damn it!) Today's consumer marketplace offers us thousands of chances to get exactly what we want—but the dark side is that it also gives us thousands of opportunities to screw up.

The Anxious Communitarians are the most overwhelmed of the four Boomer tribes. They may like making choices at the mall, but the proliferation of other kinds of decisions weighs on them more and more. Although the autonomy that ordinary people are now *expected* to exercise might be liberating for some, to the Anxious Communitarians it can feel like a burden. This tribe isn't signed up for the Connected Enthusiasts' program of experimenting with everything that comes along in health and wellness: aromatherapy, new forms of exercise, new vitamin supplements, and new meditation practices. The Anxious Communitarians would be grateful for a few simple answers: Is this good for me or bad for me? What does my doctor say?

Unfortunately for this tribe, the number of doctors who operate on a command-and-control basis is shrinking all the time. Most old-fashioned, just-trust-me doctors are now retired or helping the dead manage their arthritis in purgatory.

As the medical field has evolved alongside society during the past several decades, many health care practitioners have changed the way they relate to patients. Medical schools are increasingly emphasizing an egalitarian, give-and-take approach, where listening to patients is as important as prodding them, giving orders, and writing prescriptions. The term "doctor's orders" was common in my youth: the doctor was the expert, and the patient's job was to submit to his (almost always *his*) recommendations. Today, many patients arrive in their doctors' offices with printouts from the Internet, pharmaceutical companies' ads from magazines, and a sense that they're fully entitled to robust discussion of the options available to them, whether they're managing a chronic illness, treating their allergies, or trying to restore their sexual mojo. ("So, Doc, what do you think about this one?" "Well, Michael ...")

Although many Canadians celebrate this change, and in theory this more egalitarian approach empowers the patient, for some Anxious Communitarians it only exacerbates their fear of illness. Generally happy to defer to experts and authorities, the Anxious Communitarians used to find comfort in good old-fashioned doctor's orders. For these Canadians, "Take two of these and call me in the morning" is vastly preferable to "Let's discuss whether a pharmaceutical response is more appropriate for you than some changes to your diet and a reduction in your stress level." With their low scores on values associated with decision-making, adaptation, and confronting change, Anxious Communitarians aren't usually energized by opportunities to exercise autonomy; they're more likely to be overwhelmed.

Part of this sense of being overwhelmed can be attributed to values and temperament, but there's more at work here: Anxious Communitarians have the lowest levels of education of any of the Boomer tribes, and some may be intimidated at being expected to engage their doctors as equals in considering their treatment. "What do you want *me* to say? You went to medical school; I started working at the plant right out of high school. By the way, that's why my back hurts."

A 2009 article in *The New York Times* quoted Dr. Rebecca L. Sudore, assistant professor of medicine at the University of California, San Francisco, who has researched the implications of patients' "health literacy." "Over the years," she says, "the health care system has gone from a paternalistic, doctor-centered model to one that is patient-centered, with shared decision-making on every level. I think it's great, but that really places high literacy demands on patients. We expect them to go home with diabetes or congestive heart failure or an organ transplant and just take care of themselves."[4] For many people, and for

Anxious Communitarians in particular, this is a huge and unwelcome expectation.

The kind of dialogue and exchange between doctor and patient that Anxious Communitarians find stressful is precisely what the Autonomous Rebels are after. While the deferential Anxious Communitarians want to be taken care of by an authoritative figure with degrees on the wall and a crisp white coat, the Autonomous Rebels would feel frustrated and insulted if their doctor assumed a "just trust me" attitude with them. For Autonomous Rebels, being put in charge of some portion of their own care—even in a way that demands a lot of new learning—is more likely to be a relief than a burden. These Boomers trust themselves more than anyone else to make good decisions; just three in ten members of this tribe believe that doctors always know better than their patients—the lowest proportion of any Boomer tribe. Because they're relatively confident in their ability to make decisions and navigate challenges, Autonomous Rebels are comfortable taking the reins in managing an illness or rehabilitation. The feeling that they're contributing to their own recovery by making sound choices and exercising discipline may be the best medicine of all for the hyper-independent Autonomous Rebels.

Like the Connected Enthusiasts, the Autonomous Rebels believe strongly that individuals should take responsibility for promoting their own good health. But the Autonomous Rebels are skeptical of some of the wellness measures Connected Enthusiasts believe in, such as "positive thinking" as a tool for fighting illness. Autonomous Rebels accept that some link exists between physical and mental health, but they scoff at the notion that a can-do mindset can have any meaningful impact on real illness. "Quit chanting and get thee to a physician" is the most likely Autonomous Rebel response to anyone who thinks they can meditate their way out of sickness.

This tribe also diverges from the Anxious Communitarians and Connected Enthusiasts in their attitude toward alternative therapies like acupuncture. With their high and growing scores on the value *Hyper-Rationality*, the Autonomous Rebels are becoming increasingly insistent on logic and reason as they age; if the efficacy of a treatment hasn't been proven through the most rigorous application of the scientific method, they don't want to hear about it—unless, perhaps, their condition is life-threatening and they've run out of mainstream options.

Although they may doubt the value of some "alternative" health practices, Autonomous Rebels are willing to accept a fairly holistic conception of how individuals can achieve health. For instance, they take food seriously, saying that they read articles about nutrition and try to buy their food locally from responsible producers. As for what they drink, I suspect the Autonomous Rebels' fermented beverage of choice is wine. These Boomers cling to every scientific study that reports on the health benefits of a glass or two of red wine each day and are likely the backbone of the upscale winer market. In *vino* these Boomers have found pleasure, if not *veritas*. Wine is to the Autonomous Rebels what Scotch and cocktails were to their parents, with the provenance and vintage of the wine you drink being a more significant status symbol than the price of the car you drive.

The Autonomous Rebels are becoming much more focused on their health over time. Today, this tribe is only about average on the value *Effort for Health*, while Disengaged Darwinists are below and the other two tribes above average. But over the last eight years, the Autonomous Rebels' commitment to good health has surged; their growth in health-related values has exceeded that of any other tribe. They seem to be feeling the results of whatever lifestyle changes they're making: their reported sense of *Vitality* has also gone through the roof in the past decade or so.

Autonomous Rebels and their American counterparts have probably had a major hand in the success of websites like WebMD, which let people punch in symptoms and learn about what might be ailing them. With their high levels of education—and their growing enthusiasm for technology—members of this tribe are able to navigate sometimes complicated medical language with reasonable confidence; they're also motivated to understand exactly what's going on inside their bodies and the full implications of their doctors' recommendations.

Autonomous Rebels are grateful for the wonders of modern medicine and respectful of their doctors, but this is a tribe that's used to making informed decisions about pretty much everything. Autonomous Rebels think hard about which stock to invest in, which restaurant to visit, which wine to sip, which computer to buy, and which country to visit on their next vacation. They're not about to get lazy while making the most important decisions of all: those concerning their own health. Autonomous Rebels don't expect to be fully in control of their medical treatment, but they want to know enough so that they can participate in a substantive conversation about whether to take a prescription medication or undergo a procedure.

Like the Autonomous Rebels, the Connected Enthusiasts believe that their health is mainly in their own hands. They reject the idea that there's "not much they can do" to promote their own health aside from deal with illness as it comes. They're the most likely of the four tribes to say that they go out of their way to make lifestyle choices they believe are good for their health. (Majorities of all the tribes respond in the affirmative to that question, but in the case of the Connected Enthusiasts, their answers to a range of more specific questions about their day-to-day behaviour affirm their claim that they pursue healthful lifestyles.)

Indeed, the Connected Enthusiasts are the health nuts of the Baby Boom generation. These Canadians do everything they can to enhance their vitality, improve their resiliency, and make sure they live the longest, most energetic lives possible. Unlike the Anxious Communitarians' efforts toward good health, the Connected Enthusiasts' wholesome diets, exercise regimens, and vitamin popping aren't driven by any fear of illness. Rather, this tribe that thrives on experiences simply wants to make every day as rich and pleasurable as it can be. Over time, they've learned that feeling good—and having the energy to work, socialize, travel, and pursue all the other activities that fill their lives—requires staying in shape and paying attention to what their minds and bodies need.

Connected Enthusiasts lack the Autonomous Rebels' fierce insistence on maintaining control over their health care and are willing to defer to their doctors when it seems appropriate. But unlike the Anxious Communitarians, they're not about to go along with any old recommendation just because it came from an expert; the Connected Enthusiasts want to be engaged in the process of determining and managing their own care.

While the Autonomous Rebels and Connected Enthusiasts both feel considerable responsibility for their own well-being, the Connected Enthusiasts draw from a larger toolbox in promoting their good health. Connected Enthusiasts express considerable faith in alternative therapies like acupuncture and chiropractic, and they put more stock in the power of positive thinking to manage serious illnesses.

One aspect of retirement that Connected Enthusiasts are most looking forward to is having more time to devote to exercise and active living: this tribe is the most likely of the four to say that regular exercise will be a very important part of the next phase of their lives. Since these Boomers are also the most likely to say that spiritual growth is on the agenda for them in the years to come, the Connected Enthusiasts will be a key market for activities such as yoga and Tai Chi that engage body, mind, and spirit. When the time comes, this tribe will be on the lookout for retirement facilities that offer plenty of opportunities for age-appropriate fitness activities, as well as fresh, healthful food.

This tribe is the most likely of the four to report taking nutritional supplements like calcium or vitamins, and the most likely to eat foods enriched with vitamins and minerals. (If you've ever walked down the aisles of your grocery store wondering who's driving the demand for orange juice with calcium, eggs with omega-3 fatty acids, and probiotic yogourt, it's the Connected Enthusiasts. Every little bit helps, they figure.)

The food and science writer Michael Pollan wouldn't be too impressed with the Connected Enthusiasts' penchant for "healthful" additives in their food. In his book *In Defense of Food*, Pollan attacks "nutritionism," the idea that "nutrients" are a bunch of Lego blocks we can manipulate, mix, and match in order to engineer the perfect diet. Pollan argues that nutritionism is an enormous boondoggle perpetuated by food manufacturers who can make processed foods seem healthier by squirting the nutrient du jour into any old product. Real food—fruits, vegetables, grains, and to a lesser extent meat and dairy—is in fact the best way to nourish ourselves, says Pollan.

But if good-food advocates like Pollan want to fret about any Canadian Boomer tribe, it shouldn't be the Connected Enthusiasts. As it turns out, the Boomer tribe most likely to buy "enhanced" foods like omega-3 orange juice is also the tribe that's most enthusiastic about real food and the rituals of breaking bread. The Connected Enthusiasts are the most likely of the four Boomer tribes to say they cook for pleasure, and the second most likely to regularly have friends or family over to share a meal. These socially connected Boomers care a great deal about where their food comes from: they're the most likely to say they shop at small, local shops and outdoor markets (where these experiential shoppers get a kick out of buying directly from the farmer or producer). The Connected Enthusiasts are certainly the most likely of the Baby Boomers to be striving toward a hundred-mile diet: they're nearly three times as likely as the Disengaged Darwinists and Anxious Communitarians to say they regularly buy food from local or regional producers. Indeed, Michael Pollan may yet get a chance to convince the Connected Enthusiasts to abandon their "enhanced" food products: this tribe is the most apt to read articles about food and nutrition in newspapers and magazines.

The Connected Enthusiasts are almost certainly catching every issue of *Zoomer* magazine, the new project of media pioneer Moses Znaimer, who now heads the Canadian Association of Retired Persons (CARP). According to Znaimer, a Zoomer is a Boomer with zip; Connected Enthusiasts are nothing if not zippy, and they're probably hoping Moses will lead them and their fellow Zoomers to the promised land of everlasting life.

The Connected Enthusiasts' love of food—and their attention to how it's produced and prepared—makes perfect sense: this tribe is serious about health and passionate about experiences. Enjoying a delicious, healthful meal with good friends is the ultimate delight for these Canadians. Their Autonomous Rebel friends can bring the wine to the party and impress everyone with their knowledge of its unique terroir and subtle berry flavours. I suspect the Connected Enthusiasts tend to impress not with their knowledge of sophisticated cooking techniques (although they probably have a few tricks up their sleeves) but with the atmosphere of warmth and fun they create in their homes. Hangers-on or accidental invitees—the cousin from another city whose trip home was delayed by a day ("Bring her along!") or the recently divorced acquaintance who tags along with friends who are closer to the hosts—will be made to feel like the guests of honour. And when the glasses are raised for a toast, everyone will wish one another what else but "Santé!"

As Canadian Baby Boomers cruise through middle age and late middle age, health is one of those topics like family: it inspires disagreement because everyone has some direct experience, and everyone has an opinion.

The Disengaged Darwinists long to live as much like Mad Men and Mad Women as they can, reasoning that even the most scrupulous health nut isn't invincible—so you might as well do what feels good. (Many would probably agree with Joan Rivers, "The first time I see a jogger smiling, I'll consider it.") Although, naturally, Disengaged Darwinists would rather be healthy than unhealthy, on most measures they report less interest and less effort than their fellow Boomers. As a result, this tribe (constituting nearly half the Boomers) may well be on the collision course with the health care system that so many experts have warned us about. Despite their relatively weak efforts thus far at maintaining their bodies, Disengaged Darwinists are just as attracted as anyone else to long life (for one thing, these traditionalists want to be grandparents for as long as possible); public health and even marketing campaigns should aim to remind these Canadians that they can make healthier choices without being fussy hippies or vain yuppies. ("Real men eat salad—with their steak"?)

The Anxious Communitarians fear illness just as they fear so many other possibilities in life: crime, financial ruin, family breakdown. They tend to believe that everything—from clinical medicine to herbs and positive thinking—might have some benefits for their health, but they also can feel overwhelmed at having to choose among these options. These Boomers are waiting for the guru (whether in a white coat or a yoga outfit) who will cure all that ails them inside and out; in the meantime, they'll take regular doses of Oprah.

The Connected Enthusiasts feel great, and they're having a ball experimenting with all the exercises and superfoods that might make them feel even better. For these Canadians, everything is an adventure and an opportunity to socialize, and health is no different. The Connected Enthusiasts are the holy grail for anyone hoping to attract bodies to a spa, wellness centre, or other fountain of youth; these Boomers will make a trip of it— and they'll invite their friends.

In matters of health, as in so many others, the Autonomous Rebels value information more than advice. They believe they have an important role to play in managing their health, but telling them what to do tends to provoke contrarianism and resistance; giving them a range of options and pointing them to some targets for research is more likely to win their trust and loyalty. Reliable online sources will find a ready audience in this tribe—but those with something to sell (whether pharmaceuticals, fitness programs, or eternal salvation) should be forewarned that these skeptical and educated Boomers will sniff out a thinly veiled advertisement with ease. They want substance.

Despite my insistence throughout this volume that Boomers aren't all the same, the topics in these first chapters—health and family—are areas in which certain universal facts abide. People, even the highly autonomous or deeply introverted, long to connect with others. And people long to feel good, physically, mentally, and emotionally. When one or more forms of health fail, people of all backgrounds and values want to be taken seriously and treated with respect. The challenge for those who work in health-related fields, whether they are physicians, naturopaths, personal trainers, or counsellors, is to know where the universal rules end, and where catering to particular social values segments will enhance Boomers' sense of being well cared for.

four

Old Dogs and New Tricks: Boomers and Technology

"The medium is the message."

—Marshall McLuhan, *Understanding Media: The Extensions of Man*

Several years ago, the satirical newspaper *The Onion* ran a story with the headline "Getting Mom onto Internet a Sisyphean Ordeal." The article describes a fictional woman in her thirties who is trying to help her mother learn the basics of emailing and web browsing. The article's humour derives partly from the mother's difficulty in even talking about this new technology—let alone using it. ("Whenever she wants to send me an

email, she says she's going to Internet me," the daughter says.)
But another important strain is the mother's deep fearfulness
about this new online world. After receiving a spam message
inviting her to visit a porn site, she becomes convinced she's
being stalked. "And then there are the viruses," reports the exas-
perated daughter. "She said, 'I'm afraid to look at the Internet.
What if my computer gets one of those diseases I read about in
the paper?'"

A lot has changed since that piece was published in 2002. It
took a few years, but older people have enthusiastically made
the leap online—aided in part by technology that's easier for
people of all ages to use. As "user experience" has gained ground
as a technological discipline, hardware, software, and websites
have all become less intimidating. At the same time, most
people's computer literacy has grown sharply over the past
decade. The result is that older Canadians are much less fearful
of new computer technology than they once were.

Significant generational differences remain. A colleague of
mine in her early thirties feels that she grew up on another
planet from those just eight or ten years her junior; they're
"digital natives" and she's not. Indeed, some experts argue that
because of the incredibly rapid pace of technological change,
"microgenerations" are emerging among members of Generations X and Y and their younger siblings, the Millennials. Lee
Rainie of the Pew Center's Internet and American Life Project

was quoted in *The New York Times* as saying, "People two, three or four years apart are having completely different experiences with technology. College students scratch their heads at what their high-school siblings are doing, and they scratch their heads at their younger siblings. It has sped up generational differences."[1] (Personally, I feel closer to Gutenberg than to my sixteen-year-old son on issues of technology.)

For Boomers and their parents, technological change happened at an entirely different pace. The big divide between Boomers and Elders was television versus radio. The Elders' early years were dominated by radio, which was delivered in a patchwork of local signals throughout Canada during the 1920s. National broadcasting emerged in the late 1920s and access spread—slowly by today's standards—throughout the country. Within a year of the founding of CBC Radio in 1936, about three-quarters of Canadians had access to a public signal, and radio gradually became a source of both news and entertainment during the 1940s, especially as the public became hungry for reports about World War II.[2]

When television became mainstream during the 1950s, the Elders understandably saw it as an exciting development: radio with pictures! It was like vaudeville right in the living room. For Boomers, television was immensely appealing—as the source of the American popular culture we loved—but not miraculous. It simply was.

A telling factoid: by the time the first Canadian television signal was broadcast in 1952, there were already over 200,000 TV sets in Canadian homes.[3] Why would a Canadian have one before there were any Canadian broadcasts? Because they could watch American television, of course: Canadian homes close to the U.S. border were receiving signals from our innovative neighbours, and a handful of early adopters (Boomer children among them) were beginning a Canadian love affair with American boob-tube content that's still going strong today: *Lost, The Sopranos, American Idol* ... you name it, we watch it.

I can vividly remember my brother and me watching Saturday morning children's programs (the Three Stooges were our favourite stars) beamed all the way north from Buffalo, New York, to the rotating antenna our father had installed on the roof of our ranch-style house. The highlight of the television week was, of course, *The Ed Sullivan Show*, which our whole family would assemble to watch on Sundays at 8 p.m. Sullivan's guests ranged from the silly "Italian" mouse puppet Topo Gigio to the smouldering singing sensation from Memphis, Tennessee, who first appeared in 1956 when I was a pyjama-clad ten-year-old.

Today, the idea of a generation having their media experience transformed by a single device—and often one transmitting a single image that everyone was watching, like Elvis swivelling his hips or Jack Ruby shooting Lee Harvey Oswald—seems quaint.

In the past ten years, Canadians have gone from early Black-Berrys (so sleek when first released, they now look like bricks) to new BlackBerrys, iPods, iPhones, iPads, Kindles, eReaders, and a proliferation of other devices, each of which has its own potentially "game-changing" properties. There's no doubt that growing up with the Internet has been the key difference between Millennials and their parents, but the "Internet" is not something we really experience; what we experience are GPS tools that post your coordinates to the web, VoIP phones, mobile devices that will tell you whether to buy the 2004 or '05 vintage of that wine you're considering, and various "clouds" of searchable information—from the life-saving to the inane. Even on the web, the landscape is shifting massively. Young people now sniff that email, which geezers like me have finally mastered, is passé: "Why don't you just Facebook me or IM me? What are you, like, a million years old?!" (That's what I'm aiming for, smart guy.)

Along with the technological transformation, massive changes in our socio-cultural modus operandi are underway. We've moved from broadcast—Walter Cronkite telling his silent audience "the way it is" every night—to the most multi-vocal and tumultuous conversation in history. This change has implications (whose boundaries no one has yet fully discerned) for every aspect of the way we relate to one another: news-papers, government, television, law enforcement, activism, entertainment, scholarship. Prognostications about computer software and hardware, platforms and protocols are far beyond this pollster's margin of error. I will say, however, that tools that promote transparency and accountability among leaders, easier and cheaper horizontal communication among like-minded peers, and richer self-expression for everyone are adding rocket fuel to the social changes that have been unfolding in Canada over the past half-century. Just as rock 'n' roll helped to erode the Iron Curtain by sheer cultural magnetism (especially for youth), online platforms like Twitter exert influence in societies like Iran not only because they can tell people where and when to protest, but also because they give people a relatively unmediated window onto their like-minded peers—both within their society and around the world. Certain forms of affinity and communication seem to have the power to zap even the most entrenched hypocrisy.

Amid all this change, the radio generation (Elders) and the television generation (Boomers) are gamely trying to keep up. Baby Boomers were often forced to adopt personal computers, PDAs, and smartphones because these tools became mainstream while Boomers were in the thick of their careers. Some embraced them eagerly, but enthusiasm was generally beside the point: if you wanted to keep working, you had to start doing so with the new gadgets. Despite some foot dragging, by now computers and smartphones are second nature for most Boomers. Also, many

Boomers have children at home who introduce them to new gadgets and technologies almost daily—and occasionally condescend to help the old folks use or fix these wondrous machines.

Elders tend to be at a greater remove from new technologies. Many were retired or nearing retirement as the Internet transformed the workplace. And in any case, Elders were much less likely than Boomers to be employed as knowledge workers in information and communication firms. Elders also have less first-hand exposure to new personal technologies because they're generally not as closely connected to the young as Boomers are. Elders are aware of the tools and toys that suffuse young people's lives, but they don't witness them in daily action the way Boomers, who parent, teach, or employ youth, do.

Given Elders' lesser familiarity with new technologies, it's perhaps surprising that they tell us they're almost as comfortable with technology as Boomers are and are as optimistic about the promise of science and technology for the future. Elders score slightly above the national average on the value *Technological Anxiety*, a value that gauges the sense that technological "progress" is at this point causing more problems than it solves. This finding suggests that—true to the image of the panicked mother in the *Onion* article—Elders do feel slightly more overwhelmed by the pace of technological change. But counter to the stereotype, they also express greater hope about the possibilities that new technologies present.

Elders score higher than Boomers do on the value *Faith in Science*, meaning that they're more likely to agree with statements like "I truly believe that, with the help of scientific advances, we will solve the world's health and environmental problems." Elders also score slightly higher than Boomers on the value *Enthusiasm for Technology*, saying they are excited by the possibilities that new technologies present.

In other words, Boomers are less anxious than the previous generation about technological change, but also somewhat less optimistic about the capacity of science and technology to improve the world. More steeped in emerging technologies because of their age, career stage, and exposure to young people, Boomers are more matter-of-fact about technological change and more suspicious of any god—whether the *deus* in question be *ex cathedra* or *ex machina*. Elders are at once more intimidated and more impressed. This combination of fear and trust makes sense: if Elders feel less familiar and less at ease with new technologies (hence their high scores on *Technological Anxiety*), it follows that they would also feel that these mysterious new tools have untold possibilities (hence their high scores on *Enthusiasm for New Technology*). Arthur C. Clarke famously said that any sufficiently advanced technology is indistinguishable from magic. (Indeed, even though televisions and camera phones are ubiquitous in our society, if the movement of sight and sound over long distances doesn't qualify as magic, I don't know what would. I'm still trying to figure out how they built the pyramids in Giza.) Although Elders don't imagine that their grandchildren's iPhones are supernatural, they might find the gadgets sufficiently strange and baffling that they will sense an air of mysterious power about them. And just imagine the fun Boomers' kids are having showing their know-it-all parents the tricks of the new technologies—they can finally feel superior to people who think everything on earth is a footnote to their genius.

Boomers' and Elders' differing experiences of big-picture technological change during their lifetimes may also help to explain Boomers' lower levels of optimism about the possibilities new technologies present. Science took the Elders from the depths of the Depression, along spanking new freeways and airport runways, all the way to the moon. It took Boomers into the nuclear age, silent springs, and fields laced with toxic DDT. More recently, it has ushered knowledge-worker Boomers into an endless workday, untold quantities of spam, and the fear of their children surfing—or inadvertently *becoming*—pornographic images online.

When the Elders were young, polio terrorized children. A transatlantic phone call was a major (and prohibitively costly) event: when AT&T introduced their transatlantic service in 1927, the first three minutes of a call from the United States to London cost $75—somewhere in the neighbourhood of $900 today. Women, without the labour-saving devices we take for granted—and often without running water or electricity—spent vastly more time accomplishing basic household tasks: one economist calculates that in 1900 American women spent fifty-eight hours a week on housework, whereas by 1975 women were spending just eighteen hours weekly on the same tasks.[4] (Social changes have also affected women's relationships with household work, of course, but it's safe to say that even enlightened male partners have yet to do as much for the women of the twenty-first century as the washing machine did for the women of the early twentieth century—at least with respect to raw labour.) Over time, science and technology radically improved ordinary people's lives in terms of health outcomes, automated labour, mobility, communication, and entertainment. For Canadian Elders, Neil Armstrong's first steps on the moon in 1969 were the almost unimaginable culmination of a period of breathtaking progress.

Baby Boomers, on the other hand, came of age at a time when the public imagination was as much preoccupied by the dark side of technology as by its progressive possibilities. Environmental destruction wrought by industrialization and the use of technology for warfare rather than the improvement of human circumstances were central concerns for many Boomers. If their parents had been so enchanted by the benefits of technological progress that they were blind to its costs, Boomers took their health, safety, and affluence so much for granted that they were sometimes blind to the role industrial progress had played in providing these. The ubiquitous had become invisible, even risible. The 1967 movie *The Graduate* invited Baby Boomers to laugh with contempt at the patriarch who tells young Benjamin that he ought to pursue a career in "plastics." How square, we thought, as we headed back home from the theatre to listen to *Sergeant Pepper's Lonely Hearts Club Band* on vinyl (that is, plastic) LPs.

Michael Shellenberger and Ted Nordhaus consider this profound social change in their book *Break Through: From the Death of Environmentalism to the Politics of Possibility*. Shellenberger and Nordhaus argue that the environmental movement as we've known it since the 1960s didn't come about because the American people became newly aware of the ecological destruction human beings were wreaking—this destruction, in fact, had been evident for over a hundred years. The debris-strewn and oil-slicked Cuyahoga River in Cleveland, Ohio, for instance, famously caught fire in 1969, an event that was commemorated in folk songs and in the pages of *Time* magazine. But the river had caught fire several times in the previous century. It wasn't the newly evident toxicity of the river that caused Americans to take notice of their polluting ways, but the fact that they had sufficient material security—a state Canadian-born economist John Kenneth Galbraith famously diagnosed in his book *The Affluent Society*—that they could turn their attention to postmaterial concerns such as the quality of their air, soil, and water. (Of course, it doesn't get much more material than the health of the earth, an obvious fundamental of human survival. But given the choice between a job at the mine or factory today, with a paycheque at the end of the week, or a non-paying abstraction called "a healthier environment," for most of the twentieth century Canadians and Americans chose the paycheque.) "Environmentalist values," Shellenberger and Nordhaus write, "such as the strong desire to protect ecosystems, largely spring from higher-order postmaterial ... needs."[5] Boomers were able to cultivate these postmaterial concerns precisely because Elders had made such tremendous advances on the material front, sometimes at great cost to their own health and that of the planet.

Today, the Elders feel they have science and technology to thank for much of the good in their lives. They express slightly above-average optimism about the capacity of science and technology to lead us into the future: fighting disease, extending lives, and even cleaning up some of the messes that the industrial economy has produced. The Boomers, by contrast, are slightly below average on the value *Faith in Science*: they maintain their belief that scientific progress is a mixed blessing.

But if their enthusiasm for scientific and technological progress at the macro level remains muted, Boomers' excitement about using the new gadgets in their own lives has grown considerably. Baby Boomers are catching up with the Elders in their enthusiasm for technology, expressing considerably more interest in its possibilities than they did in 1992. This change in attitude is directly linked to the kinds of technologies that have become most prevalent in our lives over the past couple of decades. Overwhelmingly, these are *personal* technologies. As we know, Boomers are big on the personal: personal autonomy, personal style, personal choice. Nuclear warheads were in someone else's hands, perhaps those of a madman like Dr. Strangelove; our BlackBerrys and iPhones are in *our* hands.

When Boomers were kids, technology was large scale, industrial, and communal. Recall the mainframe! As Malcolm Gladwell recounts in his book *Outliers*, the young Bill Gates was able to learn how to program because some kind adults (a mothers' group at his school and then a local business) gave him and his junior high cronies access to huge, expensive computers that only institutions could afford. Today's technologies are profoundly personal. Some of us treat smartphones as appendages, keeping them never more than an inch or two from our bodies; they don't go in our purses or briefcases, where we can't hear them buzz or feel them vibrate, but on our belts, in our pockets, or (often) right in our hands. (My BlackBerry stares me in the face even as I edit this sentence by hand with my favourite silver pencil, a cherished gift that I've been writing with for twenty years. I don't want to be in front of my computer all the time, but I *do* still want to bang out drafts, receive and send emails, and verify remembered dates, people, and places with Google.) Marketing campaigns by Apple and Microsoft feature people (quite plausibly) identifying themselves as their machines: "I'm a Mac," or "I'm a PC." These people don't *own* or *use* or *prefer* their kind of computer. They *are* their computer: their photos, music, blogs, email, interface preferences, calendars, research, and designs are all here. What's the difference between that stuff and "me"? Nothing, really; they are extensions of my voice, senses, hands, and memory (as Marshall McLuhan observed, a few decades ahead of the marketers, in the title of his book quoted at the beginning of this chapter: *Understanding Media: The Extensions of Man*).

In some sense, Boomers' relationship with technology parallels their relationship with religion: the more personal it has become, the more willing they've been to explore it. The mainframe was like the Catholic Church: it could help you in some important ways, but there was only one way to use it, and you had to play by the rules laid out by a central authority. The personal computer is more like an individual spiritual quest: it requires an investment of learning and attention but pays off in ways that are intellectually and emotionally resonant for the user.

There may be a couple more reasons for this change in Baby Boomers' perceptions of new technology. First, Boomers get more pleasure—and less frustration—from gadgets than they once did. During the 1980s and 90s, a huge array of new technologies became available to ordinary consumers, from microwave ovens to cellular phones, personal computers, VCRs, DVD players, and PVRs. In its early stages, much of this technology was seen as appealing—but complicated. Take the VCR, for instance. For years consumers complained about their inability to set their machines to record their favourite TV shows. They saw the value of the VCR—and were sufficiently convinced of the value of the Platonic ideal of time-shifting to buy one—but in daily life, the VCR wasn't a magical time-shifter. It was just a hunk of machinery that was tricky and frustrating to use. Similarly, the personal computer has transformed the way we live but yielded its own litany of diseases: crashes, viruses, lost files, and so on.

In more recent years, however, a new focus on "usability" has meant that technology has become not only more sophisticated but easier to use. Baby Boomers who once cursed their "impossible-to-program" VCRs now know how to chat online with their kids who live on the other side of the world. Part of this change has been a matter of all of us getting used to new technology, but much of it has been driven by electronics manufacturers' and software developers' greater focus on the user. Boomers may be more excited about new technology today because each time they go to use a phone, a computer, or a television-recording device, it simply works better than it used to.

Another factor that may be driving Boomers' increased hopefulness about technological change is the fact that technology is being put to increasingly idealistic ends. For much of the twentieth century, marvels of engineering were designed to increase economic productivity and extract resources from the earth. The Hoover Dam powered the American Southwest and lit up Las Vegas. The airplane made transatlantic commerce and tourism much more feasible. Beyond these feats of industrialism, science led advances in both warfare and medicine—harming and healing people. Today, although people continue to make widgets, the holy grails of engineering aren't the technologies that will allow us to build bigger and better widgets. They are technologies that will allow us to conserve resources, reverse the damage we've already done to the environment, and generally make our life on earth more humane and more sustainable. Boomers may perceive a growing maturity in humanity's approach to the immense power that technology affords.

From simply getting things done—moving that rock, joining these two pieces of wood together—we moved to getting things done on a huge scale: mass production and mass communication. Having conquered the planet (too aggressively, as it's now informing us) and explored all its geographic frontiers, we're now trying to learn how to live on it efficiently and—we hope—indefinitely. One important step will be to control the numbers of our species trying to occupy this finite sphere. The first generation—thanks in large part to the pill—to produce fewer children than the rate of replacement inaugurated a revolutionary Darwinian adaptation. Their children continue their parents' reproductive restraint (no baby boom in their plans) as humans attempt to find ways to collectively survive on this planet.

In their growing enthusiasm about scientific and technological progress, Baby Boomers are becoming more similar to their parents. However, this change probably isn't driven by a sense of awe at technology itself, but rather by a sense of optimism that technology is being put to more positive, responsible, and equitable uses. If technological advancement signified for Elders the triumph of man over his environment, for Boomers it may signify the triumph of human beings' capacity for constructive creativity over their equally immense capacity for greed and violence. Ironically, although birth control and safe abortions are ostensibly ways of preventing reproduction, together with education they may actually be working to ensure that our species survives to live in harmony with our terrestrial habitat. More and more we're using our tools to sustain our own lives rather than to end the lives of other creatures, including humans, televised evidence of wars and genocides notwithstanding.

For a while, it seemed to the Disengaged Darwinists that the digital revolution in our culture would simply pass them by. When Environics first began tracking Canadians' attitudes toward emerging technologies, the Disengaged Darwinists were deeply wary. To these Canadians, the Internet sounded at first like something that mattered only to nerds. The Disengaged Darwinists, who tend to take a utilitarian approach to most things, couldn't see any direct benefit to being "online." They weren't motivated to spend money on the equipment or take the time to learn how to use it. When they heard people speak breathlessly about the sheer thrill of connectivity—"Last night I was in a chat room with someone in Helsinki and someone else in Cape Town!"—the Disengaged Darwinists looked blank. "Whatever floats your boat," they shrugged.

This tribe responded similarly when mobile phones began to penetrate the Canadian marketplace. For several years, cellular phones (often "car phones") had been the exclusive toys of high-falutin executives and the odd trailblazing real estate agent. When mobile phones began to come into use among ordinary people, Disengaged Darwinists remained skeptical. Not eager to socialize at the best of times, Disengaged Darwinists failed to see why being interrupted in the car or at Canadian Tire should please instead of annoy them. Some members of this tribe would have been early adopters of cellphones for others: more than a few Disengaged Darwinist men probably bought phones for their wives and daughters for safety reasons. And those who

needed to drive around a lot for work would have appreciated
the practical benefits of the phones early on. Most Disengaged
Darwinists, however, likely dragged their feet in purchasing
their first mobile devices.

Fast forward fifteen years or so, and the Disengaged Darwinists have undergone a surprising transformation in their
thinking. Despite their initially grudging attitudes toward the
Internet and proliferating mobile communications gadgets, this
tribe has finally begun to see what's in it for them. The Disengaged Darwinists' scores on *Enthusiasm for Technology* have
grown more sharply since 2001 than those of any other Boomer
tribe. These Canadians remain below average in their embrace
of new technology, but the speed at which their views on technology have changed suggests that something significant is
going on among them in the way they connect and communicate—especially online.

Given that they tend to feel somewhat cut off from the
changes happening in society, Disengaged Darwinists are accustomed to feeling a little excluded. These Boomers often feel out
of step with the trajectory of mainstream culture, as though they
were born a generation too late. When we measured their attitudes toward technology through the 1990s and in the early
part of this century, it seemed that the new tools for connectivity that others were embracing would be one more point of
divergence between Disengaged Darwinists and mainstream

socio-cultural change in Canada. Once again, the Disengaged Darwinists would reject change and be left behind.

Instead, Disengaged Darwinists appear to be catching up to the rest of the culture. They sense that new technology holds possibilities and opportunities for them, too. Although we don't know what precisely has changed about the way this tribe sees technology—only that they feel more excited and optimistic about digital tools than they did before—I think there's one very likely explanation for this shift: the Disengaged Darwinists have finally begun to connect with their own tribe online.

One of the major consequences of the spread of the Internet has been the growing self-awareness, connectedness, and organization of a huge variety of interest groups and affinity groups. Political activists, hobbyists, fans of particular celebrities, researchers and scholars, fetishists, genealogists, religious movements—all have found ways to share information, socialize, and define themselves online. The formation and proliferation of niche groups has had tremendous implications in a wide range of areas. In his book *The Long Tail*, *Wired* editor Chris Anderson argues that marketers can now efficiently access niche markets that would have been too small to target through broadcast media and traditional distribution methods. Security experts have found that a small number of angry young men can connect across vast distances and plot violence together online. And as open-source software communities have long known, people who've never met can work together on large-scale projects that would otherwise have required a massive organization and millions of dollars.

Whereas in its early days the Internet itself was seen as a niche territory, where young people or technology enthusiasts would congregate, it's now more likely to be seen as everyone's territory—a widely accessible space where niches take shape. For Disengaged Darwinists, the consequence is that a group that has felt culturally excluded for many years is finally able to talk to itself in terms it understands. Disengaged Darwinists used to watch the evening news and shake their heads at the stupidity and cupidity of the bigwigs in government and business. Now they can visit a favourite blog or YouTube channel and hear a kindred spirit rant about the very things they might once have fumed about privately (or occasionally on a radio call-in show): the government, monopolies, the cable and telecom companies—pick your poison. Instead of feeling isolated by their distaste for the prevailing social norms, they can now use that distaste as the basis for social bonds.

Just as American liberals during the Bush years felt huge emotional release in watching Jon Stewart skewer the administration's arrogance and absurdity, a growing number of Disengaged Darwinists are likely to delight in blogs, podcasts, and homemade videos that pillory bureaucratic waste, sociocultural norms, urban hubris, feminism, environmentalism, multiculturalism, and political correctness. Although anger will be the dominant mood online for many of these disenchanted Boomers, some will use their free, easy-to-access platforms to discuss areas of personal enthusiasm; our data suggest that plausible topics include cars (both antique and racing vehicles), sports, and crafts.

Some Disengaged Darwinist wags will channel their critical, sometimes cranky, observations into humour related to sports, sex, and, for those who push this tribe's *Ethnic Intolerance* scores up above average, ethnicity. Even many women in this tribe will enjoy a forwarded email full of jokes about stereotypes such as women's vanity and lust for shopping. (Blonde jokes that were rejected by most Canadians decades ago are still in fashion for some of this tribe.) All in good fun, say Disengaged Darwinists of both genders. And if an Autonomous Rebel sister informs them these jokes aren't funny, the Disengaged Darwinist will chalk it up to politically correct paralysis. Loosen up, girl!

Many Disengaged Darwinists remain loners who are unlikely to start a blog or pound out a podcast any time soon. But some will be sufficiently energetic—and sufficiently dyspeptic—to want to trumpet their opinions to the world. And the fact that this tribe has felt excluded from the Canadian mainstream for so long means they will probably be ready to embrace their new online communities with considerable zeal. Finally, somebody to agree with other than Don Cherry. And finally a tool the little guy can use to bite back when institutional authority (government, banks, celebrities) gets caught doing something stupid. Retirement will afford plenty of time for the Disengaged Darwinists to plot non-violent—but noisy and delicious—revenge.

If the Disengaged Darwinists were slow to appreciate the possibilities new technologies presented for people like them, the Connected Enthusiasts recognized those possibilities instantly. Indeed, the Connected Enthusiasts have been waiting their whole lives for Facebook, Twitter, MySpace, email, smartphones, blogs, webcams, and Skype—and they're delighted that the world of technology has finally caught up with their lust for emotional connection and rapid communication.

In their enthusiasm for the opportunities new technology offers, the Connected Enthusiasts beat the rest of the Boomers by a mile. And this tribe's excitement is only growing over time: since 1992, the Connected Enthusiasts' sense of optimism and curiosity about technology has increased more than any other tribe's. (Disengaged Darwinists have grown more since 2001— which is a sign of the reluctant Darwinists finally beginning to catch up. The Connected Enthusiasts are much more technologically engaged today and have been growing steadily on this front for close to two decades.)

Like everyone else, the Connected Enthusiasts had to navigate a learning curve as they figured out the uses—and perils—of emerging technologies. But with each step they took the rewards were obvious, and their motivation to try new things grew even stronger. The curious Connected Enthusiasts were happy to spend a little time fiddling at the keyboard if it meant they could keep in closer touch with family and friends, plan trips, shop online, and simply have new experiences—like instant messaging with a child away at university or using a webcam for the first time. The Connected Enthusiasts are the kind of parents kids complain about: their kids invite them to join Facebook so they can swap a few photos. "Okay, I'll try it," the parents gamely say. Within a week, the Connected Enthusiast parent has over nine thousand friends and the top score worldwide on Farmville; the kids don't know where to hide.

Today's online and communications technology is sometimes described in fairly utopian terms: we're told these new tools will enable us to connect more often with people we love, pursue our hobbies and explore our creativity, find the products that match our tastes and needs, express ourselves, and so on. The Connected Enthusiasts are the Boomer tribe for whom this dreamy vision most closely resembles reality. This isn't because the Connected Enthusiasts are the computer and media whizzes of their generation (although they're curious enough to explore the features of the things they buy). It's because the Connected Enthusiasts were bursting with interests, relationships, questions, and ideas before all this technology came along; when tools like social-networking platforms and ingenious smartphones finally arrived, they fit perfectly into—and became powerful enablers of—the Connected Enthusiasts' modus vivendi. Their forebears had to be content with social institutions and organizations like church groups, service clubs, and assorted associations to unite them with kindred spirits. Technology lets Connected Enthusiasts make connectivity a 24/7 romance, not just on Tuesday evenings and Sunday mornings, or at the annual convention.

Consider this tribe's strongest values. First, they actively pursue powerful emotional experiences, believe in introspection and empathy, and delight in interacting with people different from themselves. Social media and communications technologies let them nurture relationships with those they know, and give them access to an even wider web of interesting individuals. Second, the Connected Enthusiasts also score high on a range of values associated with self-expression and creativity. When a computer manufacturer tells them that with the software on their new machine they'll be able to make a digital slide show of their trip to Mexico—with mariachi music!—or even make the feature-length film they've been waiting to spill forth, the Connected Enthusiasts tingle with anticipation. (They might not get around to the film, but they'll certainly churn out some fun slide shows and home videos of parties, vacations, and special occasions. And they will delight in sharing their creations online.) Third, this is a tribe of enthusiastic—but increasingly careful—

consumers. These Canadians love that the Internet enables them to find new products and small, quirky producers; they also appreciate that it enables them to do in-depth research about purchases they're excited about, like a camera or a kitchen gadget. Research is anticipation, and anticipation is half the fun. In short, the Connected Enthusiasts' orientations to social life, creativity, and shopping make them perfect candidates for many of the tools that have become available over the last fifteen years or so. It's little wonder that this tribe's *Enthusiasm for Technology* continues to grow.

The one thing that gives Connected Enthusiasts pause when they consider how quickly communications technology is pervading their lives is the matter of privacy. Although this tribe is the most enthusiastic about the positive possibilities of new technology, it's also the most anxious about all the personal data that governments and corporations hold about ordinary people—not to mention all the information about family, friends, home, and lifestyle they voluntarily post to the web. Because they're naturally experimental and open to change, the Connected Enthusiasts are prone to jumping into new experiences with both feet. Some members of this tribe (like many Canadians of all ages) may have created extensive online photo albums and later realized with a sinking feeling how much personal information they've made public.

The Connected Enthusiasts are congenital networkers; just as they like to cultivate relationships with a great number of people, they also want to form relationships with the businesses from which they buy products and services. But much as they enjoy learning from and communicating with businesses they like, the Connected Enthusiasts are extremely wary of having their information stored in some huge corporate database. This tribe is the most likely of the four to say that if they had a choice, they wouldn't allow databanks to store information about them: six in ten Connected Enthusiasts (59 percent) feel strongly about this position, compared to roughly four in ten, give or take a few points (36 to 42 percent), among all the other Boomer tribes.

Like the Connected Enthusiasts, the Autonomous Rebels have relatively high levels of educational attainment, are affluent enough to afford the latest gadgets, and tend to be fairly engaged with the world around them. (They're tied with the Connected Enthusiasts for the Boomer tribe most likely to report an intention to vote, for instance.) But this tribe, despite its history of seamless adaptability to change, expresses relatively little excitement about new technology. Why?

It's not that Autonomous Rebels are overwhelmed or baffled by the pace of technological change; with their predominantly professional careers, these Boomers juggle laptops and smartphones with the best of them. Indeed, the Autonomous Rebels have the lowest score of the four tribes on the value

Technological Anxiety. Autonomous Rebels are the least likely of all Boomers to agree that "new technologies are causing more problems than they're solving"; just a third of them (32 percent) support this statement.

Autonomous Rebels have the wherewithal to navigate technological change—and accept that new tools and gadgets get a lot of good work done—but they simply don't feel a sense of excitement about the next slick release from Apple or the latest social-networking platform. This lukewarm attitude toward developments in consumer technology likely stems from the fact that Autonomous Rebels have relatively little interest in many of the activities that thrill Connected Enthusiasts. Autonomous Rebels are less sociable than the Connected Enthusiasts. (They're the most likely to say they anticipate spending a lot of time with friends when they retire; however, this may be driven not by a stronger-than-average appetite for company but by their high divorce rates and the fact that they're most likely of all Boomers to live alone.) The Autonomous Rebels also care little about shopping, whether online or in the flesh: this tribe scores much lower than the Connected Enthusiasts on a whole range of consumption-oriented values. Finally, the experience-seeking zeal that leads Connected Enthusiasts to try new things online—simply for the sake of trying them—is absent from the Autonomous Rebel psyche.

This focused tribe (whose members are taking themselves

more seriously with age) doesn't care to poke around online and see where the links lead. Autonomous Rebels are more likely to use the Internet as a tool for research and planning—and leave the multimedia jamboree to their kids (and the Connected Enthusiasts, of course). In other words, just as the Connected Enthusiasts' excitement about new technology isn't about technology per se but about the activities they love (socializing, shopping, exploring, and so on), the Autonomous Rebels' relative lack of enthusiasm about new devices is rooted in the fact that the Internet, cellphones, and other digital tools are handy but not life-altering. This tribe would rather read a book, cook a meal, or watch a good movie than send a tweet. Digital devices are essential tools for most Autonomous Rebels—and an integrated part of their lives—but not something they feel impassioned about. They have the same utilitarian attitude toward their cars, which are just appliances to get them from A to B, not symbols of their masculinity, femininity, family role, or personal style.

The Autonomous Rebels, with their loner streaks, also sometimes feel bombarded by technology and the sense of always being "connected." During their careers, they've gone from workdays that contained perhaps ten phone calls to days (and nights) filled with hundreds of emails—plus all the effort required to find information on the web for work, play, kids, and the minutiae of daily life. Scoring above average on the value *Need for Escape*, the Autonomous Rebels are increasingly aware of their need to simply turn off once in a while.

There's another reason for the Autonomous Rebels' reluctance to make a joyful noise about the wonders of the digital age. This tribe feels skeptical about the promises of science and technology. Autonomous Rebels doubt that science will really be able to solve as many problems as we expect. For instance, with their high scores on *Primacy of Environmental Protection*—a value that holds that protecting the planet has to be a top priority for human beings, even at the expense of economic growth—the Autonomous Rebels are probably doubtful that scientific innovation alone can save us from our own carbon-spewing folly. Such reservations certainly haven't caused the Autonomous Rebels to reject new devices or hide from the online developments that are so obviously reshaping society. This tribe is too smart to go Luddite. But skepticism about whether science and technology can really fix the world might go hand in hand with their skepticism about whether consumer technology can fix their own lives (schedules, relationships, productivity, communication, and so on). Just as with their health, Autonomous Rebels believe that the moral, ethical, and intellectual choices that people make are the real keys to outcomes—not the technological or pharmaceutical aides they happen to have on hand at their particular moment in history. Technological progress produces both good and ill—but its most consistent output, say the Autonomous Rebels, is unintended consequences.

Finally, in considering the Autonomous Rebels' outlook on technology or any other topic, it's important to remember the "Rebel" side of their mental posture. Although many Autonomous Rebels have come to positions of power, this group maintains a good dose of its distrust of the rich and powerful. The Autonomous Rebels score higher than any other tribe on the value *Skepticism Toward Big Business*, although the Disengaged Darwinists are not far behind. (If the Disengaged Darwinists fall asleep at night grinding their teeth about the neutering of their culture, the Autonomous Rebels count the sheep that have been slaughtered by Wall Street, Bernie Madoff, bonus-fattened bank presidents, and overpriced consultants milking the public purse.) And since big business is rolling out many of the empowering tools that ordinary people supposedly are using to take over the world, the Autonomous Rebels, who've always been contrary souls, might feel that some of the excitement about new technology is just so much noise about the latest, flashiest toys in the marketplace. In this worldview, Bill Gates is a greedy monopolist before he's a world-saving innovator, and Steve Jobs uses a countercultural posture for the most unctuously self-serving ends.

In the summer of 2009, customers who had purchased George Orwell titles for their Kindles from Amazon.com were dismayed to find that Amazon had remotely deleted these volumes from their devices because of a copyright problem. Amazon refunded the users' accounts for the cost of the books, but some online commentators—notably Hugh D'Andrade of the Electronic Frontier Foundation—pointed out that if a bricks-and-mortar bookseller came to your house at night, took books off your shelves, and left the appropriate amount of money on your kitchen table, there would be hell to pay. Naturally, this story was made all the more striking because of the author of the books in question. In Orwell's *1984*, after all, the state seizes problematic books and sends them down an incineration chute called "the memory hole."

When Autonomous Rebels hear stories like this—and all the others that emerge from the American economy and the Canadian bureaucracy—they can only sigh, "Plus ça change." Powerful interests will find ways to control whatever is most valuable, they reason. It's nice to think that the democratizing power of the Internet will change everything, but most likely it will just set our existing foibles against a new backdrop.

As the Disengaged Darwinists, Connected Enthusiasts, and Autonomous Rebels demonstrate, most Baby Boomers have become at least comfortable, and even passionate, about new technology since the Internet has become mainstream and gadgets have become more intuitive. The exception to this trend is the Anxious Communitarian tribe, where fear and anxiety about technology remain widespread—and have actually grown slightly over time. The Anxious Communitarians feel overwhelmed by many aspects of life: they're time-stressed, worried about their finances, and fearful about crime, illness, and everything else the nightly news tells us might get us if we're not careful.

The Anxious Communitarians' generalized fearfulness is very much in evidence when we look at their feelings about technology. This tribe is about average in its enthusiasm for new technology's possibilities, but by far the most likely to have a sneaking sense that technology is creating more problems than it solves. This sentiment is surely connected not only to the Anxious Communitarians' fearfulness, but also to their high scores on the value *Aversion to Complexity in Life*: this overwhelmed tribe is looking for simplicity—and when gadgets promise to make things easier and then implode, the Anxious Communitarians are tempted to give up and join the Amish.

These Boomers' world-gone-mad feeling about new technology has more to do with their frustrations about consumer technology—computer crashes, dropped cellphone calls, viruses, spam—than with any sweeping skepticism about human progress at large. Indeed, Anxious Communitarians are up there with the Connected Enthusiasts in their far-above-average belief that science and technology are capable of solving the most urgent problems facing humanity—from pandemics and food shortages to climate change.

The fear (of things going wrong) and faith (in scientists and "experts") that coexist in the Anxious Communitarians' attitudes toward technology are part of a larger pattern. Anxious Communitarians may be the most afraid of illness, but they're also the most confident that doctors know how to make things right. They're the most likely to believe in hell, and the most likely to believe in protective forces like angels and miracles. Fear and deference go hand in hand for these Baby Boomers, who see the world as a dangerous place and trust strong leaders to help society navigate the risks of life: doctors manage illness; nerds (and big corporations like Microsoft) protect us from viruses and online scammers; mutual fund managers shield us from the vagaries of the stock market; police protect us from bad guys. For every threat, Anxious Communitarians hope to find some trustworthy authority figure to protect them. This tribe's attitudes toward technology are part of a larger mental posture. The Anxious Communitarians' high scores on the value *Cynicism* reflect the sense that leaders too often let them down—but they keep holding on for a hero.

One reason why Anxious Communitarians are moderately open to technological change—despite their worry about the pace of that change—is that some technologies offer comforting security features to them and their families. Many Anxious Communitarians now shudder to think of the days when they had to drive without a phone in the car. GPS devices offer protection against wrong turns into dangerous territory. Technologies like OnStar promise that they will never find themselves alone in an accident, carjacking, or some other nightmare scenario. Home security systems offer similar comfort.

Although not to the same extent as the Connected Enthusiasts, Anxious Communitarians are decidedly social animals. They describe family as their top priority, and they feel responsible for keeping in touch with relatives near and far. Anxious Communitarian parents were quick to buy their kids cellphones so the kids could call home and, of course, so the mother ship could keep track of them. But with regard to social media and other new frontiers the Connected Enthusiasts are exploring, the Anxious Communitarians take a pass. Indeed, when we ask Boomers how frequently they visit social media sites like Facebook and LinkedIn—as well as other popular online hubs like Wikipedia and YouTube—Anxious Communitarians are not only the least likely to visit frequently, they're almost invariably the most likely to reply "don't know/not applicable" to the question, which probably indicates that they've never even heard of some of these sites.

The Anxious Communitarians may not be the most savvy tech consumers in the marketplace, but they know a sexy gadget when they see one. This tribe is home to the most enthusiastic consumers in the Baby Boom generation. They delight in buying new things, and report that the way things look makes a huge difference when they're considering a purchase. This tribe is likely to be attracted by colour variations and superficial bells and whistles that don't add complexity to a device but do add a little sizzle, attracting compliments from friends and relatives.

Overall, we find Baby Boomers more or less at ease with new technologies. The Autonomous Rebels know what they're doing but try to keep gadgets and "the cloud" at arm's length. The Connected Enthusiasts experience ubiquitous connectivity as a warm social bath. The Disengaged Darwinists were wary at first but are finding their feet—and their voices—online. The Anxious Communitarians feel overwhelmed but will probably find ways to manage their anxiety and at least maintain a baseline rate of technological adoption so they can continue to connect with the social circles (especially family) that anchor their identity.

The consistent early adopters in this segment are likely to be the Connected Enthusiasts. Not only is this tribe naturally exploratory and more enthusiastic about consumption than the Autonomous Rebels, but it holds the largest proportion of entrepreneurs and small business owners. If a gadget looks as though it might help them work better or have more fun, the Connected Enthusiasts are likely to give it a try. Moreover, the Connected Enthusiasts score high on *Consumption Evangelism*, saying that when they find a product or service that works, they delight in spreading the word.

But the other tribes shouldn't be discounted as potential fans of new devices. Particularly as Boomers age, sheer pragmatism will probably become more powerful in their consumption decisions. For instance, although robust data are hard to come by, some online surveys and anecdotal evidence suggest that a disproportionate number of electronic readers such as the Kindle, eReader, and Kobo are being purchased by older readers who appreciate the fact that they can enlarge the text. Similarly, older readers with arthritis reportedly find it easier to push a button than to physically turn a page. In these cases, physical circumstances appear to drive early adoption of electronic readers even among a population (seniors) that might otherwise have been inclined to give the whole product category a pass. Of course, for some of these readers it might have taken a Connected Enthusiast friend, spouse, or child to convince them to try the device. One can imagine a Disengaged Darwinist burning through a detective novel in large print on a Kindle purchased for him by his son and exclaiming, "You were right: this stupid contraption is terrific."

five

They Still Have a Dream or Two: Politics and Idealism

"Ask not what you can do for your country, but what your country can do for you."
—How Canadian Baby Boomers interpreted President Kennedy's famous inaugural aphorism, 1961

T he political views for which Baby Boomers are best known—and for which they're both loved and reviled, depending on the constituency—are progressive ones. In the United States, the words "Boomer politics" bring to mind feminism à la Gloria Steinem, civil rights à la Martin Luther King, Jr., and peace activism à la John Lennon and Yoko Ono. (None of these people were Boomers, but all were Boomer icons.) In Canada, for the early Boomers at least, Boomer politics meant Trudeaumania: a powerful attraction to the dashing, perfectly bilingual intellectual who took post–Expo 67 Canada by storm in 1968—the first federal election in which I and my postwar peers voted, since the voting age then was twenty-one.

Although Trudeau resonates as a Canadian icon for me today, I wasn't, in fact, a Trudeaumaniac in 1968. Indeed, I joined the Progressive Conservative club at Queen's University in 1965, having been inspired by philosopher George Grant's nationalist tract *Lament for a Nation*. My memorable political moment from that period was not sniffing the rose in the prime minister's lapel, but accompanying Conservative leader Robert Stanfield to a performance of the musical *Hair* at Toronto's Royal Alexandra Theatre in 1970. Believe it or not, I was recruited to enhance Bob Stanfield's image; party staffers thought that if I and my date (a friend of my girlfriend, who herself refused to come) were seen entering the theatre with our fearless leader, he might appear slightly more youthful and hip despite his baldness and unerringly dour demeanour.

For Boomers who came of age after Trudeaumania had died down, politics was a combination of state activism, increasing social liberalism, and a growing realization that Canada was distinct from the United States and developing its own narrative. This sense of distinctness was manifest, for instance, in the

Canadian literature of the 1970s, when (slightly pre–Baby Boom) writers such as Margaret Atwood, Dennis Lee, Leonard Cohen, Mordecai Richler, and Gwendolyn MacEwen were, with varying degrees of self-consciousness, carving out a new literary identity for Canada—separate from the British motherland and the American behemoth next door.

If one of the key characteristics of American Boomers was wondering whether their country was always right—resisting the war in Vietnam, holding President Nixon to account for Watergate, questioning what they saw as the excesses of the Cold War—then one of the key characteristics of Canadian Boomers was questioning whether their country was really as trivial and vacant as many Canadians seemed to assume.

Most commentators who look at the Baby Boomers through a political lens see this generation as a watershed cohort—either for better or for worse. Some, like Leonard Steinhorn in his book *The Greater Generation*, argue that the Baby Boomers practically invented civilization. Boomer-centric thinking often seems to concede that the Greeks dreamed up democracy before we came along and the Magna Carta made a few waves in 1215, but every good and just aspect of our contemporary political culture was wrought (or at least advanced) by the Boomers: gender equality, racial equality, diminished homophobia, and so on. This analysis ignores the fact that many heroes of the Baby Boom generation were not themselves Baby Boomers:

John F. and Robert F. Kennedy; Martin Luther King, Jr.; Pierre Trudeau; Gloria Steinem; Bob Dylan—all were born before the end of World War II. (Similarly, in my list of CanLit stars above, one notable absence is Al Purdy, a patriarch of Canadian poetry who was born in 1918.) Slightly older than the Boomers, these figures catalyzed some of the generation's activist inclinations, but they're testament to the fact that social changes were afoot in North America due to a host of social and economic factors. The truth is, the Baby Boomers didn't invent progressive politics.

Since Steinhorn's *The Greater Generation*, American activist Tom Hayden (co-founder of the 1960s political group Students for a Democratic Society) has come out with a book entitled *The Long Sixties: From 1960 to Barack Obama*. If Steinhorn claims for the Boomers some of the achievements of the generation that preceded them, Hayden seems to lay claim to the idealism and political achievements of those who come after. For Hayden, the pro-Obama movement—including even its youngest members—is a subset of a Boomer-enabled movement toward a more civilized planet. Although certainly the Obama presidency would have been impossible without the civil rights movement, claiming Obama's election as a Boomer achievement seems a little simplistic, given that one of Barack Obama's many distinguishing features is that he was the first candidate with a post-Boomer outlook to get close to such a high office. Born in

1961, Obama is technically a Boomer according to our own definition (people born 1946 to 1965), but his approach to technology, his thinking about the American "culture wars," and plenty of intangibles made Obama's candidacy feel like a generational departure from the Bush–Kerry, Bush–Gore, and Clinton–Dole contests. Obama's post-Boomer status was perhaps most forcefully signalled by the fact that he was the first presidential candidate in many years who didn't have to account for his activities and whereabouts during Vietnam, not because he was too old (like Bob Dole in 1996) but because he was too young: he was fourteen years old when that war ended.

While progressives claim Boomers as their generation and trumpet their many enlightened causes and accomplishments, conservatives—especially those in the United States—look on Boomers as the source of nearly every (by their lights) pernicious cultural change of the last half-century: divorce rates, urban crime, fatherless children, uncritical tree-hugger environmentalism, ostentatious homosexuality, over-the-top anti-male feminism, multiculturalism without limits, bloated government, school curricula that underemphasize civics and basics and overemphasize sex education and mushy political correctness, diminished respect for history and the military, and a general flouting of authority, tradition, and religion. Although the axes of these debates are more sharply defined—and the tone is more acrimonious—south of the border, these currents are nevertheless at work in Canada.

But the binaries through which these debates are portrayed in the media often obscure not just the opinions that Canadians actually hold, but the range of values that might underpin those opinions.

Consider the debate, for instance, about whether Canada should follow France's lead and prohibit the wearing of the niqab and burka (the full face- and body-covering garments some Muslim women wear) in certain public places. Some Canadians favour the ban because of passionate secularism: they dislike overt displays of religious submission, including those associated with the religion in which they were raised. The same people might approve of many other accommodations for immigrants and members of minority groups: they're anti-religious but not xenophobic. Some Canadians, meanwhile, would likely favour the ban because of sheer xenophobia: they don't like to be confronted with such "foreign" practices in "their" country. For them, nuns in habits are okay; Muslims in niqabs are not. Although these two groups (the secularists and the xenophobes) might agree on the niqab and burka question, they'd surely disagree about a range of related issues, from immigration policy to minority rights. Throw in some feminists who see the niqab and burka as signs of women's oppression (within Muslim communities and beyond there's considerable debate about whether these veils signify submission to God or to men who claim to represent the divine will), and you have a very mixed bag of people who agree on a specific policy but probably wouldn't care to have dinner together.

On the other side of the debate are those who would oppose the niqab and burka ban because they are protective of the right of religious people to practise their faith without state interference. These people wouldn't want earthly authority to get in the way of the edicts of the Almighty. Another group might oppose the ban on feminist grounds, holding that the state has no business regulating women's clothing. Here again, those concerned with the rights of the religious and those concerned with the rights of female citizens might disagree on a range of issues connected to gender equality and the state's role in upholding that equality—but on the issue of the burka and niqab, they would agree. Our political positions are often complicated, and the stews of reason and emotion from which they arise can be even more complicated.

The disparate political orientations of the four Baby Boomer tribes show us that no single political outlook represents every member of this generation of 9.1 million Canadians. Plus, as the burka/niqab example reminds us, even on issues about which large proportions of Boomers superficially agree, the underlying ideals and orientations that give rise to their positions might vary widely.

The political outlook most often associated with Canadian Baby Boomers—egalitarianism, a robust role for government, environmentalism, and so on—can be seen as an amalgam of Connected Enthusiast feeling and Autonomous Rebel thinking. The Connected Enthusiasts strive to be open, compassionate, and responsible. Their sense of connectedness with other people—in their own communities and around the world—is both powerful and visceral. And many of their attitudes flow from their natural inclination toward curiosity and empathy.

The Autonomous Rebels, meanwhile, go out of their way to avoid having their opinions swayed by emotion. (They may sometimes delude themselves, as any human who insists on purely rational calculation runs the risk of doing.) If they give to charity, it's because an ethical principle is at stake—not because they saw a starving child in a television ad. Human civilization, they believe, is built on compassion, empathy, trust, and generosity that in the long run will be reciprocated, a social contract of the intelligent. If they accept homosexuality, it's because they've read, reflected, and determined that to do so is fair and appropriate. They have decided that same-sex relationships between consenting adults don't victimize anyone or lead to any immutable principles being broken (besides religious superstition); they support gay rights on principle, not because they fret about hurting someone's feelings. Together, the empathic politics of the Connected Enthusiasts and the more calculated egalitarianism of the Autonomous Rebels form the double helix that has been the DNA of Canadian politics over the past four decades.

The 1960s were an exciting and turbulent decade for Canada, but the politics of that decade were the products of the generation that preceded the Baby Boomers. The Baby Boomers were affected, and in some cases inspired, by the Quiet Revolution in Quebec, the beginnings of medicare, the Canada Pension Plan, the country's new flag and national anthem, and the liberalization during the 1960s of laws relating to divorce, abortion, and homosexuality. (Boomers were thrilled to have the state out of the bedrooms of the nation. "More room for us," we figured.) But Boomers themselves didn't make these changes. It was only in the 1970s that the Boomers reached the stage at which they began to exert some direct influence over the country's policies. Canada's abolition of the death penalty in 1976, the patriation of the Constitution in 1982, and during the past decade the legalization of same-sex marriage and the refusal to join George W. Bush's "coalition of the willing" in invading Iraq could more accurately be called products of values concentrated among Baby Boomers who think like the Autonomous Rebels and Connected Enthusiasts. These two tribes, like the niqab and burka critics and defenders discussed above, agree on a wide range of issues but come to their positions by different paths.

The Connected Enthusiasts and the Autonomous Rebels agree strongly, for instance, on issues of gender and family. Both tribes are ardent in their commitment to sexual equality.

Both are markedly more likely than the average Canadian to believe that men and women should have the same professional opportunities, share household duties, and have equal authority in the family. For instance, when presented with the statement "In a household where both partners are working, it is not right for the wife to earn more than the husband," 86 percent of Connected Enthusiasts and 88 percent of Autonomous Rebels register the strongest possible disagreement. (The Disengaged Darwinists score about 20 points lower on this measure, at 65 percent, and the Anxious Communitarians score lower still, at 51 percent.) In their youth, these tribes had downright utopian ideas about gender equality and believed that the deeply felt feminism of their generation would be powerful enough to right the lopsidedness of society. And Canada did make considerable progress during Boomers' early years of political engagement, having gender equality codified in the 1977 Human Rights Act and then in the Charter of Rights and Freedoms in 1982.

"In a household where both partners are working, it is not right for the wife to earn more than the husband."

	Autonomous Rebels	Connected Enthusiasts	Disengaged Darwinists	Anxious Communitarians
Strongly Disagree	88	86	65	51

Canada's feminists drew inspiration from the vocal movement south of the border, complete with charismatic figures like Gloria Steinem, Betty Freidan, and Kate Millett. (Indeed, in a perfectly Canadian flourish, three Montrealers— Nicole Brossard, Luce Guilbeault, and Margaret Wescott— produced a well-regarded social history of that movement in their 1977 documentary, *Some American Feminists*. As ever, Canadians were keeping a close eye on their American counterparts—and often cheering them from the sidelines.) But while Americans inspired Canadian feminists, less recognizable women from Canada, like Judy Rebick and Doris Anderson, made more progress north of the border than those brilliant Americans (who became household names) did in their country. The U.S. Equal Rights Amendment was defeated because of lack of support from the states, while at around the same time the Canadian Constitution enshrined the equality of men and women.

Older and wiser today, Connected Enthusiasts and Autonomous Rebels are likely to acknowledge that the work of promoting gender equality is more complicated than federal laws and the policies of human resources departments. People's assumptions and habits concerning gender are remarkably stubborn, as the data on who disproportionately runs corporate Canada and who continues to perform the bulk of household labour (guess!) remind us. Moreover, as evolutionary biology reveals more and more about the hard-wired differences between men and women, these Boomers might smile to think back on some of their youthful ideas about breaking down gender distinctions over time, building a superspecies of perfectly equal men and women with identical haircuts, like the J'naii on *Star Trek*. But no scientific study will convince the Connected Enthusiasts and Autonomous Rebels that full gender equality—in work, play, government, and the family—is not the goal Canadian society should be working toward. Maybe some ancient neural pattern makes men better at estimating the volume of a container or makes women better at perceiving the meaning of facial expressions—so what? Women can be scientists and CEOs and men can be nurturing parents and friends. The capacity of both sexes to perform a range of nontraditional activities—and embrace a range of non-traditional identities—is proven by millions of Canadians every day. Gender differences will persist (and in many cases bring us a lot of pleasure), but thoughtful social policy can help members of both sexes to be more fulfilled and more fully human.

Just as the idea of gender equality strikes the Connected Enthusiasts and Autonomous Rebels as self-evident, the idea that some Canadians relate to their gender differently—being attracted to people of the same sex, or simply dressing and behaving in ways most Elders would have found eccentric—elicits little more than a shrug from these two tribes. But the

Connected Enthusiasts and Autonomous Rebels arrive at their respective shrugs by different paths.

The Connected Enthusiasts are thrilled by the world's diversity. When they meet someone different from themselves, their immediate inclination is to reach out, understand, and connect. They might shake their heads at the gay pride parade, but not so much out of disapproval as out of a sense of amazement at the range of self-expression on display. Confronted by an Anxious Communitarian neighbour who says, "Those people just aren't like you and me," the Connected Enthusiast is likely to reply, "Isn't it wonderful?" If one of their children came out to them, the Connected Enthusiast's first reaction—after a hug—would be "Thank you for telling me." Relief that their relationship with their child was open and trustful enough to transmit this news would far outweigh any impulse to judge.

When Connected Enthusiasts hear their gay friends or even people on television talk about experiences of exclusion or discrimination, they're genuinely upset. They don't see why some tradition or abstract principle should prevent people from being kind to one another. Confronted with a social conservative's rationale for his or her condemnation of "the gays" as unnatural, the Connected Enthusiast will probably reply not with a point-by-point rebuttal but with people: "But have you met Kevin and Max? They're our neighbours and they're the nicest young men you could ever meet." The two "arguments" are incompatible, but the correctness of the Connected Enthusiasts' position is obvious to them—they can just feel it.

Not surprisingly, given that the Connected Enthusiasts are more religious than the other tribes, a portion of this tribe dislikes the idea that same-sex couples should enjoy the same political rights as straight couples. But overall, this tribe is more likely than average to accept nontraditional expressions of gender identity, including gay relationships. And considering this tribe's deep sociability and openness to difference, I suspect that even those who oppose same-sex marriage are extremely unlikely to rant on talk radio phone-ins or be less than friendly to gay acquaintances.

Autonomous Rebels are even more supportive of gay rights than their values cousins, the Connected Enthusiasts. But whereas the Connected Enthusiasts' acceptance of sexual diversity is rooted in their general openness toward others, the Autonomous Rebels' gay-positive outlook is rooted in their rejection of what they see as irrational prejudice; gays and lesbians are simply the latest minority to liberate themselves from the discrimination of the powerful majority. The Autonomous Rebels grew up questioning assumptions and authority— and their identities and self-images have coalesced around this practice. They love being the contrarians in the conversation. So when a social conservative says the state shouldn't sanction same-sex marriage, the Autonomous Rebel is likely to reply not

"Yes, it should," but rather "Why should the state sanction any marriage?"

Autonomous Rebels are especially likely to reject hostility toward homosexuality that they see as knee-jerk or rooted in anachronistic religious ideology. It's one thing to be strongly religious (Autonomous Rebels will disagree with you but acknowledge that your views cleave to some framework), but the idea that "being gay just isn't right" according to some long-dead authority (or living televangelist) holds no water with this tribe. Indeed, it's likely to incite a contrarian riposte: "Don't knock it till you've tried it" or something equally dismissive.

Confronted with children who come out of what used to be the closet, the Autonomous Rebels are less likely than the Connected Enthusiasts to see this as an opportunity for extensive emotional sharing. Instead, the Autonomous Rebels will probably congratulate their children on their bravery and encourage them to maintain that bravery as they move through other parts of their lives. "And don't let anyone make you feel bad," the Autonomous Rebels might counsel in closing. "You're smarter than any homophobic, dogma-spewing drone. You have been since you were a little kid—I could tell. Stick to your guns, but please don't shoot anybody!"

For the average Anxious Communitarian, and especially for the average Disengaged Darwinist, "sexual diversity" is an uncomfortable topic. Both tribes score below average on the value *Flexible Definition of the Family*, the Anxious Communitarians moderately and the Disengaged Darwinists more markedly. Coming out to a Disengaged Darwinist parent will be no easy task. Although many will grudgingly accept this news (and eventually even grudgingly accept their children's partners), some Disengaged Darwinists will likely so strongly reject homosexuality that they might go so far as to alienate their children rather than rethink their attitudes. A Vanier Institute study conducted by sociologist Reginald Bibby, for instance, found that although 77 percent of parents would accept their gay child, and 35 percent say they would even approve of this news, 23 percent of parents say they wouldn't accept a gay child.[1]

Women on average are more comfortable with sexual diversity, so while a Disengaged Darwinist mom might be able to live with the news that her child is gay, a Disengaged Darwinist dad would more likely feel that the kid is (perhaps deliberately) joining the opposing team: those who have no respect for the traditional virtues of Canadian society. The "opposing team" looks to some Disengaged Darwinists like a lot of simpering urbanites who don't like resource jobs ("not green"), don't like men who act like men ("too aggressive"), don't like boys who act like boys ("ADD"), don't like the armed forces that provide them with their freedom ("too violent"), and don't like big trucks ("too polluting")—until they need a real car to pull their

Minis and Priuses out of the ditch in the middle of winter. The Disengaged Darwinist might reflect that whereas most Canadians could once be relied on to appreciate heroes like Gordie Howe and Rocket Richard, today we're supposed to stand up and cheer for some kid skating around in a sequined jumpsuit. And now my kid wants to be one of them. To the most frustrated Disengaged Darwinists, "Dad, I'm gay" sounds like "Dad, I hate you and everything you stand for." The only response that seems appropriate to such a deep betrayal is "Well then don't call me 'Dad.' You're not my kid." Translation: "I can't have a gay kid—what would that say about me?"

Anxious Communitarians could never bring themselves to disown a child, no matter how baffled and dismayed they might be by a revelation of gayness. Although the Anxious Communitarians are traditional in many ways, and often uncomfortable with diversity, they're only slightly below average in their acceptance of homosexuality and nontraditional family models, presumably because gays and lesbians are the least of their worries. The Anxious Communitarians have so much to fear that the idea of some strangers having a baffling romance somewhere ranks low on their anxiety agenda.

A child who came out would elicit compassion from an Anxious Communitarian parent, but also a lot of sadness and concern. The Anxious Communitarian's first reaction would be to ask, "What did I do wrong?" Guilt over having "made" the child different—and potentially subject to ridicule or abuse—would be the dominant feeling in the Anxious Communitarian household for some time. Worry over the discrimination the child might suffer would also rank high on the emotional agenda. Embarrassment at having to tell neighbours and relatives, or stress about how to avoid this unpleasant revelation, would be further down the list. Finally, regret at the evaporation of hopes for grandchildren would weigh heavily. (And if anyone suggested to the Anxious Communitarian parent that lots of gay couples have children, they would throw up their hands and say, "Oh, it's all too complicated—I can't keep up.")

When most Canadians hear the word "diversity," it's not sexual diversity but ethnocultural diversity that first comes to mind. And in matters ethnocultural, as in matters sexual, the Connected Enthusiasts and Autonomous Rebels share some common ground, while the Anxious Communitarians and Disengaged Darwinists occupy other values territory.

Just as Connected Enthusiasts and Autonomous Rebels agree on sexual diversity, having come at the issues from different angles, they express similar attitudes toward ethnocultural diversity but for different reasons. Both tribes score very low on the value *Ethnic Intolerance*. They reject completely the idea that Canada's immigration policy should be based on ethnicity, for instance, and they express little enthusiasm for an aggressively assimilationist approach to the integration of newcomers. Their views on the nuances of multiculturalism might differ somewhat, but the Connected Enthusiasts and Autonomous Rebels share an attitude toward immigrants (including those with an ethnocultural heritage different from their own) that is fundamentally accepting.

But while they're equally open to ethnocultural diversity, these two tribes approach that diversity with markedly different sensibilities. The Connected Enthusiasts are always on the lookout for new relationships and experiences. They're off the charts on the value *Social Learning*, which measures the inclination to learn by interacting with people from a range of backgrounds. Connected Enthusiasts not only take a live-and-let-live approach to cultural diversity, but they also take a live-and-tell-me-all-about-it attitude. These Canadians are thrilled by the diversity of Canada's cities and are eager to hear everyone's stories of migration and intercultural experience. When the members of this tribe who have European heritage ask someone whose ethnicity is different from theirs, "Where are you from?" it's not a veiled suggestion that the other person is out of place; rather, it's an attempt to embark on an authentic exchange where each participant's stories are shared and common ground is quickly found.

When they go to a restaurant featuring cuisine from elsewhere in the world, Connected Enthusiasts are most likely to say, "Bring me the house specialty: whatever you recommend" or "What's on this menu that I wouldn't find anywhere else?" Although the Connected Enthusiasts are strongly inclined toward fair treatment for everyone, their openness to cultural diversity is not so much a matter of justice as it is of pleasure and curiosity. The Connected Enthusiasts feel lucky to live in one of the most diverse countries on earth. If you can't spend all your time exploring the wider world, there's plenty to explore in your own backyard. The idea that one would see the arrival of people from different parts of the world as an encroachment rather than an opportunity is Greek to these Boomers.

Autonomous Rebels agree that immigration is a boon to Canada and believe that everyone should be treated fairly. But they don't feel the Connected Enthusiasts' temptation to meet newcomers at the airport and hear their life's story. Autonomous Rebels score well below average on *Social Learning*. Often, a rejection of *Social Learning* and a sense of *Ethnic Intolerance* go hand in hand—but not for this tribe. The Autonomous Rebels are positive about immigration and comfortable with the idea of people from different backgrounds mixing, up to and including being married and having kids (they score high on the value *Cultural Fusion*). If one of their children came home with a partner of another ethnicity, members of this tribe would be much more focused on whether this prospective family member could handle Autonomous Rebel–style irony as a blood sport than on the latitude and longitude his or her grandparents hailed from. If this relationship led to marriage, the Autonomous Rebels would go along with whatever ceremonial gestures were deemed appropriate by the young couple. Although they'd be too polite to say it, the Autonomous Rebels would think the other family's rituals every bit as arbitrary and silly as their own. They would participate respectfully, however, knowing that gestures of respect are usually more important than any specific songs, dances, or oaths.

While the Autonomous Rebels and Connected Enthusiasts see themselves as citizens of the world (the former because they believe their rationality makes them immune to tribalism and prejudice, the latter because they feel attached to almost everyone), the Anxious Communitarians feel tightly connected to a small number of people whom they know extremely well and who are much like themselves. These Boomers say that family is a huge priority, and they're intent on having deep emotional connections with those close to them. The Anxious Communitarians are much less comfortable than are the Connected Enthusiasts with people who are different from them—people of diverse ethnicities, religions, sexual orientations, and even ages. (The Anxious Communitarians are less likely than Connected Enthusiasts to say they feel at ease with people much younger or much older than them.)

Feeling strongly connected to relatively small, homogeneous

groups—but disconnected from more dispersed communities—gives rise to a number of the Anxious Communitarians' political orientations. These Boomers feel a strong sense of Canadian identity, but unlike the Connected Enthusiasts, they also feel a sense of national superiority—and a desire to show other countries that Canada is better. Therefore, the Anxious Communitarians' above average scores on *Ethnic Intolerance* likely suggest that they don't like the idea of people from "inferior" countries coming to Canada. Far from seeing immigrants as offering valuable infusions of skills, energy, global experience, and youth, Anxious Communitarians are likely to see newcomers as a drag on Canadian society—people who, as the expressions go, "take our jobs," don't adapt to "Canadian norms and values," and "expect us to do things their way." Given this sense of separation from diverse others, the Anxious Communitarians are not at all keen on the idea of people of different ethnic backgrounds mixing romantically or producing children together.

Unlike the Anxious Communitarians, who feel alienated from the growing diversity of society but close to their families and immediate communities, the Disengaged Darwinists don't discriminate. These are equal-opportunity curmudgeons. The Disengaged Darwinists score way above average on *Ethnic Intolerance* and have the lowest scores on *Cultural Fusion*; of the four Boomer tribes, this is the most hostile to cultural difference. But immigrants and people of non-European heritage shouldn't take this hostility personally; Disengaged Darwinists don't think much of people like themselves either. These Boomers are the least likely to say they derive a lot of meaning from communing with their families, participating in their local communities, or simply connecting emotionally with those close to them.

What about minority ethnic groups within this Boomer cohort? Are they concentrated in any particular tribe? The short answer is they may be—but we can't generalize about these groups with much confidence. One reason for this is that they are diverse: Canada's minority ethnocultural communities hail from well over a hundred countries. As a result, we might be able to say that one tribe had the highest proportion of foreign-born Canadians, but most of the immigrants concentrated in that tribe might be Brits who've been here for over forty years. That would be a finding, but it wouldn't tell us much about the values of Boomers who belong to ethnocultural minorities. We could examine the tribes according to their ethnic composition, but because of the diversity of Canada's foreign-born population, it's difficult to capture members of ethnocultural minority groups in our sample in large enough numbers to allow us to analyze them robustly.

As I discussed in the Introduction, one in five Canadians (19 percent) is foreign-born, and an even higher proportion of Baby Boomers (23 percent) were born outside Canada. Most foreign-born Boomers immigrated early in life; over half arrived in Canada prior to 1980. And almost half of Boomer immigrants arrived from the United States or from source countries in Europe. That means they likely had considerably different experiences from today's immigrants arriving mainly from Asia, Africa, and Latin America. As a result, although our Boomer sample does contain many foreign-born respondents and a fair amount of ethnocultural diversity, it's difficult to generalize about the mental postures of minority groups or foreign-born Boomers, or to talk usefully about the social values tribes to which they belong. Significantly, however, the tribe that stands out as having the smallest proportion of foreign-born members, the Disengaged Darwinists, also reports the highest levels of *Ethnic Intolerance*.

While Connected Enthusiasts and Autonomous Rebels are more or less simpatico in their attitudes toward social issues like sexual diversity and multiculturalism, on economic issues these tribes disagree on some notable dimensions. Both are below average in expressing resignation to serious economic inequality. They generally believe that in a society as affluent as Canada there might be relative winners and losers—but there's no excuse for the "losers" being hungry or homeless, or for their children to be insurmountably disadvantaged. They believe that Canada should have a strong and reliable social safety net, and that everyone who has the ambition to get an education and improve their economic circumstances should be able to do so. Simply put, people with low incomes should have as much chance of raising good kids as their more affluent counterparts do.

From that shared starting point, however, the Connected Enthusiasts and the Anxious Communitarians begin to diverge. The Connected Enthusiasts feel a strong sense of personal responsibility to help others, while the Autonomous Rebels are a little more individualistic in their outlook. In their daily lives, Connected Enthusiasts are attracted to direct, personal modes of contributing to their communities (indeed, this is the highest-scoring tribe on the value *Community Involvement*). These are the Boomers who volunteer at a soup kitchen on Christmas Day, or visit people in nursing homes, sometimes with pets, children, or musical instruments in tow. They want to see and speak to the people they're reaching out to—they don't just want to send a cheque.

The Autonomous Rebels, by contrast, are likely to believe in the principle of helping others, and they will put their money where their mouth is by writing cheques to (thoroughly researched) charities, paying more for green (Bullfrog) power, and even voting themselves into higher tax bills in the name of a strong social safety net and sustainable medicare. But these Boomers feel little need for emotional connection with their struggling brethren. If you ever find yourself panhandling and you come across a Connected Enthusiast and an Autonomous Rebel, make a beeline for the former. The latter will give you a speech about "Band-Aid solutions" and explain that there's a web of United Way social service agencies (to which they donate generously each year) that will help you find your way to self-sufficiency. The Connected Enthusiast will nod in agreement—but will slip you a toonie or a fin before moving on.

Another factor that contributes to Connected Enthusiasts' sense of responsibility toward others is their powerful sense of belonging to a number of overlapping communities: their local community, their region, their country, and indeed the whole human species. Of the four Boomer tribes, the Connected Enthusiasts score highest on both *Canadian Identity* and *Regional Identity*, reporting that they feel their personal identities are closely tied to both their nationality and to the part of the country in which they live. (It's important to note that *Canadian Identity* isn't associated with chauvinistic nationalism; it simply gauges whether people *feel* Canadian. Our battery also measures values like the desire to demonstrate national superiority.) I've already noted this tribe's high scores on *Community Involvement*, a value that suggests a propensity to volunteer and get involved in neighbourhood issues. Finally, the Connected Enthusiasts outscore all their age peers on the value *Belonging to the Global Village*, which suggests a sense of emotional connectedness to people around the world—a sense that when a tsunami strikes

South Asia or an earthquake hits Haiti, those are *my people* suffering. They might not be my family or friends, or belong to my ethnic group or religion, but I know about them and therefore have an obligation to care and (if at all possible) act. The Connected Enthusiasts' attitude toward the world is a powerful expression of Marshall McLuhan's statement "Too many people know too much about each other [to ignore each other]. Our new [digital] environment compels commitment and participation. We have become irrevocably involved with, and responsible for, each other."[2] One can almost hear the Connected Enthusiasts sigh: "Tell me about it."

Just as they feel at least slightly responsible for every human being on earth, the Connected Enthusiasts tend to feel more than their share of duty toward the planet itself. This Boomer tribe is deeply worried about the ecosystem and will have a knee-jerk inclination toward any product that claims to reduce waste, diminish emissions, preserve the habitat of some endangered species of exotic frog, or otherwise tread lightly. Although the Connected Enthusiasts tend to be a reasonably savvy tribe, they're probably the most vulnerable to greenwashing simply because their concern for the environment—and their longing to live more sustainably—is so great.

While the Connected Enthusiasts, on a bad day, probably feel tied down like Gulliver by the thousand Lilliputian ropes of their feelings of attachment to others, the Disengaged Darwinists on a bad day probably feel isolated by their lack of sympathy for the rest of the world. Just as the Disengaged Darwinists have less patience for people of different ethnocultural backgrounds than their fellow Boomers do, this tribe's response to others' economic vulnerability tends to be a little more standoffish. ("Don't come crying to me," about a third of them shrug. "I've worked every day of my life and you should too.") This tribe has by far the lowest score on *New Social Responsibility*, a value that gauges Canadians' sense of personal responsibility for people living in poverty. Although the Disengaged Darwinists are reasonably secure financially, they are the most likely of the four tribes to insist that they have their hands full dealing with their own problems and have little time or energy to devote to other people's worries—whether those worries belong to the poor, to Aboriginal peoples in Canada, or to immigrants struggling to gain a foothold in the economy. As the accompanying chart shows, majorities in all four tribes say they feel a responsibility to those worse off than them, but there's a significant range here, with Connected Enthusiasts preferring this sentiment by a ratio of nine to one, and Disengaged Darwinists preferring it by a ratio of two to one.

"Which of these two options do you prefer?"

	Connected Enthusiasts	Autonomous Rebels	Anxious Communitarians	Disengaged Darwinists
"I feel I have a personal responsibility to help those worse off than me."	90	79	75	66
"I have enough trouble taking care of myself without worrying about the needs of the poor."	10	20	25	33

The Anxious Communitarians, whose financial circumstances are on average worse than those of the Disengaged Darwinists, fall a little closer to the Autonomous Rebels than to the Disengaged Darwinists: three-quarters say that whatever their own worries might be, they still feel they have a role to play in alleviating the difficulties of those who are even worse off. These Boomers might even find comfort in their ability to spare something for others, reasoning that their budgets may be tight but others are in really dire straits. "There but for the grace of God go I," they mutter as they drop a loonie into the Salvation Army urn. Whereas the Anxious Communitarians' sense of community obligation is driven primarily by emotion (sympathy and guilt), the Disengaged Darwinists, who pride themselves on rationality, actively resist these feelings, not wanting to be taken for a ride.

With regard to their political partisanship, the four Boomer tribes hold some surprises. For instance, although the Connected Enthusiasts' values related to diversity and income redistribution might make them sound passionately left-leaning, one-third (32 percent) of decided voters in this tribe say that if a federal election were held tomorrow they would vote Conservative. Similarly, while Disengaged Darwinists' devotion to tradition and tough individualism might make them seem like natural Conservatives, about a third of decided voters in this tribe express support for the Liberals, NDP, or Greens (37 percent combined). As anyone who has ever canvassed a neighbourhood on a political topic knows, the road from beliefs to the ballot box can be a convoluted one.

Disengaged Darwinists, who tend to be frustrated if not disgusted with the whole range of leadership options on offer, are the most likely (22 percent) of the four Boomer tribes to say they're undecided about whom to support in the next election. Anxious Communitarians are also indecisive, and this tribe has the highest proportion (9 percent) of people who say they will abstain. (One can picture the fretful and fearful Anxious Communitarians wringing their hands while surveying the candidates and deciding to stay home for fear of casting their ballot incorrectly.) In Quebec, the Disengaged Darwinists and Anxious Communitarians are likely to support nationalist candidates who claim that they will drive home the concerns of the distinct society to the self-serving blokes in Ottawa. Outside of Quebec, the Disengaged Darwinists tend to feel the strongest allegiance to the Conservative Party; Stephen Harper and his crew favour low taxes, small government, and law and order, and they don't seem to buy this tree-hugger hogwash about climate change. Sounds all right—assuming they're not lying, which after a few years in office they probably are, like all politicians, according to the Disengaged Darwinists. Among those Anxious Communitarians who have managed to make a choice, 37 percent favour the Conservatives, who seem strong and are tough on criminals, while a quarter (24 percent) still cleave to the Liberals, who once upon a time promised to take care of them when they got old or sick.

The Autonomous Rebels and Connected Enthusiasts tend to congregate disproportionately in Liberal and NDP territory— but like other Canadians, their support is split. Connected Enthusiasts are slightly less likely to support either the Liberals (22 percent) or NDP (22 percent) than the Conservatives (32 percent). In the case of the Autonomous Rebels, support for the Liberals (28 percent) exceeds support for the NDP (25 percent) and Conservatives (21 percent). Within these Boomer tribes, as within the Canadian population at large, federal politics remains a horse race—although the NDP horse fares better among Autonomous Rebels and Connected Enthusiasts than it does in the national race. Notably, contrarian Autonomous Rebels are the most likely of any Boomer tribe (13 percent) to support the Greens, a party that has perhaps benefited from the conclusion some in this tribe seem to have drawn that the Liberals are hypocrites and the NDP are anachronistic.

It's remarkable that despite their concern for the environment (on which the Conservatives have a less-than-aggressive record) and their shared belief in a relatively robust role for the state, about one in five in each of these two progressive Boomer tribes says they would support the Conservative Party if an election were held today. These people are likely a combination of holdovers from the party's Progressive Conservative days and those who were so disgusted by Liberal corruption and complacency that they jumped ship and decided to give the Conservatives a chance—especially if they live in long-neglected Western Canada or rural areas. The Canadian Conservatives of the early part of the millennium might not be the party of the Autonomous Rebels' and Connected Enthusiasts' dreams, but they seem to be competent managers who can even show occasional spasms of compassion, as in the case of the Haiti relief efforts. Might as well park my vote here, these Boomers reason, and wait patiently for Canada's Obama to come along.

In Canada, the Boomers heralded an era in which values emerged as an important ingredient of political results. But this being Canada, and not a real country (as Lucien Bouchard once famously observed), values often take a back seat to other forces.

Our concerns are riven by Quebec nationalism and competing regional economic interests and resentments. (For instance, as commentator Andrew Potter wrote with necessary—but impressive—pith on Twitter, "Quebec is Canada's bastion of lefty social justice, but its primary export to ROC [the rest of Canada] is conservatism.") Growing immigrant and Aboriginal constituencies are also exerting more force in the federal political landscape. Boomer values will continue to be important considerations for politicians for at least a couple more decades, but Boomers' immediate needs for health care and pensions may soon begin to displace this generation's higher-order collective aspirations (for Quebec independence, a multicultural utopia, a reformed Senate, or a severing of relations with the British monarchy). Just as comfort and affluence gave rise to the powerful assertion of Boomer values in the political sphere during the 1970s, discomfort and diminished financial means in later life might cause these values to recede somewhat from the public arena. One can imagine some of my decrepit cohort caning their way up Parliament Hill and bearing banners that read, "The personal mobility device is political" and "Don't trust anyone under sixty."

six

The Life Stage Formerly Known as Retirement

"Retirement at sixty-five is ridiculous.
When I was sixty-five I still had pimples."
—George Burns

The first state-run pension program for retired workers was set up in 1889 by German Chancellor Otto von Bismarck; Prussians became eligible for benefits at age seventy. An old-age pension was by no means intended as a universal entitlement: at the time it was invented, average life expectancy in Prussia was forty-five. Because so few people lived to age seventy, hardly anyone was expected to claim the new pension benefits.

Bismarck presumably figured that if you somehow managed to live that long, you'd likely be pretty decrepit and should probably just stay home until the Grim Reaper finally got around to knocking on your door.

In Canada, the original thinking about pensions was similar: retirement age was set at seventy in the 1920s, when life expectancy for a Canadian man was sixty and for a Canadian woman, sixty-two. It was a few more decades before our leaders changed the pension system such that benefits were scheduled to kick in, on average, before the worker's death. In 1951 the federal government introduced a means-tested pension plan from which workers could begin to draw benefits at age sixty-five; average life expectancy was sixty-eight and a half, which meant three and a half years of state-sponsored ease for Canadians as they approached the end of their lives. (This paragraph has been authored by a sixty-three-year-old male who thinks he has the body of a forty-year-old, the mind of a twenty-year-old, the spirit of a child, and a life expectancy close to infinity.)

The idea that nearly everyone should expect to retire is very recent. Just a couple of generations ago, it was assumed that you would work until you were physically incapable of doing so. If you needed to convalesce for a few months before actually dying, perhaps you could prevail upon a kind-hearted daughter to put you up. But the notion that every Canadian should have a few decades of robust good health at the end of life, to be filled not with economic productivity but with travel, tinkering, gardening, golf, reading, and lying around watching *I Love Lucy* reruns, is quite new.

It's interesting that Canada's national state-sponsored compassion protects the elderly, but we have no universal national program to assist the poor. Throughout much of the twentieth century, our economy evolved from agriculture to industry, our population moved from country to city, and our culture shifted from more communal to more individualistic values. Especially since the 1950s, aging parents have increasingly expected to live on their own until they need to be accommodated in residential care facilities geared to their needs. Between the 1950s and the 1980s, three-generation homes became less common in Canada; it was less often assumed that the elderly would move into their children's homes, at least not permanently. (Since the 80s, this trend has been partly reversed, a shift driven mainly by Asian immigrants who tend to be more open to three-generation households.) Moreover, many elderly people didn't aspire to a spare bedroom or granny suite in their children's homes; everyone's expectations were changing. All these trends contributed to the pressure on the government to provide pensions and state-sponsored nursing homes. Religious communities and some secular volunteer organizations still helped elderly people maintain their independence through Meals-on-Wheels and home-visitation programs. And families still cared for their oldest members according to an updated set of rules. The big change was that the state had stepped in to ensure universal access to at least a base level of care for the oldest members of society.

Today, the idea of retirement as a universal reward for a lifetime (or at least a few decades) of hard work, although relatively recent, might already be in decline. It reached its high-water mark a couple of decades ago when financial planners began encouraging their clients to dream of retiring in their fifties—and living into their nineties. The pitch went something like this: Put in a few good decades; work hard and invest wisely (our experts are standing by to help); and by fifty-five you and your spouse will be free as birds and holding hands on a beach somewhere. According to the television ads, the retiree's hair would by that stage be taking on a distinguished silver patina, and his biceps would still be perfectly capable of lifting his surfboard. And all this was before Viagra.

But that dreamy vision of a luxurious, decades-long retirement is, we're told, a thing of the past (if it ever really existed at all). Government pension plans throughout the rich world are beginning to crack under the pressure of increased demands on benefits and diminished contributions (because generations entering their prime working years are smaller than those beginning to draw their pensions). Personal retirement savings are pretty lean, even setting aside the financial crisis that exploded in late 2008, doing damage to Canadians' retirement cushions. About a third of all Canadians tell pollsters they have no retirement savings at all, and of the remaining two-thirds, only a minority believe they've saved enough to ensure that their retirement is comfortably independent. By way of hard data to back up this self-reported financial worry, journalists often remind us that household savings rates have declined dramatically from the early 1980s, when they were about 20 percent of annual disposable income, to under 5 percent today. (Saving used to be a top-of-mind priority for most Canadians; I remember my grandmother sending me letters when I was in university with a $5 bill tucked inside the envelope. After a lifetime of working in the general store, she and my grandfather had accumulated enough savings to live on, so they distributed generous chunks of their Old Age Security cheques to their children and grandchildren, often with helpful advice about how to use the funds, such as "Go buy yourself a steak. You're too thin.")

In our own surveys, we find that early Boomers (born 1946 to 1955) actually report levels of retirement savings similar to the Elders': 22 percent of early Boomers and 20 percent of Elders say they have $250,000 or more in retirement investments, while 38 percent and 34 percent in each group have less than $100,000. The thing that really differentiates early Boomers from the Elders is not their reluctance to save, but rather their willingness to take on debt. Early Boomers are twice as likely as Elders to have more than $50,000 in debt (21 percent versus 8 percent). Among early Boomers who are already retired, 22 percent have more than $50,000 in debt. This is the first generation to enter retirement owing large sums of money.

Despite these gloomy signs, at the end of 2009 experts advised us that Canada may be in reasonably good shape. According to a report[1] commissioned by the federal government and delivered by the Research Working Group on Retirement Income Adequacy, headed by distinguished University of Calgary economist Jack Mintz, nearly eight in ten Canadian households (78 percent) are saving enough to maintain about 90 percent of their current household consumption during retirement. As for retirement income, the general rule is that 70 percent of working income is sufficient for a comfortable retirement, and some say the number is even lower since a retiree's cost of living is much lower than a younger adult's (with kids, commuting costs, and the "convenience fees" that busy workers pay for things like takeout meals). As the Mintz report acknowledges, however, considerable variation occurs across households in how much "replacement" income is necessary. A household with an annual working income of $150,000 might be able to fund a very agreeable life with retirement income that replaced only 60 percent of that sum. But a household with an annual working income of $22,000, even if it achieved 90 percent replacement, would dip below the poverty line. According to the OECD, Canadians at all income levels tend to reach acceptable levels of income replacement—and those with low incomes sometimes even exceed income replacement levels of 100 percent, meaning their standard of living actually improves in old age.

Today Canada has one of the lowest rates of elder poverty in the world: 4.4 percent as compared to an OECD average of 13.3 percent. (Only Luxembourg, the Czech Republic, New Zealand, and the Netherlands have lower rates of elder poverty.) The OECD found that as of the mid-2000s, Canada's seniors trailed only their counterparts in France and Germany in the extent to which they were keeping up with the average disposable incomes of their society at large.[2]

Most Canadian seniors are currently eligible for Old Age Security and Canada Pension Plan funds, a base that is worth up to $17,413 per person aged sixty-five or older. Those with low incomes are eligible for Old Age Security and the Guaranteed Income Supplement, which is currently worth $14,033 per person. For a married couple, that means a base income in retirement—with no work at all, and no added support from private pensions or personal investments—of up to $34,827 or $28,067. These amounts are not altogether luxurious on their own, but for most Canadians they will cover many of the basics—so add one partner with a private pension plan through work, and/or a solid RRSP, and things begin to look fairly manageable. Clawbacks on Old Age Security don't kick in until the retiree's income from work or investments reaches $62,000 per year. Today, many Canadians find their lifestyle actually improves after retirement; the challenge for individuals (through work and savings) and for our governments is to maintain this relatively rosy picture as the Baby Boomer population ages.

Even if our public pension system continues to chug along, our personal savings don't totally fail us, and our debt loads remain manageable, it's clear that we're in a time of transition in terms of our individual and collective approaches to retirement. While we can quibble about adjustments to our savings patterns and investment vehicles, it's our lengthening lives that are the heart of the problem (and for more and more of us, longer life is indeed a "problem"). If we still died at sixty-five on average, pension funds would easily be able to support the few long-lifers among us. But the math we used decades ago simply doesn't hold up if the average age surges up to eighty, ninety, or a hundred. Is it practical, or even desirable, to fund a large cohort of people for thirty idle years between the day they retire and the day they die, especially given that the government will also be paying the cost of health care and other professionals who are needed to hold our hands as we drift across the River Styx? Although cutting retirement benefits is undoubtedly a possibility in the years to come (and in the financial turbulence of the last few years, some Canadians dependent on private sector pensions have already been given a taste of this bitter medicine), I suspect that changes in our health and in society's expectations about later life will simply lead us to work longer.

How do Canadian Baby Boomers feel about the prospect of giving up the dream of being silver-haired surfers enjoying Freedom 55? On the whole, not as cranky and grudging as one might have expected. Most Canadian Baby Boomers are open to continuing work in some form after their so-called retirement. Half of the Boomers (54 percent) say it's their intention to do at least some paid work after they retire, and an entrepreneurial (and presumably still energetic) 9 percent plan to finally start the small business they've been dreaming of during their years as working stiffs toiling for someone else. We also find considerable enthusiasm for post-retirement volunteerism, including volunteerism that leverages the Boomers' career backgrounds. The substantial majority of the Baby Boomer population intends to stay professionally engaged—whether for money, fun, satisfaction, or all of the above. Just 16 percent of this generation aspires to do "no work whatsoever" after they punch the clock at their full-time job for the last time.

Notably, although a large majority of Boomers hope to continue working after their retirement, only a very small proportion (8 percent) say they plan not to retire at all. It seems that retirement remains a desirable milestone for most Baby

Boomers. Although they may wish to maintain the intellectual stimulation, the social contact, and a reasonable proportion of the remuneration they currently derive from employment, the fact that Baby Boomers still plan to "be retired" suggests that they want to build a new relationship with their work—making their work look and feel different from what it was when they were in their thirties and forties. I suspect they want satisfaction from a job well done and the social stimulation of co-workers, but not the stress nor the irritants, like pushing meaningless paper and taking orders from some jerk. I for one intend never to retire and never again to work, work being defined as doing something for money that I don't want to do. God knows I'm not writing this book for the money; I'm doing it because it interests me and might interest others—and because it reminds me that my brain and I are staying alive.

As older workers want and need to keep working, a challenge for employers will be to find models that work for both businesses and employees. Some employers worry that employees in later life may not perform as well as younger people, or that they may not adapt as well to new technologies and new business circumstances. (*The Economist* wonders, on the other hand, whether older employees adapt to new technology with less ease because companies invest less in training them, assuming that they won't "get it" or will leave before the training investment has yielded a return.[3])

As questions about older workers' capabilities become increasingly important to businesses, researchers are beginning to deliver useful data. In the summer of 2009 two economists published a paper in the *American Economic Review* that called into question some common assumptions about older employees' efficacy. The researchers gave "senior" (over fifty) and "junior" (under thirty) workers a series of tasks.[4] The older participants were slightly less competitive overall, but the seniors outperformed the juniors in a number of tests and were more co-operative with one another. Perhaps most interestingly, the researchers found that teams with a mix of older and younger workers outperformed teams that included just one age group. This finding dovetails nicely with the argument of Axel Boersch-Supan at the Mannheim Research Institute for the Economics of Aging that in the modern economy, team productivity matters more than individual productivity—and teams whose members offer youthful vigour and the experience and judgment of age might be the best of all possible worlds.

Moreover, regardless of whether older workers are cognitively superior or inferior to the young upstarts in the next office or cube, they're uniquely positioned for at least one job: relating to customers their own age. McDonald's and Wal-Mart have reportedly already begun hiring older workers because customers find them friendly and helpful. Other firms that are not slinging burgers and household goods but addressing more age-specific issues have also begun to harness the power of front-line Boomer staff.

In January 2009, for instance, a financial services company that administered retirement savings plans hired a group of Baby Boomers to man their Denver call centre after quarterly statements went out: they knew they'd be receiving calls from a lot of terrified and angry older adults who were watching their retirement savings go up in smoke. The company's managers reasoned, wisely, that the last thing these clients wanted was some thirty-year-old telling them to calm down; a mature voice on the other end of the line was likely to be a comfort in itself, if only a small one.[5]

Human resources managers who are interested in employing "post-retirement" Boomers—both temporarily and part-time—have reason to be especially attentive to the needs and aspirations of Autonomous Rebels and Connected Enthusiasts, who are markedly more enthusiastic than the Disengaged Darwinists and Anxious Communitarians about flexing their professional muscles after their so-called retirement. The Connected Enthusiasts, in particular, can't begin to imagine their lives without work: just 5 percent plan to do no work whatsoever as they enter the next phase of their lives. The Connected Enthusiasts are the most likely to plan to do paid work during their retirement, and they're the most likely to plan to volunteer in an area that makes use of their professional expertise.

Connected Enthusiasts are also the most likely (at 13 percent) to say they hope to start their own small businesses after they retire. This entrepreneurial aspiration is not surprising, since members of this tribe are the most likely to already report that they own a small business or work for themselves. Presumably the Connected Enthusiasts who hope to start a business in retirement are among those who currently work for someone else. But perhaps a few of those who are already entrepreneurs hope to put their current business on autopilot and start a new shop based on their latest interests or idea for the next big thing. South of the border, although some of the most spectacular start-ups of the last decade have been headed by twentysomethings like Facebook's Mark Zuckerberg, entrepreneurial activity has actually been concentrated in older cohorts; between 1996 and 2007, the fifty-five to sixty-four age group had about a third more business start-ups than those aged twenty to thirty-four.[6]

The Connected Enthusiasts, as energetic and curious as ever, are horrified by the idea of a "restful" retirement. (These Boomers plan to rest when they're dead—if it turns out there's nothing better to do.) When asked to choose between two statements, "Retirement is a time to relax after a lifetime of hard work" versus "Retirement is a time to take on new pursuits and activities now that work obligations are lighter," the Connected Enthusiasts choose the latter statement by a ratio of nearly three to one (74 percent versus 24 percent).

	Connected Enthusiasts	Autonomous Rebels	Anxious Communitarians	Disenaged Darwinists
"Retirement is a time to relax after a lifetime of hard work."	24	29	45	47
"Retirement is a time to take on new pursuits and activities now that work obligations are lighter."	74	71	51	50

Since the Connected Enthusiasts are among the most affluent of the Baby Boomers—and are in line with the Boomer average in terms of their confidence about their retirement finances—their stated intention to continue working probably isn't driven by a financial imperative. The Connected Enthusiasts love activity, stimulation, feelings of accomplishment, and, above all, social interaction. Since their work may provide them with some or all of these benefits, the Connected Enthusiasts want to keep doing it for as long as they can. Given the choice between the statements "I would be happy to do some work [in retirement] to keep myself active, social, and mentally sharp" and "I will have spent my whole life working and would like to avoid work in retirement," the Connected Enthusiasts choose the first by a ratio of five to one (81 percent versus 16 percent).

At the other end of the spectrum are the Disengaged Darwinists, who are more than twice as likely (38 percent) as the

Connected Enthusiasts to agree that "I will have spent my whole life working and would like to avoid work in retirement." This is perhaps not unexpected, given that the Disengaged Darwinists are below average in saying that their job is important to them. This tribe's above-average likelihood of feeling perfunctory about their work is also evident in their thinking about post-retirement volunteerism. We asked Baby Boomers whether they hope to volunteer after they retire, and if so whether they would like that volunteer work to be in an area related to their professional lives or in another sphere entirely. Four in ten Disengaged Darwinists (43 percent) said they would be interested in volunteering in areas unrelated to the work they've done to make a living. This put them very close to the Boomer average (44 percent). By contrast, just a quarter of Disengaged Darwinists (25 percent) said they would be open to volunteering in their areas of professional expertise, which puts them behind the other Boomer tribes—especially the Connected Enthusiasts, 47 percent of whom hope to leverage their professional skills for the greater good in retirement. One can envision a Disengaged Darwinist wanting to coach a hockey team or volunteer in a community safety group, activities that, given their traditional values and male skew, would provide some postmaterial satisfaction after a lifetime of working just for the money.

"In retirement, would you like to volunteer in an area that uses your professional background?"

	Connected Enthusiasts	Anxious Communitarians	Autonomous Rebels	Disengaged Darwinists
Yes	47	33	30	25

When we ask Anxious Communitarians to describe their aspirations for retirement, the patterns we find are somewhat more surprising. These Boomers are about as likely (40 percent) as the Disengaged Darwinists to say they hope to avoid work after they retire since they will have spent their lives working. But despite wanting to run for the hills after their last day of work, the Anxious Communitarians are actually the most likely of the four Boomer tribes to say their job is a very important part of their lives. If work is so important, why would the Anxious Communitarians be so eager to leave it? I suspect that Anxious Communitarians' relationship to their work is informed by the same feelings that underlie their relationships with family: they feel comforted and affirmed by the sense that they're needed. At work, as at home, the Anxious Communitarians probably relish those rare moments when someone notices their contributions and says, "What would we ever do without you?" This tribe is also markedly more likely than other members of the cohort to work in sales and service; with their nurturing tendencies, the Anxious Communitarians would derive satisfaction from helping others find the products and support they need. At the same time, with high scores on *Time Stress* and a general sense of being overwhelmed by the complexity of the world around them (as evidenced by their high scores on *Aversion to Complexity* and *Technological Anxiety*), the Anxious Communitarians likely anticipate that it will be a relief to leave their jobs and no longer have to keep up with the pace of a business or the stresses and frustrations of some underfunded, overstretched public sector bureaucracy.

The Autonomous Rebels have in some ways been the material winners of the Baby Boom generation. Here we find the highest incomes and the highest proportions of people who describe themselves as "professionals." (The Connected Enthusiasts have somewhat lower incomes and are less likely to have professional occupations, but they certainly feel like winners; with their trades, skills, and high rates of entrepreneurialism, the Connected Enthusiasts take pride in their work. Those who run their own shops feel lucky to deal directly with the people who need their help.) But the Autonomous Rebels show signs of taking a "been there, done that" approach to their professional lives. This tribe is the least likely (22 percent) to say their work is very important to them, scoring even lower than the disillusioned Disengaged Darwinists (27 percent). Presumably the Disengaged Darwinists at least take old-fashioned pride in putting in an honest day, whereas the Autonomous Rebels too often have "Dilbert" moments that call into question the intelligence and integrity of their professional enterprises. Having watched business fads and organizational buzzwords come and go over the years, the Autonomous Rebels are starting to wonder how many more meetings they can sit through in which people say, "At the end of the day, going forward, the bottom line is that the only thing that can optimize these synergies is outside-the-box thinking. So get that on your radar screen if you have the bandwidth." When this sort of argot comes out, the Autonomous Rebels roll their eyes and drift back to the language of a simpler time, like when the Animals sang in 1965, "We gotta get outta this place."

These Autonomous Rebels will remain active in their retirement; they're below average in saying that they hope to do "no work whatsoever" after they retire. By a factor of nearly three to one they prefer the statement "Retirement is a time to take on new pursuits and activities now that work obligations are lighter" (71 percent) over "Retirement is a time to relax after a lifetime of hard work" (29 percent). (The Disengaged Darwinists, however, are about evenly split on this choice.) The Autonomous Rebels see plenty of opportunities to be active that don't involve work; for instance, they're the most likely to say they hope retirement will afford them time to explore exotic places in other parts of the world. Some Autonomous Rebels will try to combine these explorations with volunteer work, hammering boards on a Habitat for Humanity project somewhere or bringing their professional skills (medical, linguistic, creative, or infrastructural) to the challenges of another society.

Overseas volunteer-placement agencies like the Canadian Executive Service Organization (CESO) reach out to Boomers with reminders that they have plenty of time left to revive and live out the idealistic dreams of their youth. The fact that Boomers can make meaningful contributions to the greater good while enjoying fascinating travel and intercultural experiences makes for a powerful pitch. Two of my Boomer friends have turned on, tuned in, and dropped out of their Toronto day jobs and headed off to build a YMCA in the Caribbean—a dream come true for aging Autonomous Rebels looking for the next challenge in life. Another pair took a one-year sabbatical to work on a range of Habitat for Humanity projects around the world. After this interlude, they returned to their old jobs, which they loved, refreshed and ready to settle in for several more years of professional stimulation.

We asked Boomers a lot of serious questions in our battery on retirement. Will they have enough money? Will they have to work? Which investment vehicles are they using? Are they prepared to care for their ailing spouses? But we also wanted to give the Disengaged Darwinists, Anxious Communitarians, Connected Enthusiasts, and Autonomous Rebels a chance to have a little fun contemplating the next phase of life. We invited them to formulate a bucket list of experiences they'd like to have before they die—the term "bucket list" having been popularized by the 2007 movie of the same name starring Morgan Freeman and Jack Nicholson as two old codgers dying of cancer who embark on the mother of all road trips to do everything they'd always wanted to do before kicking the proverbial bucket.

Survey data can often be abstract, forcing individuals' responses into categories and percentages. But on this open-ended question of what Boomers want to do before they die, we received answers as intimate as "Stay in love" and as poignant as "Make up with my son."

Although naturally a great deal of variation occurred in each tribe, many of the answers were emblematic of the psychographic profile we found in the group. For instance, seven of the fatalistic Disengaged Darwinists said they hoped to win the lottery before they died; just one Autonomous Rebel said the same. Some members of every tribe wanted to visit a far-flung destination before the end (and many chose specific famous sites like the Great Wall of China), but the homebody Disengaged Darwinists were more likely to list sunny English-speaking locations like Australia and California, and several Anxious Communitarians named dramatic but accessible spots like Banff and the Grand Canyon. The Autonomous Rebels and Connected Enthusiasts more often chose European or Asian destinations.

Several Disengaged Darwinists wanted to show their love for their families by building them homes or cottages, a legacy of heroic traditionalism: Dad building the sturdy hearth where the family will assemble even after he's gone. One felt he could show his love without the bricks and mortar: his bucket-list item was "Continue being a good dad." Another, perhaps taking a DIY approach to his mid-life crisis, wanted to build himself a race car.

The Anxious Communitarians' love of home and family came through strongly in their answers to this question. More than one wanted to return to the town or even the very home where they were born. Others said that before they died they wanted to "see my son married" or "see my son happy with his own son." One eternal optimist in this segment hoped to see the Toronto Maple Leafs win the Stanley Cup. (Here's a sign that I report our data faithfully; if I were making this up, I would have attributed that wish to one of my Disengaged Darwinist relatives.) Another Anxious Communitarian (perhaps of the opposite sex, perhaps not) expressed a lofty hope of another kind: "Sleep with George Clooney."

Our Connected Enthusiasts showed their sense of adventure, their social appetites, and their idealism in describing their bucket-list dreams. Several wanted to learn one or more languages. Every travel destination on earth—and a few in outer space—came through with this tribe, but perhaps the most personal was the Connected Enthusiast who wanted to "visit the two children I sponsor." Many wanted to improve the world before they left it, some working on a small scale ("Help a young person succeed") and others working on a huge canvas ("End poverty in Canada"). And of course, some wanted to have fun, to see Cirque du Soleil and "faire le clown."[7]

The Autonomous Rebels had their own ambitions, many of them intellectual. Several of these Boomers wanted to publish novels before they died. One had a rather specific creative project in mind: "Finish my film on Ukrainian socialists in Canada." (Does everyone in Canada originally come from Winnipeg?) A second political junkie wanted to "be involved with a political think tank" while he or she could still think. Here again travel destinations were extremely diverse: Machu Picchu, the Amazon, safaris, China, Brazil. Other adventure destinations were closer to home: "Drop acid (safely)."

As you'll know if you've read this far, I tease my fellow Boomers relentlessly. But the answers that came through in this creative section of our survey reveal how diverse, interesting, lively, and even sometimes lovable these Canadians are. I find myself hoping they all have the retirement they are dreaming of.

The Anxious Communitarians will strive to make themselves useful to those they care about most, especially their families and close-knit communities—but they will also try to take a little more time for themselves after a lifetime of non-stop duty.

The Disengaged Darwinists will try to relax into hobbies and recreational activities, and along the way perhaps try to be role models for young people, who, they figure, see too much stupidity on television and around town and could use an infusion of common sense. The Autonomous Rebels will try to stay intellectually engaged and will probably have to force themselves to engage socially. If these natural loners can stay connected with a workplace or volunteer organization that maximizes opportunities to think and contribute while minimizing bureaucracy and useless chatter, they will be happy. The Connected Enthusiasts will be hopelessly overprogrammed and will love it; their "retirement" is likely to be busier and more stimulating than the peak of many people's careers, since they will effectively add a full-time job (in the form of learning, travelling, socializing, and personal projects) to their lives without really eliminating their "real" work. Eventually they will have to slow down the pace—but not yet.

seven

Religion, No Religion, and Meaning

"Imagine ..."

—John Lennon

When at the age of fourteen I declared to my father my intention to abandon the Catholic faith, he warned me of the pain and dismay this move would inflict on a higher power: my mother. My father's suggestion that I reconsider my plans to break with the church had little to do with my own spiritual health (privately he probably applauded his son's independent-mindedness) or prospects for an agreeable afterlife (a state of being he too doubted). My dad knew that if I stopped attending church, my mother would worry. And he didn't want his beloved wife to worry—at least not about her son's soul, when earthly concerns like mortgage and car payments were more pressing. If I left the church, my mother would worry some about the state of my character, and she would also worry (although this went unspoken) about her reputation as a good parent, a good Catholic mother.

For my parents' generation, religion, responsibility to the community, and overall respectability were very much entangled. Did the parish priest or the women at my mother's church care what she really believed about heaven and hell, angels, and the Eucharist? I suspect not. But turning up at mass every Sunday morning and volunteering for Catholic Women's League activities in the church basement mattered a lot. Keeping one's children in the fold mattered too. My mother's sense of mission about raising me and my brother as Good Catholic Boys, a former altar boy in my case, was perhaps made more intense because my father was Protestant. Their mixed marriage had caused a serious stir among Team Catholic and Team Protestant in Walkerton, Ontario, in 1945. She may have felt the need to compensate, to show that she kept as good a Catholic home as anyone else in the parish.

My own nascent sense of engagement with my community and my society had almost nothing to do with church. I cared about politics and current affairs, not religion. I wanted to read the *Toronto Star* every day and *Time* magazine every week. I wanted to start a UN club at my high school and try to decipher the Russian and American strategies during the Cuban Missile Crisis. I also enjoyed shaking things up a little: once, in grade ten and in a fit of national pride, I urged my school principal to replace "God Save the Queen" with "O Canada" during the morning announcements—long before the latter song became our official national anthem in 1980. In a classic Canadian compromise, the temperate administrator met me halfway: we agreed to alternate between the two. (This was the high-water mark of my political activism to date; I peaked politically at age sixteen.)

Two years earlier, twitching with curiosity about the world, I had asked our parish priest about an article I had read in *Time* that discussed overpopulation. Was it wise, I wondered, for the church to forbid contraception when Malthusian demographers were warning us that the earth would soon be completely overwhelmed by swarming humanity? In return, the priest asked me whether I thought God was stupid. In retrospect it seems obvious that this was a rhetorical question; that was less obvious when I was fourteen. Confused, I restated my question, inviting God's man in Rexdale (our family left Bruce County for better prospects in the Toronto outskirts in the late 1950s) to illuminate the reasoning of the Almighty. I was asked again, more firmly, whether I was accusing my Creator of stupidity. We were at an impasse, one of many where my church made me feel more and more like a pubescent version of the heretic Galileo, a suburban avatar of the Enlightenment in conflict with closed-minded religious orthodoxy. But instead of a telescope and a passion for astronomy, I had the newspaper and a passion for questions.

For my mother, like many Canadians of her generation, serving God and serving the community were a single endeavour. For a "social butterfly," helping at the church reinforced the social fabric of the neighbourhood, offered some support to the poor and the elderly, and generally expressed engagement with and care for others. It also seemed to be a natural extension of her work as a nurse. For me as a teenager, confronted with an irritable priest who saw questions about the world from a curious kid as inherently impious, involvement with the Holy Catholic Church seemed not only separate from but opposed to any real engagement with the world. The religious dogma I was being inculcated with seemed implausible, almost laughable. (Plenary indulgences, days off time served in purgatory in return for a few Hail Marys ... give me a break, I thought.) I couldn't believe that adults seriously believed this superstition, and I was even less convinced that the church was the best way to learn about the world, connect with other people, and contribute to my society, let alone hone my moral sensibilities.

I wasn't alone in deciding that religion wasn't the best vehicle for expressing my youthful idealism—or the best way to engage with other people in meaningful ways. Millions of Baby Boomers—whether they were interested in gender equality, the anti-war movement, environmentalism, gay rights, reproductive rights, or any number of other movements—had found meaning in principles and communities that religious institutions tended to reject. (A notable exception was the church-led civil rights movements in the United States, where religious belief and social justice were powerfully connected. But churches fighting Jim Crow in the American South were a long way from the religion middle-class white kids experienced in Canada.)

When leading-edge Baby Boomers abandoned religion and embraced the political movements of the 1960s, they made a break between religious belief and community involvement. There were ways of finding meaning, advancing worthy causes, and certainly of connecting with their communities that didn't involve the church. Baby Boomers found a range of new social outlets through which to express their values, and for many, their youthful break with religion became permanent. These Boomers chose rebellion and "revolution" over faith-based activism. Their idealism was secular, not religious.

Environics' values data show that Baby Boomers who were secular two decades ago largely remain so today. In 2008 Baby Boomers were the same age as the Elders were in 1992. We can assume that, having reached late middle age, these Boomers were beginning to confront more or less the same sense of urgency about existential issues as their parents were in 1992. But even in our most recent surveys, the Baby Boomers fail to show signs of flocking back to religion as they age, making amends for myriad religious transgressions and starting, as it were, to bone up for their finals. Pas du tout. Whereas Elders in 1992 were nearly three times as strong as the population at large on the value *Religiosity*, as of 2008 Baby Boomers were slightly less likely than the average Canadian to express strong religious faith. Notably, Boomers tend to diverge most sharply from Elders on the social (as opposed to the theological) dimensions of religious practice and belonging.

For instance, we asked Boomers and Elders about aspects of their spirituality they would like to pursue in retirement. Boomers are only slightly less likely (21 percent) than Elders (25 percent) to say they hope to explore their own personal spirituality. Boomers and Elders are about equally likely (4 percent versus 5 percent) to say they plan to spend time reading about different faiths, while Boomers are more likely (8 percent) than Elders (4 percent) to say they intend to devote some of their time in retirement to trying spiritual practices that fall outside of their own religious traditions. On the question of whether they hope to be involved in a religious *community*, however, one in five Elders (19 percent) names this as an aspiration, compared to just one in ten Boomers (10 percent of all Boomers, and

8 percent of "late Boomers" born between 1955 and 1965). Even among Boomers who aren't completely disengaged from spiritual pursuits, many prefer to find their own path instead of joining a congregation.

This social and ritual side of religion remains the biggest difference between Boomers and Elders. In terms of their actual belief in religious concepts like God and heaven, the two cohorts are quite similar: Boomers are only five points behind Elders (80 percent versus 85 percent) in saying they believe in God, four points behind in believing in heaven (63 percent versus 67 percent), and even with their parents' generation in reporting a belief in hell (37 percent in each case). Incidentally, Baby Boomers are considerably more likely to believe in supernatural concepts *not* sanctioned by traditional Judeo-Christian religions: 40 percent of Boomers say they believe in ghosts, for instance, compared to 20 percent of Elders. Both cohorts are exceeded in this regard by the post-Boomer generation: 51 percent of Canadians aged forty-three or younger believe in ghosts. Maybe the spectres of Baby Boomers like Mick Jagger and Keith Richards have convinced young Canadians that the undead walk among us. As for my own beliefs on this front, if Keith Richards outlives me, my post-corporeal spirit will take this as unequivocal proof that there is a God and that she has a wicked sense of humour.

The relative similarity of Boomer and Elder beliefs about major religious concepts suggests that it's not an altogether atheistic worldview that keeps Boomers out of religious communities, but something about the way these communities behave and organize themselves. Statistics Canada data lend some weight to the idea that non-belief isn't necessarily what keeps Boomers away from temple, mosque, synagogue, and above all church. A study released in 2006 found that although only about a third (32 percent) of Canadians attend church at least monthly,[1] about one in five Canadians (21 percent) engages only in private spiritual practice. That is, one in five Canadians prays, meditates, or reads sacred texts at home—but for some reason never darkens the door of a religious building. Any number of reasons—from illness to introversion—could be keeping these people away from religious organizations. But for some, it may be the way those organizations do business.

One of the most alienating behaviours of conservative religious communities for egalitarian Baby Boomers has been their reluctance to accept gender equality. Although mainline Protestant churches have made moves toward greater gender parity, the Catholic Church—still Canada's largest denomination—has remained steadfast in its insistence that women not be ordained as priests. Reform and Reconstructionist synagogues tend to espouse egalitarian ideals, but in Conservative and Orthodox Jewish communities, women are structurally excluded from important aspects of religious practice. In some communities, women don't "count" as congregants—so in Jewish prayers where ten people are needed to form a prayer group, or *minyan*, women can't be part of the tally. "I have had the extraordinary experience," political scientist Janice Stein wrote in an essay for the *Literary Review of Canada*, "of sitting in a chapel and watching the leader of prayers count the men in the room, his eyes sliding over me as he counted. For all intents and purposes, not only did I not count, I was invisible."[2] Stein acknowledges that in some other local congregations she would indeed "count" and that she could vote with her feet and move to one of those synagogues— but it's hard to believe that as a distinguished professor at the University of Toronto who commands immense respect in virtually any room she enters, she should have to.

Gender inequality exists to varying degrees in different quarters of Canada's other substantial religions—Islam, Sikhism, Buddhism, and Hinduism—but since these religions are practised predominantly by foreign-born Canadians, the dynamics of religious belonging are often different. The imperative for people to belong to religious groups is stronger when those groups provide either valuable cultural moorings or substantial material support (such as settlement assistance). If when I was fourteen my priest had been the linchpin of a minority community that provided essential support to me and my parents, I might not have posed such cheeky questions— or if I had, I might have found the "Father's" scolding harder to dismiss.

The fact that religious communities have moved more slowly than the population at large to embrace gender equality may underlie one of the patterns we find in Boomers' evolving attitudes toward religion. That Boomers rejected both religion and patriarchy at roughly the same time is no coincidence, because in the minds of many Boomers the two are the same. This is at least part of the reason why those among the Boomers who most vociferously rejected religion, Quebec Catholics, are exactly those Canadians who have the most difficulty accommodating the new "Other" in their midst, Muslims, and in particular Muslim women in hijabs, who eerily resemble the nuns who ruled their elementary schools in the 1940s and 50s. A few Quebecers with a penchant for alarmism worry that their fragile francophone enclave in North America is headed back to the religious future: Catholic past, secular present, Muslim future? Ooh la la!

Since 1992 Baby Boomers overall haven't grown stronger on the value *Religiosity*—they have continued to score much lower than Elders on this trend. But that apparently steady average score hides an interesting finding: since 1992 Baby Boomer men have remained quite stable in their views on religion, while Baby Boomer women have grown notably less attached to religious ideas and communities. Baby Boomers haven't become their parents in matters religious, but the men who were religious in the early 1990s are holding fast, whereas the Boomer women are exhibiting diminishing levels of interest in religiosity. For instance, in 1992, about four in ten Boomer women (39 percent) considered themselves to be members of a religious faith;[3] by 2008 that proportion had declined to 30 percent. Boomer women today are less likely than they were in the past to say that they hope to have a religious funeral, that their religious beliefs are important to them, and that it's important for children to have a religious education. Boomer men, by contrast, have remained stable or gotten stronger on each of these measures.

In my own experience growing up, it was the women—my mother and grandmothers—who were the most pious and observant, while the men assumed a perfunctory, even standoffish attitude toward church. Their attendance seemed intended to please their wives rather than God or earthly religious authorities. Boomers' more egalitarian relationships in a more secular age mean that spouses are likely to follow their own spiritual paths.

Religious patriarchy leaps out as one likely explanation for the divergent patterns we have seen between Boomer men's and women's approaches to religion since 1992. Boomer men on average tend to be very supportive of gender equality, but they probably find it easier than their wives, sisters, and daughters to overlook the biases and prejudices embedded in some religious communities; it's understandable that Boomer women may have a harder time turning the other cheek when they're treated as second-class citizens.

There's another possible reason for the growing gap between men's and women's acceptance of religion. If in the past religious communities acted as key sources of social connection, and if Boomers moved away from religion partly because they found other kinds of social sustenance, perhaps Boomer women are happier without religious communities because they're better than Boomer men are at finding and fostering social bonds. On average, our studies show women's values to be more extroverted and men's more introverted; Boomers fit this pattern. Not only are Boomer women more likely than men to say that their friends are a very important part of their life (35 percent versus 28 percent), but women seem to derive more satisfaction from almost every aspect of life than men do. When asked to state whether various things are "very important in my life," women score slightly higher on every dimension. Work, family, friends, hobbies—a greater proportion of women than men name all of these as important in their lives. Only on "faith or spiritual beliefs" do Boomer men and women score the same, with 29 percent in each group saying this part of their lives is very important to them. The fact that men are growing stronger on organized *Religiosity* while women grow weaker—even as both groups remain equally likely to say their spiritual beliefs are important to them—reminds us that there are many forms of spiritual engagement, both public and private.

Women's low scores on *Religiosity* aren't explained by a more indifferent attitude toward existential and spiritual issues: Boomer women are more likely (44 percent) than men (33 percent) to say they reflect regularly on the meaning of their lives, and more likely (50 percent versus 38 percent) to say that finding time to reflect on this existential question is very important to them. Women are more likely (24 percent versus 18 percent) to say it's very important to them to explore their own spirituality when they retire, and slightly more likely to say they plan to read about and even try certain elements of different spiritual traditions.

Oprah, that relentless entrepreneurial genius, has been attuned to the particularities of American Boomer women's quest for meaning for years. "O" has repeatedly hit the self-help sweet spot in offering her questing flock suggestions for reading, ritual, and community. Through her talk show, magazine, and web presence, Oprah has directed her (mostly female) devotees to a range of accessible spiritual thinkers who demand no particular allegiance or rule-following, but offer gentle, pragmatic advice about finding "spirit" in daily life. In 2008 she championed Dutch-born Canadian Eckhart Tolle, who promotes a Buddhism-flavoured approach that involves being "in the moment." Oprah also gets spiritual with a woman named Marianne Williamson, whose podcast on Oprah.com, "Miracle Thought," offers "an idea, a quote or an insight to help you miraculously navigate your day." Deepak Chopra is Oprah's mind-body-spirit guy, who says he offers insights on spirituality, sexuality, well-being, and peace—all drawn from science, including the surprising world of quantum mechanics! The church of Oprah will not appeal to every Baby Boomer woman—but the fact that the Oprah media empire is cultivating "spirit" among its advice-giving categories is significant.

When we look at the Boomer tribes' orientation to religion, we find that people's attitudes toward their inner lives vividly mirror their perspectives on the world around them. Those who are curious, open, and exploratory toward travel, food, and people different from themselves also tend to be curious, open, and exploratory toward seeking spiritual fulfillment. Those who feel most comfortable when surrounded by the familiar tend to stick to the script in their spiritual lives: they might practise the faith of their parents in a tepid way or reject it in an equally tepid way.

The Connected Enthusiasts, who are relentlessly engaged in every area of life, take the quest for meaning very seriously. These Boomers are most likely to say that their spiritual beliefs are very important to them (50 percent), and that they reflect frequently on the meaning of their lives (56 percent). For these Baby Boomers, religious and spiritual pursuits are opportunities for learning and self-discovery. The Connected Enthusiasts are the most likely of the four tribes to express enthusiasm for learning about different faiths, and trying spiritual practices that they didn't grow up with. (Since they're also the most likely to be serious about exercise and healthful living, it's a good bet that these are the Boomers who are buying the largest number of yoga mats, finding that soulful sustenance and stretching, physically and spiritually, go together rather well.)

Very often, commentary about religion and spirituality—particularly in the United States, but also in Canada—assumes a binary. On one side of this binary are people who are committed to a religion and practise that one faith deeply. On the other side are people who are ardently secular, rejecting all religion as hocus pocus. In this model, the more spiritually engaged you are, the more likely you are to cleave to a single set of ideas about God, ethics, death, and the good life. The spiritual orientation of the Connected Enthusiasts puts the lie to that simplistic picture of religious life in Canada: the Connected Enthusiasts are at once the most spiritually interested tribe *and* the most curious about a range of faith practices. These Boomers are seeking meaning and fulfillment in every area of life—from people to cultural experiences, travel, food, and ideas—and spirituality is an important part of the picture.

In traditional terms, the one tribe that barely edges out the Connected Enthusiasts in religiosity is the Anxious Communitarians. These security-seeking Boomers, who favour traditional ideas about gender and social roles, also express the highest levels of belief in a number of religious concepts, including God, heaven, and miracles. The Anxious Communitarians are the most likely of the four tribes to say they believe in Jesus (77 percent). And not surprisingly, these Boomers who thrive on fear and guilt in every area of life (from the environment to finances, food, and sexuality) are the only group in which nearly half (47 percent) believe in hell.

But despite their above-average levels of belief in these religious concepts, the Anxious Communitarians seem to derive little sense of personal sustenance from their spirituality. Just 30 percent say their faith or spiritual beliefs are very important in their lives. This is higher than the secular Autonomous Rebels and the indifferent Disengaged Darwinists—but nearly twenty points lower than the Connected Enthusiasts (50 percent), who seem to find considerable satisfaction in their curious, questioning approach to spiritual life.

Of the four Boomer tribes, it's the Anxious Communitarians whose relationship with religion most closely mirrors that of the Elders. The Anxious Communitarians are the most likely to say that belonging to a religious community is important to them; like their parents, these Boomers see social belonging and mutual support as a crucial aspect of religion. (The Connected Enthusiasts, by contrast, are powerfully spiritually engaged but see spirituality as more of a private quest for meaning than a matter of Sunday service, church bazaars, and bake sales.) And like the Elders, the Anxious Communitarians have little interest in exploring faith traditions other than the ones their ancestors cleaved to. In short, while the Connected Enthusiasts are spiritual explorers finding deep fulfillment in reinventing religion and spirituality on their own terms, the Anxious Communitarians are finding moderate fulfillment in upholding the old-time religious traditions (and belonging to the communities) embraced by their parents and grandparents. While the Anxious Communitarians might not be having transcendent spiritual experiences, they likely find comfort in communing with others like themselves, sharing rituals, and, of course, carrying out their duties as the glue of their families and communities (which might alleviate a little guilt).

Although their love of tradition leads many Anxious Communitarians to stick to their parents' faiths, some members of this tribe probably feel that they were abandoned by mainline Protestant churches such as the United and Anglican denominations—that today these are no longer the churches their parents would have recognized. Those who are dismayed by their old churches' efforts to somehow accommodate modernity (by moving toward greater gender equality and softening—if not outright rejecting—condemnations of homosexuality) may migrate to more conservative flocks, whether the Catholic Church or an Evangelical congregation. Indeed, in the autumn of 2009 the clever marketers at the Vatican made a bold move to draw disaffected Anglicans worldwide back into the Catholic fold: the Holy See created a new set of canon laws that would enable whole congregations of Anglicans to join the Catholic Church. Although the official purpose of the move was to heal the wounds created by the church schism five centuries ago, most observers acknowledged that it had more to do with welcoming Anglicans who were dismayed by the changes within their church, from the ordination of women priests in the 1970s to the election of an openly gay bishop in the United States in 2003.[4]

Anxious Communitarians are the Boomers who feel least in control of their lives and therefore may feel the greatest longing for some otherworldly consolation. The other Boomer tribes reject the threat of eternal damnation—a revolutionary move—and would rather focus on the ideas and behaviours that make sense to them here on earth. They generally prefer the carrot to the stick, the pursuit of both meaning and pleasure instead of the avoidance of punishment. In the lives of Anxious Communitarians, the concepts of duty and self-sacrifice remain powerful. As the realization dawns that their families' chronic underappreciation of their sacrifices may continue indefinitely, Anxious Communitarians are justified in hoping that they'll receive compensation for all their good deeds on some other plane. For the Anxious Communitarians, whose fatalistic values suggest they feel they can do little to change their lives, religion is solace. For Connected Enthusiasts, who believe that life is made good or bad by choices and attitude, religion is a means of improving life here and now—perhaps dramatically.

The Autonomous Rebels are the most ardently secular Boomer tribe. They are exceptionally skeptical about many of the religious concepts the Anxious Communitarians and Connected Enthusiasts find compelling. Most Autonomous Rebels, who pride themselves on clear, rational thinking, consider heaven a fantasy: 43 percent believe in life beyond the pearly gates, compared to 74 percent of Anxious Communitarians and 62 percent of Boomers overall. But Autonomous Rebels are even more likely to eschew that less-appealing fiction: hell. Just 21 percent of Autonomous Rebels believe in hell, and 28 percent believe in the devil. This means that at least 7 percent of Autonomous Rebels believe there is a devil who has no permanent infernal residence. Perhaps they think he walks among us in the form of their first husband or wife.

Although they're the most likely to reject religion and its institutional trappings, the Autonomous Rebels do express interest in some form of spiritual practice. They're second only to the Connected Enthusiasts in expressing an openness to trying spiritual practices other than those with which they were raised. (For many nominally or formerly Christian Autonomous Rebels, this will mean meditation, fasting, and yoga. For the male members of the tribe, it might mean crying at their father's funeral.) True to their autonomous natures, however, the Autonomous Rebels want nothing to do with religious communities; just 4 percent of this tribe say that belonging to a religious community is important to them—the lowest score of any group. If spirituality can mean reading a book, visiting an exotic location with a rich religious history, or breathing deeply while sitting on the floor at home, fine. If it means getting together with a bunch of other people for gooey conversation about love and understanding—or, worse, about God and His fiery punishments—the Autonomous Rebels want no part of it. Besides, when Autonomous Rebels look around the world, they see religion as a source of evil (the Taliban) rather than good, foolishness (Sarah Palin) rather than wisdom, and more often than not just a convenient rationale for killing other people and not losing any sleep over it. The fact that a Michigan-based company named Trijicon was discovered to have been inscribing references to Bible verses on the sights of rifles it supplied to the U.S. Army and Marine Corps would have caused Autonomous Rebels to snort knowingly over their morning newspapers.

Skeptical as the Autonomous Rebels are of religious concepts and communities, the Disengaged Darwinists appear to be even less spiritually engaged. This tribe isn't quite as emphatic in its rejection of religious trappings as the Autonomous Rebels are: the Disengaged Darwinists are less likely to avoid religious communities altogether, for instance. But this is most likely a sign that Disengaged Darwinists are willing to go with the flow on the odd Christmas or Easter—put on the tie and show up to please the family, as my father and grandfather did. Disengaged Darwinist men and women will certainly do this without hesitation for the funeral or wedding of a family member or friend. For this tribe, irritated by many of life's demands but respectful of tradition, showing a certain amount of deference to a religious community is a question of manners. It's probably not about finding enlightenment or fulfillment: the Disengaged Darwinists are the least likely of the four tribes to say it's important to them to explore their own spirituality. Making an appearance at a religious service or ritual meal is one thing; earnestly lifting one's soul unto the Almighty is quite another. Religion for these quintessential cynics is just one more institution that has let them down, like the government, the company to which they gave their blood and sweat for forty years, and the NHL.

The Disengaged Darwinists tend to be about average in their levels of belief in Christian religious concepts like God, hell, and miracles. They are neither as believing as the Anxious Communitarians, nor as doubtful as the Autonomous Rebels. The one concept on which the Disengaged Darwinists stand out as exceptionally skeptical falls outside the Christian tradition: reincarnation. Members of this tribe, who tend to be wary of ideas and practices from cultures other than their own, are the least likely to believe that after death, beings may return to earth for another go-round. It's no coincidence that while the Disengaged Darwinists are the least likely (32 percent) to buy reincarnation, the Connected Enthusiasts are most likely to believe in it (57 percent). This may be wishful thinking on both their parts: the Connected Enthusiasts are probably hoping to be reincarnated as themselves so they can take this delightful ride all over again (perhaps winning the spiritual lottery and coming back as an Angelina Jolie or Brad Pitt), while the Disengaged Darwinists are hoping to be transported to some other spiritual plane, free of the crooks and idiots who run the world as we know it. Maybe by the time I die and come back, they grumble with a twinkle in their eyes, the Leafs will have finally found a way to win a hockey game.

eight

The Long Goodbye:
Boomers Plan Their Exit

*"It is possible to provide security against other ills,
but so far as death is concerned we men all live
in a city without walls."*

—Epicurus

In the fall of 2009, Cirque du Soleil founder and billionaire clown Guy Laliberté became the first Canadian space tourist. On September 30, Laliberté (a Quebec Baby Boomer par excellence) blasted off from the Baikonur launch pad in Kazakhstan, shot into orbit in a Soyuz rocket, and went on to spend nine days aboard the International Space Station.

Although Laliberté has shown tremendous business savvy in other aspects of his career, he seems to have cut a rather bad deal on this particular trip. Had he deferred gratification only slightly (until after his death), a Houston-based company called Celestis would have been willing to launch him into space for just $2500—a fraction of the $35 million he paid to blast off in his current, uncremated form.

Celestis, whose slogan is "A Step into the Universe," enables the bereaved families of adventurers, geeks, and space enthusiasts to have a portion of their loved one's "cremains" (cremated remains) launched into Earth's orbit, shot to the moon, or sent into deep space on a "permanent celestial journey"—destination anywhere. This last option is what the son of *Star Trek* creator Gene Roddenberry has settled on for his parents, whose ashes will strike out for the final frontier in 2012. Indeed, a portion of Gene Roddenberry's ashes already embarked on their own star trek in 1997, along with the cremains of 1960s counterculture icon Dr. Timothy "LSD" Leary and a number of others. (We may never know whether the hippie psychiatrist's journey into space was the ultimate high, but for a man who advised others to tune in, turn on, and drop out, it was certainly a spectacular way to slip the constraints of mainstream America.) Since only a few grams of Roddenberry's molecular dust went on that first trip with Leary, there's plenty left for a second launch with his spouse.

Proponents of cremation suggest that the possibility of dividing up a person's ashes and dispatching them to multiple final resting places is a significant emotional benefit. This concept will make perfect sense to those Baby Boomers who have embraced the concept of multiple identities and will love the idea of their physical presence on earth being distributed among several meaningful sites, not just buried whole next to Mom and Pop. Only the children of the Boomers stand to suffer from this practice, since they'll probably be the ones tasked with travelling the world to deposit spoonfuls of Dad's ashes everywhere from Machu Picchu and the Galapagos Islands to Stanley Park, the family cottage, and the rough on that tough par four at the golf club.

Boomers—especially Boomer women—stand out noticeably from Elders on the question of burial versus cremation. Among Elders, a modest majority of 58 percent say they intend to be cremated (a radical departure from the preferences of *their* parents, a story in itself), while 36 percent express a desire to be buried when their time comes. Boomers, on the other hand, prefer cremation by a ratio of nearly three to one: 72 percent versus 25 percent. A five-point difference occurs between men and women on this question, with Boomer women more likely (74 percent) than Boomer men (69 percent) to wish to hasten the fulfillment of the "ashes to ashes" aphorism. One possible explanation of women's greater inclination toward cremation is that they've spent years having their appearance evaluated and don't wish for friends and family at their final encounter to peer into their caskets and privately judge the quality of their makeup or the final state of their wrinkles (the finish lines?). For women more than for men, the idea of having their earthly form incinerated might seem like a dash for freedom. Consider how giddy the disembodied spirit of Nora Ephron might be, for instance, upon the annihilation of her problematic neck.

Boomers' greater preference for cremation may be rooted in a number of shifts that have characterized this generation. First, and most obviously, there's the Boomers' more secular outlook. Some religious traditions, notably Hinduism, favour cremation. (Indeed, discussion has taken place in recent years over designating the Niagara River as a waterway where ashes in symbolic quantities and flowers might be deposited as part of Hindu funeral rites.) But in the Judeo-Christian tradition, burial of the dead has been the norm.

The comedian Lenny Bruce (who wasn't a Boomer, but defied categorization in any case) performed a bit that reflected the conventions of human burial according to his Jewish mother: "I got a tattoo on my arm. My mother screamed when she saw it. She says, 'Now you can't be buried in a Jewish cemetery!' I said, 'It's okay, Ma. I'll be buried in a Jewish cemetery. They can amputate my arm and bury it in a Catholic cemetery. It can wave to my body.'" As the power of religious rules and conventions has receded among Baby Boomers, millions have become less attached to the idea of keeping their lifeless bodies as intact as possible and ready to be transported to heaven for an after-party with Jesus, Moses, John Lennon, and the other greats.

Instead of disposing of their bodies by religious rote, Boomers have become free to consider the return of their flesh to the earth in more personal and pragmatic terms. On the pragmatic front, they're now able to weigh the costs and environmental implications of their choices. On the personal front, many Boomers, with their penchant for customization, will wish for the disposal of their bodies to reflect their personal interests and styles. Lying in a cemetery alongside a thousand strangers, many of whom were probably jerks, would be an affront to some Boomer egos. Even more outrageous would be to rest in or near one of the monuments or mausoleums that for some families— especially those of old Upper Canada—signified their positions as lesser nobles in the colonial hierarchy. "Please," think individualistic Boomers, "scatter my ashes in the garden; I'm not King Tut."

Celestis, the company that rockets human cremains out of the atmosphere, may seem to offer a distinctly contemporary service because they use technology that, even decades after the moon walk, still seems miraculous. But the changes that have brought this firm into being are as much social as they are technological. The spread of secularism in Europe and North

America has effectively erased the scripts for many of life's major passages. The implications of this change go well beyond the disposal of bodies and affect every aspect of memorializing the dead. Birth and baptism no longer go together automatically. Marriages once included a single set of fixed and sober scripts, shared by millions of co-religionist couples across time; today's vows are creative writing exercises in which couples rework their expressions of commitment until they fit like a tailored suit. Marriage vows are now expressed in colloquial language. In some cases they're burbled underwater in a scuba ceremony or shouted over the roar of a plane's engine as the newlyweds prepare to skydive hand in hand into the first moments of their union.

Death and its once staid rituals haven't escaped the deep forces of socio-cultural change that have reshaped life in North America. And of course, the fact that Boomers (45 percent) are less likely than their parents (59 percent) to want a traditional religious funeral doesn't mean that members of this generation are about to let their expiry go unobserved. Indeed, for the millions of Boomers who have spent their lives exploring the nuances of their personal identities through their relationships, consumption habits, political convictions, and aesthetic tastes, a universalizing ashes-to-ashes send-off obviously will be too mechanical. As is often the case, the nimble American market-place has been especially quick to respond to emerging demand for nontraditional memorial services. But Canadian members of what is now called the "death-care industry" are also making more and more concessions to new trends in the rituals of death.

If you were to die today, for instance, it would probably be easy to find a funeral home willing to play a video message from you during the visitation. Some people choose to have their recorded address play next to their open casket, so their virtual face speaks just a few feet from their fleshly face (presumably silent). A growing number of funeral homes are familiar with this request and can easily furnish the requisite technology.

You might have to go farther afield to find a facility with "themed viewing rooms" like the ones designed by the Wade Funeral Home in Louisville, Kentucky. One award-winning room, "Big Momma's Kitchen," is meant to evoke the warmth and hominess of a Southern matriarch's mission control centre—a fully outfitted kitchen, complete with a tray of real fried chicken sitting on the stove. If you did need to travel to Kentucky or elsewhere to get precisely the send-off you wanted, you wouldn't have to go in a hearse: you could ride in the customized sidecar of a Harley-Davidson Road King (with the help of Biker Burials of Wrightsville, Pennsylvania).

Not everyone thinks a flamboyant funeral is a good idea. Joe Queenan, author of a rather scathing book on his own cohort entitled *Balsamic Dreams: A Short but Self-Important History of the Baby Boom Generation*, scorns Boomers for having "transformed the traditional funeral service into a ludicrous stage show, a slapdash mixture of performance art, stand-up comedy, and karaoke."[1] Queenan understands the Boomer impulse toward intimacy and personalization. In the late 1980s he wrote an op-ed piece criticizing a friend's funeral because it felt empty:

> I sneered at the service's generic quality, lamenting its dependence on hollow, formulaic rituals. I wished the service had been more honest, emotional and personal.
>
> Like many others before me, I have now learned the truth of the old saying, "Be careful what you wish for." Since my friend died, I have attended any number of honest, emotional, personal funerals, most of them so foolish they made my blood run cold. Between the nitwit eulogist, the farewell home video, the flatulent sign-off music and the inappropriate clothing, funerals have devolved from sacred bonding rituals into commedia dell'arte farces. And it's only going to get worse as more Boomers pass from the scene.[2]

But while some Boomers will turn their ceremonial farewells into truly theatrical affairs, this will by no means be the norm— neither in Canada nor in Queenan's native United States. Our own data suggest that among Canadian Boomers, the spread of secularism has simply meant that a larger proportion will feel free to do their own thing at their funerals, as they did at their weddings. For some, "their own thing" will be as modest as having a favourite cello suite played during the service instead of organ music. For others, it might be something slightly zany. In death, as in life, Boomers' values relating to religion, family, tradition, and ritual will determine how they want their passing marked. Boomers don't anticipate many more weddings; their funerals are the one truly personal rite of passage that's left for them to contemplate and plan. They want it done right. As in so many other spheres, they're determined to do it their own way.

The traditional ceremony won't be abandoned overnight; indeed, a plurality of Boomers (45 percent) tell us they hope to have a traditional religious ceremony. Many will see this as a kind of religious homecoming—perhaps especially if they haven't been particularly observant as adults. Even for those who aren't religious, sentimental attachments rooted in family or culture can still produce feelings of kinship with the church. Consider Quebecers, who are proud to be a secular—even anti-religious—society, but still insist on having a cross prominently displayed in the National Assembly as an assertion of their tradition and cultural heritage. Who knows—perhaps the Latin high mass will become *de rigueur* at the funerals of Quebec Catholics (whether lapsed, divorced, gay, or part-time Buddhist) in ten, twenty, or thirty years. Nostalgia can be a powerful emotional force that easily slips the bonds of reason and principle.

This may be especially true, Quebec filmmaker Denys Arcand seems to suggest, if traditional religion has been replaced with spiritual vacuity.

Quebec folk music icon Gilles Vigneault (he of "Mon Pays" fame) captured this ambivalence about religion but passion for cultural heritage in remarks he made prior to the performance of his "High Mass" in Quebec City in 2008. "A mass," he said, "is the occasion for gathering together to borrow a being who sometimes one invents, who at other times one believes in fervently, but who seems profoundly necessary for all human nature. This is about holding a mass as you would any mass, that is, with ceremony, politeness, and I would say, for my part, with faith. Faith in human beings, before having faith, pretentiously, in their god. With respect for our parents, they who practiced religion much more than we practiced writing. Which did not serve them too badly when one considers that we are here to carry on."[3]

Boomers may be markedly less likely than Elders to plan on a religious funeral, but the practice is by no means dead. The result of socio-cultural change over the past half-century simply means that those who don't feel their life will find its most fitting tribute in a Latin mass or other traditional ritual will be able to try something else. Two key factors will enable Boomers to design the funerals that they believe will honour their lives most appropriately. First, families are now more likely to comply with unconventional wishes than they were a generation ago. Second, death-care professionals are able to accommodate trailblazing Boomers with a wider range of options.

Just as there are major tribal differences in religiosity among Boomers, the four segments diverge sharply on the question of whether to invite God to their funerals. For the Anxious Communitarians, the most traditionally religious of the four tribes, a no-nonsense religious funeral is an obvious requirement: these Baby Boomers are about as likely (57 percent) as the Elders to say they plan to have a traditional religious ceremony when they die. At the other end of the spectrum are the deeply secular Autonomous Rebels, just 35 percent of whom say they will likely opt for a traditional religious send-off. Half of Disengaged Darwinists favour a religious service (50 percent), probably more out of a sense of tradition and convention than any theological conviction. The Connected Enthusiasts, although expressing strong spiritual inclinations, are in about half of all cases planning to have a memorial service that's more social than religious; 37 percent say they plan on a traditional ceremony. (The Connected Enthusiasts are, after all, the most sociable of all Boomers—and this will be their last party.) In short, Canadian Boomers who have spent their lives steering clear of church and temple show little interest in re-entering the fold at the final hour. Those who revere God, tradition, or both will tend to seek out the same sorts of rituals that marked their parents' and grandparents' deaths; these people spent their lives trying to live up to their parents' ideals, not question or reject them. Those who have migrated to evangelical denominations will want to adhere precisely to the strictures of their new faiths.

But it's not only values associated with religion and tradition that will inform Canadian Boomers' choices about their own ritualized departure. As with any other set of purchases, Boomers' *consumer* values will shape their decisions. The exit industry is broadly divided into services to do with the ceremony, the handling of the body itself, and the purchase of monuments and other lasting memorials. The recent proliferation of choices in the funeral industry has affected not only the style of memorial ceremonies—such as whether you want a selection of your favourite Beatles tunes played or prefer to go with the more anthemic "Imagine" by John Lennon—but the whole range of tasks associated with death. If you need help answering questions like "Does anyone know a good charter boat that will scatter my ashes at sea?" there are now funeral planners—like wedding consultants, but different—who are ready to help make your exit one (for others) to remember.

Values that have informed so many other decisions in Boomers' lives will be very much in operation at the end of those lives: their desire (or lack thereof) to express their personal style; their feelings about the display of status symbols; their concern for the environment; their commitment to sparing their families financial strain; their introversion or extroversion; their gritty pragmatism or their willingness to spend more for a dash of style.

Not long ago, these concerns would have been seen as totally extraneous to the process of arranging a funeral, purchasing a casket, and ordering a headstone. Grieving families would be ushered into a hushed funeral home where they were invited to choose mahogany or pine, depending on their means and the honour they wished to show the deceased (no pressure). Embalming cost what it cost and was too gruesome to discuss— let alone haggle over. A plot at the local cemetery was arranged. There was little to debate; although many people found funerals terribly expensive, the death of a loved one was no time to comparison shop. Some combination of grief, dignity, guilt, taboo, and the fear of wagging tongues kept most people from even questioning their options.

But along with growing secularism, something else came along to permanently change the world of death care: the Internet. That vast, anonymous field of information-sharing, self-revelation, and, of course, shopping hit the industry like a cyclone. As one article in *Wired* magazine put it back in 1999, just as online shopping was becoming more trusted and mainstream, "baby boomers are already online in droves, often planning for elderly parents' funerals, and, increasingly, their own. On the web, they find something totally foreign to the traditional death care industry—consumer information. Price comparisons abound, anathema to an industry that has thrived in a death-denying culture where people pay the asking price at the local funeral home and rush for the door."[4] Ten years on, thrifty shoppers can buy caskets from a huge array of online retailers, including Wal-Mart and FuneralDepot.com (slogan: "Where overpaying is not dignified").

Many Baby Boomers will delight in such opportunities for thrift. Autonomous Rebels, though the most affluent of the tribes, hate the idea of being fleeced (or having their widow or widower fleeced) because of some irrational, emotional longing for a tribute. This tough-minded tribe—particularly if they make their own arrangements "pre-need" (that is, while they're still breathing and before Alzheimer's sets in)—will likely go for thrift and simplicity, especially in the disposal of their bodies. Indeed, at 8 percent, Autonomous Rebels are tied with the Disengaged Darwinists for most likely to say they want no funeral whatsoever. For this tribe, the most valuable thing about the funeral business is how ripe it is for mockery; they still remember with relish the 1965 film *The Loved One*, an oddball (but searing) comedy that revolves around a Los Angeles funeral home. Antireligious Autonomous Rebels are likely to see the funeral business in its traditional form as merely the commercial sidekick to institutional religion: a racket that exploits grief, fear, and guilt and sells you things you don't need (like a velvet-lined, carved mahogany casket). These contrary-minded Boomers would rather see the funeral dough spent on good food and drink for the living than on an ornate box for the deceased. Better still, let the living spend their own money on food and drink and let the leftover bucks of the departed go to a charity that's combatting global warming—a mega-offset to counterbalance the emissions his or her charmed life on earth produced.

At the other end of the spectrum, Anxious Communitarians, though least able to afford an expensive send-off, are probably the most likely to wish for a final tribute in keeping with the dignified funerals of their forebears: a traditional casket (as opulent as possible) or a similarly elegant urn. A headstone near the family plot (with Mom and Dad, who remain their moral and emotional anchors) will also be compulsory; the Anxious Communitarians are unlikely to request being scattered on a mountaintop. Who, they wonder, would want to be so far from home?

The Connected Enthusiasts, the most ecologically concerned of the four tribes, will be intent on environmentally friendly ways of letting their bodies return to the earth. Although three-quarters (74 percent) intend to be cremated, those who wish for their bodies to be interred whole may opt for an eco-friendly cotton shroud for burial instead of a casket. Thousands of tonnes of metal and concrete—and thousands of gallons of formaldehyde-based embalming fluids—are used for the disposal of bodies in Canada each year. Many Connected Enthusiasts will want no part of this, and will seek out death-care providers certified by the Green Burial Council. Those most passionately concerned about the planet might even investigate "resomation," a cutting-edge body-disposal technology that uses a sixth of the energy required for cremation and has a smaller carbon footprint. ("Unlike cremation," reports *The New York Times Magazine*, "resomation doesn't vaporize the toxic mercury of dental fillings and doesn't char joint implants, leaving them clean, shiny and potentially recyclable."[5] Why let those great titanium hips go to waste, Baby Boomers? Let someone who needs them use them when your time comes, along with your donated organs!) In any case, this tribe doesn't see the disposal of their bodies as the most important part of their leave-taking process: the most likely of the four tribes to say they want a nontraditional spiritual ceremony (17 percent) or just a big party (20 percent), the Connected Enthusiasts will allow friends, family, food, and conversation to be people's final image of them—not a slick casket or a prime plot.

The Disengaged Darwinists are in line with Boomer averages in most of their death-care preferences. Seven in ten (69 percent) say they plan to be cremated. (Notably, the desire for cremation is fairly consistent across the tribes—ranging from 69 to 74 percent.) Although they're a little more likely (50 percent) than their age peers to say they favour a traditional religious ceremony at their funeral, they don't exhibit any especially strong preferences in the way the other tribes do; they seem to be going with the flow. When you're dead, you're dead; who cares? Perhaps the Disengaged Darwinists, who have the lowest scores on the value *Awareness of Mortality* (a trend that measures the extent to which people reflect on their own death and the deaths of those they love) and are the least likely to report having an up-to-date will, are avoiding the whole idea of what will happen when they die. This is surprisingly stereotypical Boomer behaviour for the Disengaged Darwinists, a tribe that usually does the opposite of what one would expect from the generation. But while the stereotypical Boomer's doubtfulness about his or her own mortality is rooted in an obsession with health—how could someone who swims, does yoga twice a week, and eats only organic food ever die?!—for the Disengaged Darwinists this is far from the case. This tribe scores low on *Effort for Health* and *Awareness of Mortality*. These Boomers have no illusions about their own mortality, but a strong current of fatalism drives both their indifference to their health and their shrugging attitude toward the angel of death.

The stereotypical Baby Boomer, of course, is in profound denial about the eventuality of his or her own death. This mythic Boomer is so narcissistic that imagining the world without all-important *moi* is like imagining the ocean without water: the very idea becomes meaningless and barren. But our own data don't indicate any strong evidence of death denial among the Boomers—or at least, nothing beyond the death denial that's already endemic in North American culture. On average, Boomers are no more and no less likely than other Canadians to say they reflect regularly on their own demise or the passing of people they love. It's more in their desire to make personal choices about the rituals of death—and not follow convention or prescribed institutional rituals—that Boomers as a generation differ from their parents.

Averages, of course, can mask important differences within groups. For instance, although women tend to live longer than men, female Boomers' *Awareness of Mortality* is higher—and growing at a much more rapid rate—than men's. It's women who are walking the halls at night rehearsing their "Alas, poor Yorick" speeches, while the men snore happily. Part of the reason for this may be that women are bearing more of the burden of caring for aging parents—their own and their spouses'—and so are more likely to find themselves face to face with the dying process, whether in their own homes or in long-term care facilities where they're confronted with a whole army of frail, demented spectres of what might be. "Why don't you go and visit my mum," their husbands say. "You're so good at that sort of thing."

But an even more fascinating gender difference emerges in men's and women's thinking about the end of their lives. When asked what kind of funeral they would prefer (religious or secular, formal or casual, and so on), a small minority of Baby Boomers (7 percent) say they would rather have no funeral at all. Boomer men (5 percent) are about as likely as the Elders (6 percent) to say that they would rather their deaths go unmarked. Boomer women stand out on this item, with nearly one in ten (9 percent) declaring that she'd rather go quietly. Although 9 percent remains a small minority, the difference between men and women on this item is statistically significant—and intriguing.

Every reader will likely be tempted to develop their own pet theory about the meaning of women's greater likelihood of rejecting any memorial tribute. My own suspicion is that men relish the idea of a funeral because they imagine that people will (finally) say complimentary things about all their accomplishments—especially their professional ones: the law firm they nurtured from the 1970s, or the fact that they were the best damn bricklayer on any job site lucky enough to have them. For many Boomer women, their heroism has been of a divided—and therefore quieter—nature. While he devoted his full attention to the law firm or the bricks, she was having her own career accomplishments, but putting them on hold as she rushed to get the kids to piano lessons. The work might have been equal (or disproportionately hers) as she nurtured parents, children, and, of course, him and received perfunctory thanks, but the line items on her CV may have been fewer. The thought of people intoning ceremonial platitudes about the passing of family "glue" or "saint" might be too cloying for some Boomer women to contemplate.

After all the trappings of Boomers' end-of-life ceremonies are put away—the candles extinguished, the Beatles albums back on the shelf, the ashes floating serenely through space in high-tech capsules—there's just one issue for the remaining earthlings to address: the money. Much has been made of the enormous transfer of wealth that is in the process of shifting from thrifty Elders to their Boomer children. What is unknown is whether Boomers will make a similar generational bequest to their own children—or blow the whole wad on fun while they're still around (or on their elaborate funerals).

Elders notably outscore Boomers on the value *Legacy*, which measures the priority people place on leaving a material legacy for their children and grandchildren. Our data on legacy don't extend back to 1992, so unfortunately we can't compare Elders' and Boomers' attitudes at the same life stage; it may be that Elders' greater emphasis on legacy can be explained by the fact that they're closer to the end of their lives. Boomers, meanwhile, are facing retirement and are strongly preoccupied—especially given the market meltdown that began at the end of 2008—with how to finance their own remaining years.

Although Elders express more enthusiasm than Boomers do

for leaving a stash of cash behind for their families, the two cohorts look very much alike when they describe how they would like whatever they do leave behind to be distributed. Both Elders and Boomers say they hope for their children to be the main beneficiaries of their estates; 48 percent of Elders and 45 percent of Boomers say that they plan to leave the bulk of their money to their children. Spouses are in second place, with about a third (34 percent) in each cohort saying their spouses will be their main beneficiaries.

There are marked gender differences on this question, with Boomer men (45 percent) twice as likely as Boomer women (22 percent) to say that they hope to leave most of their money to their spouse. This disparity reflects a sense of realism among both men and women about which partner probably will depart first: women, on average, live longer than men and so are more likely to be left holding on to the family money, in their final years doing so in a comfortable but costly nursing home. Also not surprisingly, divorced Boomers are much more likely (71 percent) than married Boomers (43 percent) to say they will leave most of their money to their children.

Despite substantial values differences between these two cohorts, which lead to an array of divergent behaviours in other areas, both groups overwhelmingly plan to leave their money to family. Boomers are only slightly more likely to say they plan to spend their money themselves while they're alive (10 percent versus 7 percent of Elders)—and these are not just selfish souls; they are disproportionately people at the low end of the income spectrum, who probably worry whether they will have enough money to make it to the finish line themselves, let alone leave anything behind. It's no accident that the more affluent Boomers are the ones more likely to have prepared a will; they have greater reason to believe there will be something left over to distribute.

Most Boomers will, of course, hope to be remembered not only for leaving bequests that helped pay off a mortgage or enabled a kitchen renovation, but also for their values, their ideas, and the message they communicated through the way they lived. As Margaret Somerville wrote in *The Globe and Mail* in early 2010, for humans as meaning-seeking beings, it is desirable "to make dying the last great act of living"—and part of making your own death meaningful is the act of shaping the meaning that others take from your life and its ending.[6] One prominent and poignant example of this behaviour in Canada was the farewell letter Toronto City Summit Alliance (TCSA) founder David Pecaut wrote to friends and supporters as he was dying of cancer. (The TCSA has spearheaded a range of ambitious and important civic projects in Toronto, bringing together leaders from a wide range of backgrounds and sectors, and operating on a principle of what Pecaut called "collective leadership"—a model he believed could be Toronto's gift to the world.) In this letter, which Pecaut initially sent to close associates but which was later published (with his permission) in the media, Pecaut described his hopes for Toronto and some of the feelings and ideas that had animated his tremendously energetic work on behalf of the city. It's hard to think of another Torontonian who has left such a powerful and explicit legacy not of material gifts but of ideas, inspiration, and ways of working together. Although Pecaut's death was premature, and it goes without saying that protracted illness is punishing, it's not surprising that this glass-half-full entrepreneur took the opportunity to craft an expression of his perspective and values that might guide and inspire others who share his vision and wish to carry on his work. I suspect that more than a few Baby Boomers will follow suit in their own ways.

Our data suggest that Baby Boomers vary broadly in the extent to which they contemplate their own deaths. The Anxious Communitarians are the most likely to report that they reflect regularly on the end of their lives, and on the deaths of people they know or have known. The Connected Enthusiasts are moderately above average on this value, while Autonomous Rebels and especially the Disengaged Darwinists are below average in their *Awareness of Mortality*. But our survey provoked at least a moment or two of reflection from all our Boomer respondents—whether this was a regular activity for them or an unheard-of glimpse into the beyond.

In our survey, just as we offered Boomers a chance to name a favourite "bucket-list" item, we invited them to articulate an epitaph they hoped would adorn their (for now) hypothetical headstone. This was another just-for-fun query and many Boomers responded in kind, like the wag who proposed, "He came, he saw, he played eighteen holes." Some didn't appreciate this frivolous question about their final monument and delivered a mild scolding in the box meant to receive their epitaph. But a great number of Boomers took this opportunity for introspection and composed epitaphs that were remarkably earnest, sometimes surprising, and often sweet.

Some similarities were evident across tribes: devotion to family, for instance, is something in which nearly all Canadians take pride. But even on this unscientific measure, some tribal differences came through quite clearly—or seemed to in the eyes of this Boomer. It's hard, for instance, to imagine the epitaph one Disengaged Darwinist proposed ("RIP—Finally!") having been written by a Connected Enthusiast. The latter tribe's epitaphs tended to focus on the brevity of life ("Life is short; enjoy it all!" was characteristic), not the idea of wearily falling across the finish line.

The Disengaged Darwinists' offerings were not without a sense of pleasure in life; the golfing epitaph above came from one of these Boomers, and another suggested that "Gone hunting" be etched into (most probably) his headstone. Many made understated, matter-of-fact statements about their efforts in life, such as "He was basically good," "A hard-working, honest individual," and "Tried his best." A few planned to go out on a sour note; "A waste of time and space" was one sad suggestion. And no exercise of this sort would be complete without the classic "Life's a bitch." A few Disengaged Darwinists, though not apparently giddy about life, did manage to transcend curmudgeon status with epitaphs that suggested self-awareness and some sly humour. "Keeping one eye open," said one. "One life, two wife," said another.

For the Anxious Communitarians, the epitaph (even this imaginary kind) was clearly no place for sarcasm or humour. This tribe tended to focus on their service to others, either in their social roles ("A good wife and mother. A good baker, too!") or in their personal qualities ("A kind, caring, thoughtful, loving person"). One member of this tribe hoped that her children would see fit to sum up her life with a simple "Thank you, Mom." Another encapsulated his or her life of migration thus: "Moved to Canada, worked hard to better myself and to provide a decent life and security for my family." Imagine the years of work and self-sacrifice that went into making those nineteen words true. Anxious Communitarians really do hold the world together for many families and communities.

While the Anxious Communitarians often defined themselves through their service to and care for others, fewer
Autonomous Rebels did so; instead, true to their name, they
tended to focus on personal development and self-awareness.
One suggested, "Lived an examined life courageously"; another
insisted, "Let it never be said she lived an unexamined life." One
member of this tribe figured there was no sense in reinventing
the wheel and crafting his or her own epitaph; might as well
hand the space over to one of the great minds: "Wisdom begins
in wonder. Socrates." Like the Disengaged Darwinists who
offered rather humble descriptions of their achievements, several
Autonomous Rebels offered un-self-important conclusions like
"Passed through, made progress" and "Shared his craft." One
member of this tribe, perhaps recalling his or her rebellion in
youth and beyond, hoped to see the headstone reflect sustained
commitment to ideals: "Never surrendered."

The Connected Enthusiasts' ideas for epitaphs reflect the joie
de vivre that's characteristic of this tribe. Many proposed
epitaphs focused on living life fully, such as "Loved life and all
its potential" and "Lived to the fullest." Like the Anxious Communitarians, many Connected Enthusiasts focused on their
contributions to others, but with a slightly greater focus on the
world at large as opposed to family relationships. "Treated
people with respect, helped build a better community," one
hoped to see on his or her headstone; "Improved the world

around her," another wrote. And like the Disengaged Darwin-ist who planned to keep one eye open, one Connected Enthu-siast thought that his or her facial expression in death might communicate something about a view of life: "Died with a smile. What was so funny?"

nine

What Have We Wrought?

"Make no mistake about why these babies are here. They are here to replace us."

—Jerry Seinfeld

Throughout most of the Baby Boomers' lives to date, the refrain from the Bob Dylan song "The Times They Are A-Changin'" could be loosely translated as "Here come the Boomers!" But after several decades of Boomer dominance in politics, economics, and culture, today's rhetoric about changing times really means, "There *go* the Boomers."

Some members of my cohort still kid themselves that they're up-and-coming rebels. In the world of Canadian politics, Michael

Ignatieff, Bob Rae, Jack Layton, Gilles Duceppe, and even Stephen Harper come to mind. In reality, however, this highly educated, outspoken generation long ago became the establishment. The cohort that aligned itself so strongly with youth and progress will soon have to step aside and make way for a new generation of geniuses who believe that they, too, know a few things about how the world ought to work. As the Boomers themselves thin out and eventually disappear altogether, it will be fascinating (for others) to observe which of their values will abide in our culture and which will disappear.

As for that next generation of prodigies and geniuses,[1] some have already made themselves known: the most celebrated entrepreneurs of the past decade and a half have been the technology mavens who figured out how to catalyze and capitalize on the mainstreaming of the Internet while they were barely out of diapers. The giants in this category are people like Facebook founder Mark Zuckerberg (age: twenty-six; net worth: $2 billion) and Google founders Sergey Brin and Larry Page (in both cases, age: thirty-six; net worth: $12 billion as of an hour ago).

One senses intuitively that no Baby Boomer, however intelligent, would have been capable of the innovations these young people produced—they were early and insightful contributors to a new kind of conversation about technology, communication, and social organization. Boomers like Bill Gates and Steve Jobs were visionaries who saw the massive potential of the personal computer both as a tool and a toy. In Canada Mike Lazaridis and Jim Balsillie of Research in Motion saw similar potential for mobile email and web browsing through their world-changing BlackBerry. But people like Facebook co-founder Chris Hughes (Barack Obama's social media strategist) grew up taking easy access to computers and mobile devices for granted and soon began to feel the social and organizational potential of the Internet in their bones. The rise of these baby-faced entrepreneurs is one important sign that the times they (still) are a-changin'—and the changes are by no means only technological.

The most famous change-monger of recent years has been Barack Obama. During his primary campaign and then his presidential campaign, Obama talked unceasingly about change. His critics derided the concept of change as ridiculously generic, but the term did double duty for Obama. The most obvious meaning of the candidate's call for change was that the party in power should change. Americans agreed: they were war-weary and battered by a terrifying economic crisis, and they were deeply disillusioned with the Bush administration.

But the Obama campaign pointed to a second and even deeper kind of change—one with more important implications for Canada. As David Eaves and Taylor Owen argue in an insightful piece in the *Literary Review of Canada*, Obama provided a glimpse of the possibilities of the "post-Boomer era":

what politics might look like when it's no longer being argued primarily by people who came of age in the 1960s. Eaves and Owen contend that engaged young Canadians were so impressed by Barack Obama in part because they were so unimpressed by the terms of political debate in their own country, which tend to be fossilized versions of yesterday's new ideas. Ironically, it's the supposedly "progressive" side of the debate (the liberal-minded and often Liberal- or NDP-minded) that's most preoccupied with conserving the political achievements of the past: the gains made by mid-twentieth-century giants like Lester Pearson, Tommy Douglas, and Pierre Trudeau.

A large segment of the post-Boomer population, argue Eaves and Owen, is oriented to "neo-progressivism"—which cares not about holding on to twentieth-century institutional and bureau-cratic structures, but about experimenting with the insights and technologies of the twenty-first century to develop pragmatic (rather than ideological) solutions to twenty-first-century problems. And this is where those baby-faced American entre-preneurs come in: platforms like Facebook, Twitter, and whatever comes next are enabling new modes of communica-tion and social organization that let people build constituencies around issues and share ideas about how to address them. "New information technologies," write Eaves and Owen, "mean the costs of democratically affiliating, mobilizing and organizing people and co-creating and distributing ideas have never been cheaper. More importantly, diversity and freedom—not control—drive innovation in a networked world."[2] Distributed ideas and distributed work mean distributed power, which by implication is the beginning of the end for representative democracy and the end of the beginning for direct democracy. This is the real meaning of declining voter turnout. Why show up to pull a lever on election day at the local elementary school when you can bring corporations and governments to their knees from the comfort of your home?

It's not that everyone under the age of forty is a brilliant innovator. (Some youth tribes in Canada fit the stereotype of the disengaged, basement-dwelling misanthrope almost perfectly.) But those who are innovating are sending powerful signals that a post-Boomer realignment is taking shape. We also see a great deal of evidence for this realignment in our values data, and we find that it's occurring not only around political debates but also around issues of identity, personal relationships, consumption, pleasure, and the quest for meaning. The post-Boomer generation will uphold some of the values the Autonomous Rebels and Connected Enthusiasts brought into the Canadian mainstream (gender and racial equality and gay rights are no-brainers for most young people), but they will reject other aspects of the Baby Boomer worldview. They are part of a new conversation—a conversation that is very different from the argument the Boomers had with their parents.

For instance, after rejecting their parents' religiosity, many Boomers remain allergic to any whiff of spirituality. Having been resentful of or disillusioned by institutional religion as they knew it when growing up, the most skeptical of these Boomers see hypocrisy in every expression of faith and suckers in every pew. (They see double hypocrisy in public expressions of faith; Sarah Palin or Mitt Romney at prayer in front of the Fox News cameras is enough to make them gag. Stephen Harper may be a religious man, but he's Canadian enough and savvy enough to keep his practice private.)

The post-Boomer generation is also fairly secular, but not as forceful in its rejection of spiritual concepts and practices. The post-Boomers are notably below average on the value *Religiosity*, for instance; they score slightly below Boomers. (The Elders are far above average.) But the same story doesn't hold with the value *Spiritual Quest*, which measures people's openness to more personal modes of spiritual engagement. Whereas the Boomers score moderately below average on this value, the post-Boomers are slightly above average, suggesting they're leaving the door open if not to traditional religious belonging then at least to some reading, talking, and experimentation. Also, while young people are the least likely of the three cohorts to believe in God and Jesus, they're the most likely to believe in miracles, angels, ghosts, and reincarnation. As it turns out, post-Boomers are also the most likely to find hell and the devil to be plausible concepts. After all, their parents, probably both of them, *were* Boomers.

It is a remarkable finding that the Boomers' children are as secular as the Boomers but more open to the idea of spirituality as a personal quest. I think the explanation for this phenomenon is that Canadians who were born after 1965 were less likely to have experienced religion as a coercive force that sought to control their behaviour and even their thoughts and feelings. Religion is still widespread in Canada, but it doesn't exert the same cultural pressure it did when the Boomers—especially the early Boomers—were young. Although majorities of Canadians express some kind of faith, church attendance is a minority practice, pursued disproportionately by the elderly, and religious beliefs tend to be private matters in this society where pluralism and politeness mix so gingerly. Whereas many secular Boomers feel they had to fight to escape the religious institutions in which they were raised—and later purge themselves of the guilt and fear those institutions had instilled in them when they were children—most post-Boomers never had a dog in that fight. Some people go to church, synagogue, temple, or mosque; others don't. Some religious people are bigots and blowhards; others are thoughtful and generous. Post-Boomers seem more likely to have a whatever-floats-your-boat attitude to religion. This level of equanimity is something that many Boomers, who are in their minds still arguing with their parents, their pastors or priests, or Pat Robertson or the Pope, will probably not attain in this mortal coil.

I once received a note via the Environics website from a Canadian living abroad who had read one of my previous books on social values. She thought I had made a few good points but that I had also made a huge error in suggesting that *any* member of her values tribe (the Cosmopolitan Modernists, the Elder precursor to the Connected Enthusiasts and Autonomous Rebels) could consider giving money to a religious organization. She reported that she'd rather burn her money than see it end up in the hands of any kind of "spiritual" organization—and that anyone who remotely shared her values would feel the same way. In fact, our data suggest that some members of even the most secular tribes donate to religious charities. I think these people continue to support such organizations for personal reasons (as a tribute to their more religious parents, for instance) or simply because they support the good works that many religious communities do, even if they reject the theological rationale behind those works. In any case, the reader's fiery (but good-natured) note offers a glimpse of the intensity with which some older Canadians—and especially Baby Boomers—have renounced the religiosity that used to weigh so heavily on their families and communities. Young people may be secular, but I suspect that few would have such a sense of anger or resentment toward the religious institutions they experienced (or, more likely, didn't experience) in the 1980s and 90s.

Given that young people have grown up with an awareness of much more religious diversity than their parents and grandparents, I suspect they're more likely to see religion as a fairly neutral fact about a person's identity—like ethnicity or gender—than as a system of belief that strictly governs behaviour. From this perspective, coming into contact with a range of religions is as natural as coming into contact with a range of ethnicities: presumably all have their nuggets of wisdom, and all have their baggage of hypocrisy, dogma, and patriarchy. The idea that these religions actually have different accounts of history and The Truth about the Universe probably doesn't keep many post-Boomers up at night.

A similar pattern of post-Boomers evolving new, more flexible articulations of Boomer values emerges on issues of equality and diversity. Baby Boomers came of age at a time when there was segregation in the United States and explicitly racist immigration policy in Canada. Intermarriage was a scandal, and employment discrimination was a given for many organizations: you hired your own kind, the only trustworthy group in town, and men took priority. The old WASP clubs of Toronto were unabashed in their exclusion of Jews who had the funds and the audacity to apply for membership. There's still plenty of inequality and discrimination in the world, but for the Boomers' children, at least the *principle* that all people are equal is taken for granted. This change has come about partly through legal and institutional changes (in Canada, the Charter of Rights and Freedoms and evolving approaches to equity in the workplace) and partly through sheer demographic reality: young people, especially those in Canada's cities, have grown up with peers from around the globe. When I was a kid, it was unusual to have a friend who wasn't born at the same hospital as you were; my son Will's best friend, Hyssam, was born in Cairo, Egypt. For Catholics in my Bruce County youth, Protestants were the enemy and vice versa. That Hyssam is a Muslim is mildly interesting for Will, although the topic of religion, he tells me, comes up only in his North Toronto high-school history classes and never after school.

People tend to migrate when they're young and hungry to improve their lot, and ready to take on the challenge of life in a new country. Canada's foreign-born population is on average younger than the population at large, as is Canada's "visible minority" population (about seven in ten in this group are foreign-born). The median age of Canada's visible minority population is thirty-three, compared to thirty-nine for all Canadians. As of the 2006 census, close to a quarter (23 percent) of the visible minority population was younger than fourteen (compared to 18 percent of all Canadians), whereas just 7 percent of visible minorities were aged sixty-five or older (compared to 13 percent of the total population). These age trends mean that people who are now in their teens, twenties, and thirties are themselves more likely to be visible minorities, or if they are of European heritage, they're more likely to have spent large amounts of time with non-European peers in school and at work. Diversity is normal for young Canadians, especially those living in cities. When urban Boomers were young, diversity meant having a couple of Italian kids in your class. (And "celebrating diversity" meant that you refrained from hurling epithets at each other in the schoolyard.)[3]

For the post-Boomers,[4] racial equality is a given. This group scores substantially below average—and below the Boomers—on *Ethnic Intolerance*. And since Canadians score low on *Ethnic Intolerance* in general, the fact that post-Boomers are below average means they reject this form of intolerance with exceptional force. Post-Boomers are also more likely than Boomers to say, for instance, that it's okay for people of different ethnocultural backgrounds to get married and make beautiful babies together (the value *Cultural Fusion*).

The attitudes post-Boomers express in our surveys are borne out in their behaviour: according to Statistics Canada, mixed marriages are on the rise in Canada, and young people are leading the charge. Although mixed unions remain a small minority overall (3.9 percent of all unions as of the 2006 census, up 33 percent since 2001) the proportions of mixed unions are markedly higher among young people and those living in cities. In 2001, for instance, people in their twenties were three times as likely as people in their fifties to be in a romantic relationship with someone of another ethnic background. Young Vancouverites are at the leading edge of this trend; 13 percent of those in their twenties who have paired off in Vancouver are sharing life with a partner of another ethnicity. They don't just tolerate the other, they savour the other.[5]

Baby Boomers believed in the fundamental equality of people, and some fought for this principle—whether in their own families ("That joke isn't funny, Dad") or in the arenas of public policy or the media. But Boomers' kids are more likely to be living the reality of equality and exchange, and doing so with an easy, nonchalant attitude. Just as Baby Boomers took for granted the economic status their parents had struggled to achieve, the post-Boomers live in a world where both relative affluence and some of the Boomers' gains in the realm of social justice can also be taken for granted.

Again, it's not that racism has been banished from the earth. But the fact of diversity and at least the *principle* of equality are givens of daily life today in a way they weren't when my generation was growing up. (When I first introduced my partner, who's partly of Ukrainian heritage, to my extended family, my uncle saw fit to say with thinly veiled condescension, "Dasko. Now what sort of a name is that?" Today's parents are much more likely to take pretty much any name in stride, perhaps repeating it a couple of times to make sure they've gotten it right but certainly not behaving as though it came from another—inferior—species.) Because the post-Boomers live in a society in which diversity is ubiquitous and respect is, in most contexts, assumed, they're able to take an easier, less cautious, and often more playful attitude toward identity, stereotype, and the quirks of their own people. Indeed, in my own anecdotal experience young people seem to find Baby Boomer political correctness slightly stilted and unnatural; in our efforts not to offend, we can be overcautious. My young colleagues and acquaintances swap good-natured jibes about one another's various minority identities with remarkable ease; when respect and good intentions are assumed, (appropriately calibrated) jokes come with the territory. "Yo Bitchez, time to pay up!" was the salutation in an email my daughter recently received from one of her university roommates announcing it was time to fork over the rent. I have yet to hear this form of address at the Boomer-led feminist gatherings that occur from time to time around my dining-room table. In my youth, epithets were intended to hurt others, not express affection or open doors of exchange.

This increased ease young people feel about their diverse social environments has led to a proliferation of cultural goodies, especially of the comedic variety. Russell Peters, a Canadian of Indian heritage (born in 1970), has made good south of the border and around the world telling jokes about and doing impressions of everyone ranging from Koreans to Nigerians to the Irish. His own ethnic group is also fodder, of course; he began tape-recording his Indian relatives as a kid so he could mimic their accents. As a profile in *Toronto Life* relates, "In Peters' mind, the world he plays to is post-racist, the battle all but won if only because the opposition went away."[6] Peters strives to remain ahead of the cultural curve and is versed in the intermarriage trends I described earlier: addressing the white members of a packed house at Toronto's 19,000-seat Air Canada Centre, Peters recently warned them about their evolving relationship to their non-white neighbours: "You can't run, you can't hide. One of these days, you are going to [have sex with] one of us."

Many American comedians are also working in a similar register, with risqué takes on the whole stew of issues associated with diversity, racism, identity politics, political correctness, and media representations of various groups. Sarah Silverman (also born in 1970) tells jokes about being a nice Jewish girl that make Joan Rivers sound like Laura Bush. Margaret Cho (born in 1968) does a recurring impression of her Korean mother that's hilariously overdrawn and deeply lovable. (In one bit, Cho impersonates her mother during a conversation in which she's trying to get her daughter to admit to being gay: "It's okay if you're gay. There are gays all over the world … all all all over the world. But not Korea.") Wanda Sykes, a black lesbian with a French partner ("I say she's French because it's a nicer way of saying she's white"), does a bit in which she says it's easier to be black than to be a lesbian because at least you don't have to come out to your parents as black. She carries the joke forward by impersonating the dismayed parents faced with such a coming out: "You're not black. It's just a phase. You're confused."

Magazines and clothing lines are also springing up to meet the desire of the diasporic young to explore and express their identities—usually with humour. *Heeb*, a New York–based magazine, speaks to young Jews about pop culture, Judaism, and much else through thick layers of affection, irony, in-jokes, and intelligence. Another magazine scratches a similar itch among Asian Americans. Its name? *Hyphen* (as in, hyphenated identity).

Perhaps you'd rather wear your identity on your chest than read about it. If you are South Asian, you might want to head over to DesiThreads.com (*Desi* being a word descended from Sanskrit for the people and products of South Asia). Desi Threads is a company that will sell you a T-shirt proclaiming, for instance, "I'm famous in Bollywood," "Desi pride," or "Brown is sexy." Cheekier customers may choose something with a little more edge, such as a shirt featuring Apu, the South Asian convenience store owner from *The Simpsons*, uttering his signature line, "Thank you, come again." (Apu has a Ph.D., by the way.) Or a shirt that says, "My other shirt has been outsourced."

Thirty years ago, playful expressions of identity like these were off-limits. Equality was serious business—no room for levity. Equality is still serious business. But today expressions of difference, including humorous takes on the quirks of one's own group or even the way that group is seen in the wider culture, are not seen as antithetical to a serious commitment to equality.

The fact that entertainers like Russell Peters have huge and tremendously diverse audiences is a sign not only of low *Ethnic Intolerance* but, more importantly, of the powerful emergence of the value *Social Learning*, which measures the belief that interacting with people of different backgrounds is fun and enriching. The *Social Learning* mindset, on which the post-Boomer generations stand out markedly, assumes that people are equal (yawn) but also that difference means great stories, great conversations, and great insights about ourselves and others. For people who are strong on *Social Learning*, we are all a bunch of walking Rorschach tests; we see our values and assumptions reflected or distorted in one another, and we delight in talking to others about what they see when they look at us. Through these conversations, we follow neural pathways in our brains that we never knew existed.

The same sense of playfulness and flexibility that leading-edge post-Boomers bring to their relationships with ethnicity is evident in their attitudes toward gender. While on racial equality the post-Boomers outscore both their parents and their grandparents, on gender equality they're more or less in line with the Boomers. Post-Boomers are about as likely as their parents to agree that men and women are inherently equal and that boys and girls should have the same opportunities, both in the family and in the workplace. Where post-Boomers outscore their parents is in their acceptance of diverse family models (especially same-sex unions) and, more broadly, on the value *Flexibility of Gender Identity*, which measures the belief people should be able to adapt gender in ways that make them feel most like themselves. Whether it's your dress, your work, your partner, your walk, your hair, or your hobbies, you should be able to live the way you want even if this involves behaviours not traditionally associated with your biological sex. *Flexibility of Gender Identity* also implies an acceptance of the idea that gender is somewhat fluid: that you might feel more masculine one day and more feminine another day, and that this is normal, not unhinged.

We see evidence of this fluidity of gender in the faddishness with which masculine and feminine identities seem to drift through fashion and popular culture—especially for men. For several years in the late 1990s, Russell Crowe was *the* sex symbol. Women had had enough of the sensitive man with soft hands and a desk job: they wanted a gladiator, someone who could win a bar fight, someone who didn't talk about his feelings or—God forbid—have a therapist. Someone straight-forward, strong, and protective: a real man. But soon the passion for Russell Crowe–type men seemed to ebb and the metrosexual turned up. Here was a man so secure in his mas-culinity that he could not only use facial moisturizer but be picky about which one he used. Here was a heterosexual man who saw socks as an opportunity for a splash of colour, who appreciated an elegant pen, who knew how to dance and didn't fear that others would therefore think he was gay. If the Russell Crowe man was a caribou whose robust antlers, ready for bat-tle, were a sign of virility, the metrosexual was a peacock whose plumage had evolved to attract. Each had his own distinctly masculine appeal. The same man might try on both costumes as fashions evolved.

A similar degree of playfulness and flexibility has been seen among women: from the *Sex and the City* ladies' "girly-girl" shoe-shopping jags (and blast-from-the-past husband hunting), to the musician Pink's six-pack abs and brazen attitude, to Lady Gaga's over-the-top costumes that are an unsettling mixture of hyper-feminine glamour and monstrous confusion, female pop culture figures have adopted a huge range of postures over the past decade.

Linguistically, the expression "man up" has taken hold in recent years. (As in "I'm sorry your car is stuck in the snow, but complaining isn't going to get you anywhere. Man up and dig it out.") Both men and women can be exhorted to "man up." Although feminist purists will object to the equating of strength and efficacy with masculinity, there's something distinctly playful about the expression, which positions "manning" as a verb—and as an activity at which men can be deficient and women can excel. (After all, if men were always and inherently strong and efficacious, there'd be no need to remind them to man up.)

One complaint about the kind of feminism championed by many Boomer feminists during the 1970s was that it placed too much emphasis on sameness as a sign of equality: women wearing pants and becoming firefighters, men being kindergarten teachers and nurses. Perhaps because women have made so much material progress over the past few decades, the Boomers' push for sameness—women being strong and men being sensitive, Mars and Venus meeting in the middle—is fading away. Women are more confident that they'll be taken seriously at work, for instance, so they see less need to wear a navy "power suit" to underscore their seriousness. Within the bounds of professional appropriateness, they can dress like themselves—whether colourful or conservative—and assume that their sartorial choices will not be scrutinized any more than those of their male colleagues. Post-Boomers seem to be more comfortable with the concept of gender as a matter of costume and performance, a part you can play with as much or as little passion, flare, and humour as you wish. They're more likely than Boomers of either gender to perceive a kernel of truth in the saucy dictum of cross-dressing performer RuPaul: "We're born naked. Everything else is drag."

Speaking of performance, when the post-Boomers perform— especially the youngest of them—they're vastly more likely than their parents or grandparents to assume that the whole world will see; everything is online, right? The differences across generations on the value *Control of Privacy* are huge. For example, we asked Canadians to respond to the statement "It worries me greatly that government and companies are storing more and more information about people's private lives." Among Elders, 44 percent express the strongest possible concern with this data-hoarding tendency, and an additional 36 percent say they're at least somewhat concerned. Among early Boomers (born 1946 to 1955), the highest level concern attracts slightly more people (48 percent), presumably because these Boomers are online more and feel more exposed to the financial and personal privacy risks of working and socializing in a networked world. Among late Boomers (born 1956 to 1965) extreme concern drops back down to 44 percent. But it's among Generations X and Y that concern about privacy drops off most sharply: just

31 percent of Gen Xers (born from 1966 to 1979) and 22 percent of Gen Yers (born from 1980 to 1993) express strong concern about their data being accumulated by institutions and private companies.

There is some evidence that as young people learn more about the possible implications of oversharing online—especially as they hit the job market—they become more careful. A telephone survey conducted by researchers at the University of California, Berkeley, found that most young adults aged eighteen to twenty-four reported being more concerned about their online privacy in early 2010 than they had been five years ago.[7] And the Pew Research Center's Internet and American Life Project finds that two-thirds (66 percent) of teens actively manage their privacy settings on sites like Facebook; this is higher than the proportion of adults who do so.[8] Most teens who post personal information online also say they give some thought to the various levels of access they grant to readers; friends may get to see all the messy details of the weekend, but parents, teachers, and prospective employers may see a smaller subset of the user's online profile.

Still, although most young people may be careful about online privacy—and even growing more wary over time as social-networking platforms like Facebook become more aggressive in sharing users' data with advertisers—the fact remains that those who have grown up with the Internet clearly have different assumptions about what it means to share information about themselves online, whether in their daily blogged pensées or photos and videos. Older people often gasp at the ease with which young people expose their lives (and sometimes their bodies) online. In more than one recent election campaign, candidates, usually young ones, have had to withdraw from their races because of blog- or Facebook-related embarrassment. In the 2008 federal election, an NDP candidate and a Conservative candidate each truncated their campaigns because of inflammatory remarks they had made online long before the election race began: the NDPer on a Facebook page, the Conservative on a blog. In the 2009 B.C. provincial election, a young NDP candidate, Ray Lam, had to withdraw from his race in Vancouver–False Creek because of racy Facebook photos.

As these cases show, excessive online sharing can be a serious liability—for now. But standards and expectations will evolve as two changes happen. First, everyone (including young people) will develop more nuanced approaches to sharing personal information on the Internet. Privacy is a much more widely discussed aspect of online life today than it was even a few years ago, and demand for privacy tools and protections will likely continue to grow. Second, young people and their mores will displace Boomer dinosaurs who would cringe at even some of the low-level sharing their kids do online. A hint of these changing standards comes from Sue Gardner, executive director of the Wikimedia Foundation, the parent organization of Wikipedia and other online free-content projects. Gardner gave the 2009 Dalton Camp Lecture in Journalism at Fredericton's St. Thomas University, covering a range of topics related to the proliferation of online content and its effect on journalism, politics, and society. Gardner acknowledged that when she first started hiring young people to work at the Wikimedia Foundation, after Facebook had become a phenomenon, she was appalled at the ways in which the candidates exposed themselves online: the silly, drunken photos surprised her, and in the first few cases, it seemed they would really hurt the candidates' chances. But that was before Gardner realized a crucial fact: *all* the candidates had those photos. Soon she recalibrated her expectations: "After I'd seen 500 applicants' drunken party photographs, I settled down and figured: it's a level playing field—I'll just try to hire whoever seems smartest."9

I will not venture a projection about where this trend toward relatively unselfconscious display might lead us. What is clear is that Canada is entering (along with various pockets of the world, depending on cultural variations and Internet penetration) a new era of both transparency and exhibitionism that has the potential to take the Boomer dictum "the personal is political" into a whole other galaxy, where the personal is professional, the personal is commercial, and the personal is, above all, public. Just ask Tiger Woods.

For all the socializing and personal disclosure young people seem to engage in, their elders often wonder whether they're in some ways worryingly cut off from society. You may have five thousand "friends" on Facebook, but what have you done for your community lately? What is the state of civic responsibility among young people? How do the post-Boomers relate to their fellow citizens, their country, and the planet they call home? Our data suggest that the generations following the Boomers are not altogether disengaged, but neither are they strongly committed to the modes of citizenship and responsibility that previous generations have embraced.

Post-Boomers score noticeably below average on the value *New Social Responsibility*, saying they don't feel especially responsible for helping other people who face difficult circumstances. But this isn't necessarily a purely callous position: post-Boomers are in line with Boomers and Elders in believing that in a society as affluent as Canada, there's no excuse for extreme poverty. If poverty is unacceptable, and if post-Boomers themselves feel no great responsibility for helping people less fortunate than themselves, what's to be done? The government should fix it, of course. Post-Boomers vastly outscore Baby Boomers on the value *Government Involvement*, which measures the belief that society is better off when government steps in to solve its problems. All but a minority of youthful idealists shrug and say, "It's not my job."

Another problem post-Boomers may be relying on government to solve is climate change. Despite young people's reputation for being passionate tree huggers, we find post-Boomers to be surprisingly fatalistic about environmental issues. They don't doubt the apocalyptic implications of the ecological damage humans have wrought since the Industrial Revolution; indeed, post-Boomers have the highest scores of the three cohorts on the value *Ecological Alarmism*, perhaps because they're the most likely to be around to see the proverbial excrement hit the fan. Remarkably, however, this alarmism about an overheated planet doesn't appear to light much of a fire under young Canadians. This cohort is the least likely to say they make an effort to buy ecologically friendly products.

One would expect young people to be working feverishly to save the planet, not just because of the stereotype of youth as ardent greens, but also because saving the planet that gives them life would be enlightened self-interest in its most basic form. (It's important to keep in mind that a couple of the six youth tribes are probably doing the hardest, most innovative work they can muster on climate and energy issues. But this doesn't change the somewhat disheartening generational portrait, at least from a progressive Boomer perspective: for every inspired "New Aquarian"—the psychographic children of the Connected

Enthusiasts—there are two "Aimless Dependants"—imagine a much more nihilistic Disengaged Darwinist—who probably think the Copenhagen Summit is the name of a brewery.)

In fact, our values data suggest that powerful life-stage effects are at work regarding ecological values—and it's older Canadians who are more concerned about the environment. Although it's difficult to say why with certainty based on our data, I suspect that older people feel a heightened sense of concern for the fates of the children and grandchildren who will have to live on this planet after they're gone. Think of the greater concern older people have about young people being in car accidents or taking silly risks with their friends; partly because of experience and partly because of the risk aversion that can accompany age, older people are often more sensitive to the dangers of the world. Young people don't *want* to die in car accidents, of course, but many of them—especially testosterone-fuelled young men, it seems—don't have a visceral sense of the real possibility of such a fate. In the absence of this deep impulse of dread and peril, some youth are more likely to speed, pull stunts, and lose their temper, ignoring the warnings and hand-wringing of their elders, who are "worrywarts" and have ideas about the world that are downright "random." Older people's greater ecological concern might be of a piece with their other forms of worry; while young people are distracted by their own pursuits, older people have begun to take the long view—and don't like what they see.

Another factor that may contribute to older people's stronger sense of ecological concern is their greater tendency to garden. Paying close attention to the changes in a micro-environment like a garden—and feeling real concern for and investment in the small ecosystem one is fostering—may help to nurture a feeling of responsibility for the larger system in which that garden exists. Fretting over the health of a single tree can inspire awe at the vastness and complexity of a forest. Observing the effects of hotter- or dryer-than-usual summer in a garden (and fretfully adhering to watering bans) is likely to make an impression; experiencing that same summer in an air-conditioned condo tower, showering at will and generally insulating oneself from its effects, is unlikely to cause any great flashes of insight.

Whatever the underlying thinking and experiences, older Canadians are indeed greener in their values (and in their self-reported behaviours) than are younger, more materialistic, and status-anxious Canadians. Currently, the areas in which young people at large report the highest levels of enthusiasm mostly involve having fun: socializing, having intense emotional experiences, and shopping for cool stuff. Does this mean that the Baby Boomers have raised a generation of superficial, hedonistic, materialistic airheads? I suspect not.

First, the diversity of the post-Boomer generations cannot be overstated: the "young people" discussed in this chapter range in age from seventeen to forty-four—everyone old enough to be in our sample as of 2008 and young enough not to be Baby Boomers. In addition to this age diversity, this generation has more psychographic diversity than any other: the Elders coalesce into three tribes, the Boomers into four, the post-Boomers into no fewer than six. Some of these tribes are tremendously idealistic, entrepreneurial, exploratory, and open-minded. Others are materialistic, angry, and aggressive; demonstrate no particular regard for themselves or others; and are aimlessly alienated from the mainstream of our evolving diversity and more tolerant social values.

Second, four in ten Canadians are either immigrants or the children of immigrants. Very often, newcomers have arrived in Canada from traditional cultures and less wealthy ones; as a result, they aspire to tasting the fruits of North American affluence and modernity. Immigrants' wish to attain the material benefits of a good education and hard work is one that generations of the Canadian-born have displayed and has been the source of a great deal of the economic growth this country and others have enjoyed. Canada's growing (and very young) population of urban Aboriginal people is likely to display some of the same aspirations. Both groups will evolve toward more post-material values over time as their basic material security becomes an assumption instead of a preoccupation. One hopes that we'll all evolve toward postmaterialism faster than the planet "evolves" toward collapse.

Third, although the average positions of young people on some values are less than inspiring, it's important to remember that our priorities change as we age. How many Baby Boomers who now dream of visiting the children they sponsor in another country once would have said their fondest wish was for a little MG to call their own? (The automotive love of my youth was a red Alfa Romeo GTV 2000. What a car!) Those Autonomous Rebels who say they want to write novels or join think tanks during their retirement—did they ever just want to find a girlfriend or boyfriend and go to that new coffee house to discuss Dostoevsky and existentialism, dreaming of eternal dyadic bliss?

Baby Boomers—and certainly their parents—are entering deeply postmaterial phases of their lives. Most have what they need and don't anticipate really wanting for the basics, even if their retirement savings fall short of their ideal. The higher rungs of Abraham Maslow's hierarchy of needs (which has food, clothing, shelter, personal safety, and other essentials at its base and climbs up to higher-order needs such as status and personal fulfillment) are within reach for most Boomers. For the most part, they have mastered their trades, built successful businesses, earned sterling professional reputations, raised good kids, or achieved any number of other more idiosyncratic goals. They feel good about themselves, and they feel good about the way others see them. With both their material needs and their quests for social belonging and status largely taken care of, the Boomers are ready to spend the rest of their lives pursuing genuinely meaningful experiences. (One emblematic bucket-list wish: "I'd like to travel with my son somewhere he would like to go." Is that them together on a Harley heading out of Saskatoon on their way to Banff?)

The average post-Boomer is just embarking on this journey: accumulating debt while pursuing an expensive degree they hope will lead somewhere, launching a career, and seeking a long-term partner. They're entering a period of striving, hard work, and uncertainty. They're trying to gain ground materially—some bearing the added pressure of having immigrant parents who made immense sacrifices for their children to succeed—and are trying to show others (often through consumption) that they're making the grade. Seen in this light, the average young person's relative lack of fire about the state of the environment is perhaps less surprising.

Over time, young people will find their places in society. Not everyone will "win" in the sense of achieving every aspiration or becoming the richest, most famous, most cited, or most technically proficient person in their circle of friends. But most will find a path that satisfies them. (And all have achieved a substantial measure of good fortune by being born in or immigrating to a society with a strong social fabric, a reasonable social safety net, and unusual physical security.) As this happens, young Canadians will slowly, incrementally begin to move beyond their material aspirations to express their postmaterial values with increasing confidence and conviction: their sense of global citizenship, their sense that identities are fluid, and their vision for whatever multicultural, multivocal, multi-faceted place Canada has become. Baby Boomers will be fortunate if they live long enough to watch their children—and their friends' children and their children's children—evolve beyond their inevitable love affairs with materialism to become more fully themselves.

I am one early Boomer who feels lucky to have the freedom—political, material, social, and emotional—to be himself, imperfect but aspiring to rise above my insecurities and be authentic. This is a gift I have been given by Canada, by my friends, by my profession, and perhaps above all by my Elder parents. My parents were small-c conservative in many ways, but they each had their critiques (rarely discussed) of the world in which they had grown up.

My dad felt he had done his duty in the war—but it wasn't the greatest time of his life (as the mythology sometimes has it). He never felt comfortable in the Legion Hall exchanging war stories, and he chose not to march on Remembrance Day. He didn't want ever to see his sons fighting in a war for their country. He hated fascism and communism across the ocean, but he also grew to hate nationalism and militarism among those on "our side." Instead of making him passionately patriotic, his experience of war made him deeply skeptical of ideology at large. He saw no romance or heroism in war. He and my mom wanted their sons to live in Canada, not die for Canada.

My mom, for her part, had wanted to be a doctor—not a nurse. Her thrifty and patriarchal father couldn't conceive of a woman doctor, and even less could he conceive of footing the bill for such a ludicrous thing as sending a daughter to medical school when motherhood would relegate her to the home soon enough. My mother was a wonderful RN, but she worked in hospitals for the rest of her life in the knowledge that sheer prejudice had prevented her from becoming an MD.

We buried (actually cremated) my mom a couple of years ago, and I found myself having great difficulty delivering the eulogy. This was perhaps because I felt that this intelligent woman should have celebrated more personal success on this planet than she did.

If a commitment to education was the crucial difference between the Elders and their parents, the most crucial differences between Elders and Boomers are the Boomers' secularism and their altered orientation to the role and status of women. My generation accelerated the shift from unquestioned patriarchy to (at least aspirational) equality between men and women, and in my view made a major contribution to the most important social revolution in the twentieth century.

Because of the social change that has transpired over the

course of Baby Boomers' lifetimes, my daughter has all the opportunities that were denied my mother; I hope she'll see the unfulfilled aspirations of her grandmother and other Elder women as fuel and inspiration—not as a weight or a source of guilt. More likely, she takes her opportunities for granted just like her Boomer parents took their middle-class affluence for granted when they were her age.

In the year this book is published, 2010, I am turning sixty-four—an age made famous by the Beatles, who saw loving someone to this advanced age as tantamount to eternal devotion. Actuaries tell me I will live for another eighteen years. If they're right in their predictions and my parachute indeed fails to open at some point in 2028, my daughter, Marion, will be thirty-six years old, and my son, Will, just turned thirty-three. Each of them will live to beyond a hundred if they manage not to kill themselves on our new Vespa.

I am, for the moment, a happy, healthy Baby Boomer, having only recently bid adieu to my beloved parents, looking forward to the second half of my adult years. Life is good, so it must be a gift, one that to be truly enjoyed must be shared with others. Like many of my Boomer friends, I'm looking forward not only to my own adventures, but to watching my generation reinvent later life—and to watching our kids remake the world in their own way.

Amen.

Methodology of the Canadian Social Values Monitor

THE THEORETICAL FOUNDATIONS OF SOCIAL VALUES RESEARCH

The Environics social values measurement system seeks to understand the structure of social values in a society and monitor changes in those values over time. The roots of the method go back more than a century and a half to a curious young Frenchman named Alexis de Tocqueville. De Tocqueville visited the United States in the 1830s in order to examine, first-hand, the social and political life of the world's "first new nation." His *Democracy in America* is to social values research what Adam Smith's *The Wealth of Nations* is to the understanding of economics. Later in the nineteenth century, economist Thorstein Veblen took another giant step forward in the description and understanding of changes to human social values with his *Theory of the Leisure Class.*

A generation ago, academic social scientists such as Maslow, Riesman, Bell, Rokeach, and Thurstone began to describe and measure social values, and to explore their dynamics and manifestations in contemporary societies. They also identified a hierarchy of social values. For example, Maslow saw a structure and evolution of values from those associated with physical survival at the base level of human needs to those associated with self-actualization at the highest intellectual and moral levels of motivation. Individuals, and even whole societies, could be roughly characterized according to this values hierarchy depending on the beliefs and concerns they displayed most strongly.

In everyday parlance, the term "values" has come to take on a rich panoply of meanings and connotations. Take, for instance, the ubiquitous "family values," whose precise nature is often assumed without articulation. In the 1960s, however, psychologist Milton Rokeach first theorized about and defined social values in more precise and scientific terms as having the following properties:

- They are beliefs;
- They are conceptions of, preferences for, and prescriptions about desirable modes of conduct or established orientations

toward living and existence (in other words, the means of living);

- They are conceptions of, preferences for, and prescriptions about desirable end-states of existence and social ideals (in other words, the ends of living).

Examples of the first type of beliefs, the means of living, include such values as honesty, hard work, or even "playing the system." Examples of the second type, the ends of living, include such values as status, health, peace, enlightenment, and power and influence.

Such formative and fundamental beliefs about the desirable means and ends of human conduct and existence are thought to be largely moulded in adolescence and early adulthood experience. Social values are informed by a person's prevalent perceptions and learning provided both in the family and in his or her close kinship group, and by exposure to the predominant sociohistorical environment and influences of the times into which he or she is born, is being raised, and comes of age (by which we mean "reaches sentient awareness of the world"). Once massively defined by institutions such as the church and state, values have never been as idealistic or ideological as they were cast in Rokeach's view, but rather can also serve, quite pragmatically, as a person's or society's adaptation to, and justification of, current personal or cultural practices. Those practices—from interpersonal honesty to Machiavellianism, and from social assistance to genocide—are more often than not framed, or even "spun," in terms of the higher-order values they serve.

In terms of today's social scientific jargon, at Environics we consider values also to be evidence of "motivated cognition." These are beliefs that both determine and reflect our responses to the world as we struggle to meet such basic psychological and sociological needs as biological survival, connection with our close kinship groups, and our species' predilection toward organizing socially in hierarchical and status-defined groups. So, beyond their definition as desirable or prescribed means and ends of living, the term "values" has come to capture the deeper motivations behind human behaviour, tendencies of thought and feelings—unconscious as well as conscious—and the intra- and interpersonal dynamics related to them.

As we peel the onion of human motivation, we see that a host of different aspects of people's worldviews are well captured by an assessment of their "values," so defined. These aspects include assumptions, perceptions, and habits of thought; attitudes, judgments, and opinions; and intentions, tendencies, and actions. Values stand in, then, as a good description for a multitude of mental, emotional, and motivational postures with which we conduct our transactions with others and ourselves. What our research really attempts, then, is a rather broadband analysis of the worldviews of individuals and of collectives, big and small.

THE EVOLUTION OF SOCIAL VALUES

For most of history, the pace of change for us humans culturally and technologically, and certainly spiritually, can only be described as glacial. A paradigm shift in worldviews happened rarely (think agriculture, iron, Christ, Galileo, Gutenberg, Luther, Darwin, etc.), and its effects played out over generations of adaptation to the new invention of things or ideas. Not so in today's rapid world of invention and cultural convergence, where knowledge is discovered so rapidly that it can double within half a single generation. Now, the main mechanism for values change at a societal level is generational replacement. Youth are a constant source of new ideas and beliefs that infuse the culture and become predominant as the values of older generations die with their cohort.

Although they are shaped by the world one experiences in one's youth, values are not unchanging things set immutably in stone. Rather, they evolve through one's lifetime, albeit usually slowly. At the psychological level, they change somewhat as a function of a person's life stage, life challenges, and experience. Which parents among us can deny an uncharacteristic but extreme authoritarian impulse or two when confronting a raging child? Moreover, values can change somewhat in response to major socio-historical events as they occur throughout people's lifespans, for example in reaction to the spread of a technology like the PC or a disease like AIDS, or as the result of insecurity born of a deep recession, the trauma of face-to-face combat in war, or the chilling aftermath of an act of terror.

With the development of democracy and pluralism, and the corresponding decline in unbending institutional regulation of people's worldviews in many parts of the world, the character of values has changed from one of imposed stability and homogeneity within a culture and across time to one of flux and variability. And with the accelerated pace of change in most aspects of our world, this trend has been further enhanced in our own time.

SOCIAL VALUES METHODOLOGY

The social values assessment methodology we employ, which was first developed in the 1960s by Alain de Vulpian and our French colleagues at his company Cofremca in Paris, was invented in response to a wish to understand the evolution and meaning of the spontaneous rejection of traditional values and institutions evident among many young people in French society at that time. Like their North American colleagues in this enterprise, such as Daniel Yankelovich, the French social scientists took their initial understanding of the societal structuring and evolution of social values from extensive qualitative research, primarily in-depth, one-on-one interviews. This research revealed new attitudes toward order, religious and secular authority, success, social status, the role of the sexes, and the place of youth in society, as well as a growing orientation of individuals toward personal autonomy, informality, and immediate gratification.

In the early 1970s, the knowledge gained from this qualitative research was used to create questions and scales designed to measure the diffusion of these new values within the French culture. This was accomplished through annual quantitative surveys of representative samples of the population. Thus was born the study of "socio-cultural currents"—the evolution of social values in a culture—and the resulting "Système Cofremca de Suivi des Courants Socio-Culturels" (3SC). The system was subsequently extended beyond France into more than twenty countries in Europe and the Americas. On this side of the Atlantic, the polling firm CROP, based in Quebec, imported 3SC to Canada in 1983, and with the help of Environics Research Group and Kaagan Research Associates, into the United States in the 1990s.

A TECHNICAL LOOK AT THE SOCIAL VALUES MAP

Each new social values map we create for a culture requires about ten steps of detailed methodology leading up to a "trackable" quantitative analysis. While we will neither go into the reasons why all these steps are necessary, nor how they are conducted statistically with the specific software algorithms employed, we will describe the most important facets in detail here.

The goal of the first quantitative study in a new country is to understand the major structural relations among the values in evidence there. As more data come in, we begin to explore the currents and trajectories of values evolution in that society. Here are the necessary steps in the workup of a full-bodied socio-cultural profile of a society.

VALUES CONSULTATION AND SENSING

The key to the development of a socio-cultural analysis for any country is value sensing. This is where we discover which values are currently prevalent, and lay the foundation for the detection of new trends that may emerge in the future. Through the qualitative research we routinely conduct in a given culture for a wide array of clients, we constantly seek to extract and abstract what is novel and potentially important in socio-cultural values terms in relation to that which has come before. We ask what is bubbling up from the many generative groups in the culture, from youth and new immigrant groups to emerging political or religious movements. We try to sniff out what is developing in terms of political counterculture, new ideologies, technology uptake and resistance, new social forms in the family, changing attitudes toward work, trends in popular culture and entertainment, evolving patterns of consumption, emerging preferences for travel and leisure, new aesthetic and design sensibilities, evolving food and drink preferences, and so forth.

In addition to our ongoing research, we conduct special studies just for this purpose of values sensing, by finding the opinion leaders, local experts, and market mavens at the sharp edge of the values change wedge in these various topical areas, and then interviewing them in depth. As part of this values trend identification methodology, we do detailed interviews, web-based research, anthropological studies called everyday life research (EDLs), and countless focus groups with both average and exceptional people. And importantly, we also interview local cultural experts, commentators, and interpreters and lean on our international colleagues, who also conduct this type of research worldwide, for their experiences and insights. When our preparation is complete, we sift through the trends collaboratively as a research team, through the benefits and biases of our training individually as sociologists and semioticians, psychologists and market researchers, prognosticators, analysts, and communicators.

In doing this work, this "search for the new," we look for what is likely to be enduring rather than faddish in cultural evolution; current fashion and hot-this-season children's toys, for example, are not something that are best viewed as constituting what we take to be values. Plus, we look for things that are likely to have multiple manifestations in people's lives. In recent years, for example, the perceived invasiveness of employers, governments, and e-commerce marketers has led to a concern for privacy that is likely to have diverse manifestations as people assert their rights to privacy across a wider spectrum of their lives. We might hypothesize about whether privacy will become more precious—or completely meaningless—as technology enhances our ability to connect with (and keep watch over) one another. Only time and empirical data will tell if, or under what conditions, people will accept or reject mandatory drug testing, workplace video monitoring, or e-commerce "leave behinds." To find out which way the cookie crumbles, indeed if it does at all, we need a quantitative survey to assess our hunches, heuristics, and hypotheses about the supposed multiple manifestations of each value.

QUESTIONNAIRES AND DATA COLLECTION

To fully understand the Environics socio-cultural system, one must understand how we create operational measures of each value identified in the qualitative phase and then analyze these together in "multivariate" (multiple variable) space. Again, we draw on both the work of other social scientists and our own empirical research to understand how best to assess each value and to explore the meaning of these values working in concert in each culture.

The first quantitative stage in the analysis is a familiar one in survey research: to develop and administer a high-quality survey to a representative sampling of the society's population so that valid inferences can be drawn, robust data patterns can be replicated, and confident generalizations can be made about various subgroups in the population. The goal is to translate the subtle and not-so-subtle values and mental postures we have sensed in the first step into a set of empirical measures that are valid and reliable, replicable, and defensible. This is where science and art really begin to comingle in our work, and where if we are any good at what we do, the solid scientific methodology underlying our values measurement system will be artfully conceived, crafted, and carried out.

Values Construction

This represents the heart of the analysis, and it is here that we both validate our hypothesized social values and discover new values that emerge from the data, using a multivariate statistical technique called principal components analysis (PCA), combined with Cronbach alpha reliability analysis. At the end of this step, we hope to have articulated a set of social values that adequately describes the culture under investigation, and from which meaningful and interesting insights can be drawn. In Canada, we typically assess and track eighty-seven such values, from those with grand and enduring sociological stature, such as the *Need for Status Recognition, Rejection of Authority,* and *Ethnic Intolerance,* to those that describe the subtleties of everyday life, such as the trends we call *Concern for Appearance, Effort for Health,* and *Personal Creativity.* Through such disparate content, we are better able to capture people's mental, emotional, spiritual, and behavioural expectations and response tendencies, and thus discern the phenomena of their everyday lives.

Each value comprises the measurement and combination of several survey items in its construction. For example, the value *Social Learning* is defined in part as "attraction to and interest in diversity" and the sense that "diversity is perceived as a source of personal enrichment." This idea is measured by having respondents agree or disagree on a four-point scale with several items in the survey, such as the item "If you want to learn and grow in life, it is essential to meet and converse with different kinds of people, who come from all kinds of backgrounds." Another item that constitutes the value *Social Learning* is "I learn a great deal from meeting people who are different from me." The items are combined mathematically to create this value measure, scores are assigned to each respondent on this and all other values, and those respondents scoring highest (or sometimes lowest) on a value are classified as strong (or weak) on the value.

PERCEPTUAL MAPPING

We again use principal components analysis (PCA), or sometimes factor analysis of correspondence (FAC), to explore the associations between individuals' standing on their many social values. From this analysis emerges a "map-space solution," a set of axes or dimensions that more generally underlie, differentiate, and explain the collection of values we have assessed among our respondents. Many such solutions are possible and considered. The axes chosen should allow us to interpret the values together on one common "map," to explore their positions relative to other values, and to track change over time in a compelling way. The axes are named to capture the main themes of the values and mental postures that define them. While there are typically three to seven axes that best describe the interrelations among the eighty-five-plus values we have assessed in our respondents, we often depict the data in only the two most explanatory and interesting dimensions when explicating and communicating our findings. (This is why our "maps" almost always look like flat rectangles with four quadrants, instead of three-dimensional galaxies with values instead of stars.)

It is important to remember that our map is about the *people* who are plotted there. Individuals are assigned a set of axis coordinates on the various dimensions, and we use these to plot each individual, or the average positions of subgroups of respondents, or indeed the entire population average of a culture, or of that culture at a specific point in time. The axes are chosen, in part, if the anchorings provided by plotting major demographic subgroups make fundamental sense across the values space. For example, older age groups are generally associated with greater conformity, and higher education is often associated with autonomy, so we use these basic markers as tests for whether the map makes sense. But these are not our only criteria for selecting the axes.

It's worth keeping in mind that any type of group, demo-graphic or not, can be defined and plotted on the map, as for example,

- Teenagers;
- Working women;
- High household income earners;
- Quebecers;
- Generational cohorts, such as Baby Boomers;
- Supporters of a political party or position;
- Early adopters of a technology;
- Heavy Brand X users;
- "Somewhat satisfied" customers;
- Dog owners;
- Particularly strong believers in the value of *Ethical Consumerism*.

The last example is of particular interest. In order to create the map that positions the eighty-seven social values in the map space, we adopt the following convention. We place the name of each value we assess at the point on the map where its strongest proponents reside. We define "strongest proponents" as approximately the top one-fifth of people who report that they agree with the value (as assessed by all its items combined). In other words, the label "Ethical Consumerism" is positioned on the map by proxy, at the average axes position points of those 20 percent of individuals strongest in their orientation toward this value, which we measure by asking how much they monitor their consumption and buy from companies with good track records in environmental and employee practices.

Each of the groups listed above can also be profiled in detail in terms of all their values to see what their particularly strong and weak value orientations are among the eighty-seven we assess. It's usually the case that a complex array of value standings characterizes any one group, such as the highly educated, but in total they must combine to give the average position for the group we show on our two major values axes. In our proprietary work, we compute a set of scores for all the values that indexes how much stronger or weaker a chosen group is compared to the national average (or any other particular comparison group of interest). The resulting "gestalt" of correlated value orientations for that group provides a rich portrait that can be used for understanding and communicating with them.

Definitions of the Socio-Cultural Trends

ACCEPTANCE OF VIOLENCE Believing that violence is an inevitable part of life. People strongest on this trend even accept violence as an outlet for letting off steam or as a way of getting what they want. For some, violence is becoming the only way they can make themselves heard in today's world.

ADAPTABILITY TO COMPLEXITY IN LIFE Tendency to adapt easily to the uncertainties of modern life, and to feel unthreatened by the changes and complexities of society today. A desire to explore this complexity as a learning experience and a source of opportunities. (Inverse of *Aversion to Complexity in Life*.)

ADAPTIVE NAVIGATION Having the flexibility to adapt to unforeseen events that interfere with the realization of one's goals. Being flexible in defining one's expectations and ways of meeting one's objectives.

ANOMIE AND AIMLESSNESS The feeling of having no goals in life. Experiencing a void of meaning with respect to life in general. A feeling of alienation from society, having the impression of being cut off from what's happening.

APOCALYPTIC ANXIETY Tendency to believe that the world is heading toward major upheavals in the future, and to anticipate these changes with anxiety.

ATTRACTION TO CROWDS Taking pleasure in being immersed in a crowd. Desire to share the collective emotions of large crowds and major public events.

ATTRACTION TO NATURE How close people want to be to nature, whether to recharge their spiritual batteries or to enjoy a simpler, healthier, or more authentic way of life.

AVERSION TO COMPLEXITY IN LIFE A desire to keep one's life simple and predictable. People strong on this trend are intimidated and threatened by the changes and complexities in modern life and values. They look for stability and simplicity. (Inverse of *Adaptability to Complexity in Life*.)

AWARENESS OF MORTALITY Awareness of and concern over one's own mortality and that of others. For people particularly strong on this trend, awareness is accompanied, at times, by a certain anxiety and fatalism combined with elements of religiosity, spirituality, millennial anxiety, and even environmentalism and belonging to the global village ("The planet is going to hell and we're going with it").

BELONGING TO THE "GLOBAL VILLAGE" Impression of being "plugged into" what's happening in other countries, that one's everyday life is similar to what people experience in other parts of the world. Also, a sense that one can feel what people in other parts of the world are feeling. A sense of being more a citizen of the world than of one's own country, of participating in an international culture, of living in Marshall McLuhan's "global village."

BRAND GENUINENESS Tendency to value authenticity and to look for a deeper level of brand experience. People strong on this trend want their brands to have a soul, a history, a founding myth, a place of origin that confers its own culture. These preferences attract them to brands that not only provide the functionality they seek, but also feed their imaginations by telling a true and compelling story.

CANADIAN IDENTITY The tendency for people to consider the fact of being "Canadian" as an important part of their identity.

CIVIL DISOBEDIENCE Legitimizing a lack of respect for the social contract, which is considered to be unworkable. Anything goes if it can help people survive in today's economy. Working or hiring someone under the table or taking liberties with one's income tax return are both expressions of this trend.

COMMUNITY INVOLVEMENT Measure of the interest in what's happening in one's neighbourhood, city, town, or region. Reflected in activities ranging from reading the weekly community newspaper to socio-political involvement in community organizations. Also an indicator of social conscience.

CONCERN FOR APPEARANCE Placing a great deal of importance on appearing "attractive," and on the image projected by one's appearance. People who are strong on this trend are image-driven; this is expressed through specific products and brands.

CONFIDENCE IN ADVERTISING Tendency to trust and use advertising as a source of reliable information. Also, a tendency to identify with the fashions and the role models promoted by advertising and the consumer society.

CONFIDENCE IN BIG BUSINESS Tendency to assume that big businesses are generally fair and ethical in their practices, committed to providing quality goods and working in the public interest. (Inverse of *Skepticism toward Big Business*.)

CONFIDENCE IN SMALL BUSINESS Tendency to assume that small businesses are generally fair and ethical in their practices, committed to providing quality goods and working in the public interest. (Inverse of *Skepticism toward Small Business.*)

CONSUMPTION EVANGELISM Desire to exercise real leadership among the peer group in adopting brands, products, and services. Consumers who are strong on this trend are enthusiastic, even passionate, about what they buy and are very well informed about product features and competitive products. These are the people others consult before buying something. Because of their large, well-maintained social network, they wield great influence in promoting a brand, product, or service.

CONSUMPTIVITY This trend represents enthusiasm for purchasing products or services in areas of particular interest (such as music or electronics), about which consumers make an effort to stay continually informed. Through books, magazines, and other means, consumers ensure that they're always up to date with the latest product offerings and market developments in their special area of interest, in order to take maximum advantage of their newest acquisitions.

CONTROL OF DESTINY Desire to escape from the domination of society over daily life. The desire to control all aspects of one's life, even those determined by forces over which we seem to have little control. Tendency to believe that not everything is predetermined, that one can influence the course of events. (Inverse of *Fatalism.*)

CONTROL OF PRIVACY   Great concern about the fact that in databases, among other ways, government and business are amassing increasingly large banks of information about people's private lives. People strongest on this trend are selective in their purchases, notably by considering the ethics of the manufacturers.

CULTURAL FUSION   This trend identifies the view that other cultures have a great deal to give us and measures people's inclination to incorporate some of these cultural influences into their own lives. The meeting and fusion of totally different cultures produces rich and varied microcultures. This phenomenon is already apparent in many areas, such as music and cuisine. Well-adapted to the complexity of the New World Order, people strongest on this trend consider themselves citizens of the global village.

CYNICISM   Tendency to systematically discredit and doubt the credibility of society's elites, whether political, economic, or institutional. Firmly believing that society's leaders are motivated by self-interest rather than by concern for collective welfare.

DISCRIMINATING CONSUMERISM   Tendency to actively adopt defensive strategies to shield oneself from the artificial needs created by the consumer society and to seek product information before making purchases.

ECOLOGICAL ALARMISM   Tendency to believe that today's environmental problems are leading the planet toward catastrophe. Conviction that industry is in the process of destroying the planet through a total disregard for the environment.

ECOLOGICAL LIFESTYLE   Giving a high priority to integrating environmental concerns with purchasing criteria. This can have positive consequences, as when consumers are willing to pay more for an environmentally friendly product, or negative consequences, as when consumers refuse to buy a product whose manufacturer has an unsatisfactory environmental record. (Formerly *Ecological Consumerism.*)

EFFORT FOR HEALTH   The commitment to focus on diet and exercise in order to feel better and have a healthy, wholesome lifestyle. A willingness to transform one's lifestyle through exercise and radical changes to diet.

ENTHUSIASM FOR TECHNOLOGY   Favourable bias toward technology. Tendency to be fascinated with the possibilities offered by modern technology, to believe that technology is the best tool for facing today's world, one that helps us adapt and respond to the demands of daily life. People who are strong on this trend have great confidence that science and technology can better their lives.

EQUALITY OF THE SEXES   Tendency to attach no importance to traditional sexual roles and images. A desire to transcend sexual stereotypes and to see an end to discrimination. The people who are strongest on this trend desire to eliminate all differences between men and women in the family, the economy, and the culture. They also favour the establishment in society of the principle of equal opportunity for all citizens, no matter what their sex, ethnicity, religion, or physical and mental abilities.

EQUAL RELATIONSHIP WITH YOUTH   A desire to reverse the traditional hierarchical and patriarchal relationship in the family. Approval of young people having as much freedom as adults. This trend also indicates a permissive attitude toward pleasure in general: giving priority to individual needs, being tolerant, favouring freedom over discipline. By contrast, those who are weak on this trend tend to see adults as guardians of youth and generally value discipline as a guiding principle.

ETHICAL CONSUMERISM   Willingness to base consumer decisions on the perceived ethics of the company making the product (whether management treats employees fairly, co-operates with governments that don't meet ethical standards, or uses testing methods that involve mistreatment of animals). A desire to see companies act as good corporate citizens in terms of these new social concerns.

ETHNIC INTOLERANCE Intolerance toward immigrants and ethnic groups. Considering immigration a threat to the purity of the country, believing that the various ethnic groups should abandon their own customs and culture and adopt our own. People strongest on this trend display conformist values and consider national superiority especially important.

FAITH IN SCIENCE Tendency to believe that scientific advances will eventually succeed in solving all the major problems facing the world today: pollution, the greenhouse effect, climate catastrophes, replacing nonrenewable energy sources, and health problems. A perception that all these problems can be fixed by future advances in science and technology. A contemporary point of view combined with a kind of magical thinking encourages this techno-fix mentality, which results in a wait-and-see attitude to the main problems of the day. (Formerly *Scientism*.)

FATALISM Tendency to believe that society is governed by forces beyond individual control and that these forces are leading society to its ruin. A sense of losing control of one's life to these forces. (Inverse of *Control of Destiny*.)

FEAR OF VIOLENCE Fear of violence occurring in today's society. Feeling insecure about personal safety, feeling vulnerable to attack in the city or in one's neighbourhood, especially at night. Tendency to believe that one must be on constant alert against gratuitous violence.

FINANCIAL CONCERN REGARDING THE FUTURE The feeling of insecurity about one's financial future, particularly in old age, and of being personally responsible in this area.

FLEXIBILITY OF AGE IDENTITY Reflects the fact that age is not a major determining factor in a person's personality, attitudes, and, most particularly, social relationships. People strong on this trend believe that they can easily get to know and have meaningful exchanges with people who are much younger or older than they are.

FLEXIBILITY OF GENDER IDENTITY The belief that one has both a masculine and feminine side to one's personality. The desire to actively explore and express these different facets of one's personality. Having the feeling of being more masculine at some times and more feminine at others. This tendency is much stronger among women than men.

FLEXIBILITY OF PERSONALITY Tendency to actively explore and experience all the different facets of one's personality (especially the ones that aren't often expressed) and to enjoy flexible, "fluid" relations with others.

FLEXIBLE DEFINITION OF FAMILY Willingness to accept nontraditional definitions of "family," such as common-law marriages. The belief that family should be defined by emotional links rather than by legal formalities or institutions. Also, the belief that society should be open to new definitions of what constitutes a family.

FULFILLMENT THROUGH WORK   A need to invest one's professional life with meaning and to find personal fulfillment through one's work. Also, a need to feel that one's work is useful to others and has some social value.

GLOBAL ECOLOGICAL AWARENESS   Tendency to believe that all environmental phenomena on earth are interrelated. A systematic vision of environmental events, a conviction that ecological problems in one area of the world can have an impact on distant regions.

GOVERNMENT INVOLVEMENT   This trend measures confidence in the ability of government to positively affect how society works. Tendency to believe that the government performs a socially beneficial function. (Formerly *Confidence in Government*.)

HETERARCHY   Tendency to think that leadership in organizations should be flexible and fluid, that a leader shouldn't take control of everything, and that initiatives and leadership should emerge from different individuals as a function of their strengths. A belief that teamwork is more effective than autocracy and that leadership must be earned.

HYPER-RATIONALITY A propensity to give priority to reason as the principal way of understanding life. A desire to keep one's emotional life "on an even keel," to use logic and reason to control one's feelings and emotions and to make day-to-day decisions. A reluctance to experience emotions. (Inverse of *Pursuit of Intensity* and *Emotional Experiences.*)

IMPORTANCE OF AESTHETICS Tendency to base purchase decisions on aesthetic rather than utilitarian considerations. Measures the attention given to the beauty of objects and products purchased. People strong on this trend often buy products purely for their appearance. Aesthetics, in this case, is a form of personal expression. (Inverse of *Utilitarian Consumption.*)

IMPORTANCE OF BRAND Giving great weight to the brand name of a product or service, a tendency to have favourite brands.

IMPORTANCE OF NATIONAL SUPERIORITY Need to prove to others, and to oneself, that one's country is superior in many ways. Tendency to see oneself as superior to foreigners.

IMPORTANCE OF PHYSICAL BEAUTY Tendency to place a high priority on a youthful and attractive body, and being willing to make a considerable effort to attain and keep such a bodily appearance.

IMPORTANCE OF PRICE Giving great weight to price as a purchasing criterion. Consumers strong on this trend always take price into account when considering a purchase, even when the product or service is a particularly desired one.

INTEREST IN THE MYSTERIOUS Tendency to reject the assumption that all valid knowledge must be logical, rational, or scientific in favour of an acceptance of facts or phenomena that remain mysteries unexplained by modern science. Openness to the influence of mysterious forces, such as fortune telling, astrology, and occult religions.

INTROSPECTION AND EMPATHY Tendency to analyze and examine one's actions and those of others, rather than to be judgmental about variances from the norm or from one's own way of doing things. An interest in understanding life rather than taking sides.

JOY OF CONSUMPTION Intense gratification through the consumption of consumer goods (other than basic necessities). Enjoying consumption for the pleasure of consumption. Keeping abreast of everything new on the market. People who are strong on this trend are often more excited by the act of buying than by the use of the products they buy.

LEGACY Desire to leave behind a legacy after death, either to one's descendants or to society at large. This legacy could be of a financial, cultural, moral, or spiritual nature. People strong on this trend tend to plan their bequests well in advance.

MEANING OF LIFE Expressing a deep need to invest one's life with meaning or a goal, and to regularly reflect on this issue. Life exploration and experimentation in general help to enrich and direct the reflections of people strong on this trend. Other dimensions of great importance to these individuals: an intensely spiritual life, introspection, social responsibility, and family.

NEED FOR ESCAPE The desire to regularly escape the stress and responsibilities of everyday life.

NEED FOR PERSONAL ACHIEVEMENT The drive to achieve personal and social success. Taking on difficult ventures to demonstrate one's ability to succeed.

NEED FOR STATUS RECOGNITION Desire to be held in esteem and respect by others and to express one's social standing or aspired status, through a display of fine manners, good taste, "class," or "chic."

NEW SOCIAL RESPONSIBILITY A deep feeling of belonging to one's community and a pronounced feeling of social responsibility, where mutual assistance places a key role. This trend is associated with a desire to be open to others, and to better understand the society and the world around us.

OPENNESS TOWARD OTHERS Need for communication and deep, affective exchanges with others. A desire for frank, warm, and spontaneous relations with people.

PENCHANT FOR RISK-TAKING Desire to take risks for the pleasure and emotional thrill of doing so. Indulging in what is dangerous or forbidden for its associated emotional high. Also, a willingness to take risks to get what one wants out of life. (Inverse of *Risk Aversion*.)

PERSONAL CREATIVITY Desire to use one's imagination and creative talents in daily life, both at work and at play.

PRIMACY OF ENVIRONMENTAL PROTECTION Particular sensitivity to the issue of environmental protection. A personal attitude that places a high priority on protection of our environmental heritage; a willingness to support strong policies, to do one's part, and to pay the costs of environmental protection; and a belief that the environment is more important than jobs or the economy.

PRIMACY OF THE FAMILY Attachment to the family, where the family takes precedence over other personal priorities. For some, especially among those strongest on this trend, there is a strong connotation of status associated with the family's success (putting the family first and identifying with it as a standard of success and social integration).

PURSUIT OF HAPPINESS TO THE DETRIMENT OF DUTY

Motivation to act and live according to one's selfish impulses rather than one's obligations to others. A need to express one's personality and pursue happiness and pleasure, in spite of the dictates of duty or morality.

PURSUIT OF INTENSITY AND EMOTIONAL EXPERIENCES

Desire to live intensely. Also, a tendency to be guided less by reason and ideology than by one's own emotions, feelings, and intuition. A need to constantly experience new sensations. (Inverse of *Hyper-Rationality*.)

PURSUIT OF NOVELTY Active desire to discover new "modern" products, services, and experiences, and to integrate them into the routine of daily life. People who are strong on this trend want to experience something new every day.

PURSUIT OF ORIGINALITY Need to feel different from others. A preoccupation with demonstrating one's individuality through original touches.

REGIONAL IDENTITY The tendency for people to consider their province or region as an important part of their identity.

People strong on this trend are very proud of their province or region and are particularly attached to its culture and traditions.

REJECTION OF AUTHORITY Rejecting unquestioning respect for and deference to those in positions of authority. The belief that authority should not be respected for its own sake. Desire to transcend the rigid framework or traditional authority. Rejection of authority in the form of institutions and as a regulating principle of interpersonal relations. Desire to participate in the decision-making affecting your life; to be informed, consulted, involved (desire for autonomy).

RELIGIOSITY Placing a great importance on having an affiliation with an organized religious faith and on religious beliefs and rituals. Measure of intensity of the feeling of belonging to a religion. Tendency to consider that religion represents the essential values and education that should be transmitted to the next generation. (Items measuring this trend do not measure conformity to ritual, but rather the "values" based on religiosity.)

REPRIORITIZING OF MONEY A desire to make money less important, being prepared to lower one's standard of living to better meet one's goals. The realization that it is possible to live well without money; that money isn't essential. People very strong on this trend aspire to a life centred more on emotion, intuition, and meaningful communications with others; they also want work to have less priority in their lives.

REPRIORITIZING OF WORK A desire to make work less a priority; to maintain a better balance between one's personal and professional lives without having to sacrifice everything for work. People strong on this trend are also strong on *Reprioritizing of Money*.

RISK AVERSION A reluctance to take risks in order to get what one wants. People who are strong on this trend desire security and stability in all areas, including the most mundane aspects of everyday life. Trend also measures conservative buying behaviours. (Inverse of *Penchant for Risk-Taking*.)

SAVING ON PRINCIPLE A tendency to save and accumulate money that is motivated by a moral rather than an economic impulse.

SEARCH FOR ROOTS Desire to preserve and maintain one's cultural and ethnic roots, and to live in accordance with one's own traditions and customs. Also, a yearning to return to one's cultural roots in order to rediscover, and participate in, the fundamental values that give meaning to one's life.

SEXUAL PERMISSIVENESS Tendency to be sexually permissive regarding oneself and others. Attaching less than average importance to fidelity within marriage or among partners, or to prohibitions against premarital sex. Also expresses a permissive attitude toward sexuality among young people, and a tendency to give priority to hedonistic pleasures in life. A willingness to ignore social norms.

SKEPTICISM TOWARD BIG BUSINESS A lack of confidence in the commitment of big business owners to the provision of quality goods and services, and skepticism toward their motives and ethics. Measures the belief that there is a conflict of interest between the public and business, and that companies are only profit-driven. (Inverse of *Confidence in Big Business*.)

SKEPTICISM TOWARD SMALL BUSINESS A lack of confidence in the commitment of small business owners to the provision of quality goods and services, and skepticism toward their motives and ethics. Measures the belief that there is a conflict of interest between the public and business, and that companies are only profit-driven. (Inverse of *Confidence in Small Business*.)

SOCIAL DARWINISM Tendency to believe that society's regulatory mechanisms and rules governing social relations are those of the jungle (the strongest prevail, the weak fall by the wayside, etc.), that the great socio-democratic ideals of recent years have run their course, and that society is in the process of accepting the inevitability of poverty and greater social inequities. A belief that one must look after one's own needs, that society has no responsibility to help those less fortunate.

SOCIAL LEARNING Attraction to and interest in diversity. Feeling that there is a great deal to learn through contact and conversation with people different from you, who come from other backgrounds and places. Diversity is perceived as a source of personal enrichment, a way to satisfy a hunger for discovery and exploration and to extend a network of contacts. This trend is also associated with a respect for other people and cultures, as well as a heightened social conscience.

SPIRITUAL QUEST Questioning the meaning of life. Aspiring to a more spiritual, richer inner life. A skeptical attitude toward the infallibility of science and the secular values of today's world. This trend borders on religiosity but is expressed without an association to a particular religious institution.

TECHNOLOGICAL ANXIETY Anxiety about the encroachment of technology. Tendency to believe that technology is progressing at the expense of our autonomy and privacy, and a desire to oppose this state of affairs. A concern that new technologies cause more problems than they solve.

TIME STRESS Feeling of never having enough time in a day to get everything done. The sense that being overwhelmed by what is to be done and of always "running against the clock" cause stress and anxiety in one's life. (Formerly *Racing Against the Clock*.)

UTILITARIAN CONSUMERISM Tendency to evaluate products and services in terms of their usefulness and to ignore aesthetic considerations. For people strong on this trend, consumption is strictly determined by the need for products, and any symbolic motivation, even hedonism, is eliminated from purchasing criteria. (Inverse of *Importance of Aesthetics*.)

VITALITY Being in touch with one's internal energy. The sense that one has a great deal of energy and that one is in direct contact with this energy. Measures an energetic, lively approach to life, a feeling that one has more vigour and initiative than most other people.

Tribes at a Glance

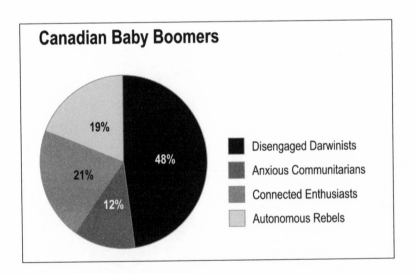

Canadian Baby Boomers

- 48% Disengaged Darwinists
- 12%
- 21% Anxious Communitarians
- 19% Connected Enthusiasts
- Autonomous Rebels

Disengaged Darwinists

POPULATION
Percentage of Boomers: **48**
Percentage of all Canadians: **13.3**
Total number: **4.4 Million**
Gender: **58% M   42% F**

OTHER DEMOGRAPHICS
Most likely to be in 1st marriage
Lowest % foreign-born

Disengaged Darwinists

STRONGEST VALUES	WEAKEST VALUES
Fatalism	Introspection and Empathy
Hyper-Rationality	Cultural Fusion
Risk-Aversion	Rejection of Authority
Ethnic Intolerance	Pursuit of Novelty

Anxious Communitarians

POPULATION
Percentage of Boomers: **12**
Percentage of all Canadians: **3.3**
Total number: **1.1 Million**
Gender: **39% M   61% F**

OTHER DEMOGRAPHICS
Below-average education, income
Older Boomers (mainly 55-64)
Disproportionately in Quebec

Anxious Communitarians

STRONGEST VALUES	WEAKEST VALUES
Concern for Appearance	Hyper-Rationality
Need for Status Recognition	Sexual Permissiveness
Fear of Violence	Rejection of Authority
Flexible Personality	Flexibility of Gender Identity

Connected Enthusiasts

POPULATION
Percentage of Boomers: **21**
Percentage of all Canadians: **5.7**
Total number: **1.9 Million**
Gender: **42% M   58% F**

OTHER DEMOGRAPHICS
Highest % of self-employed
Professionals and tradespeople
Disproportionately in Ont., Prairies

Connected Enthusiasts

STRONGEST VALUES	WEAKEST VALUES
Personal Creativity	Ethnic Intolerance
Cultural Fusion	Acceptance of Violence
Social Learning	Anomie and Aimlessness
Ethical Consumerism	Fatalism

Autonomous Rebels

POPULATION
Percentage of Boomers: **19**
Percentage of all Canadians: **5.1**
Total number: **1.7 Million**
Gender: **50% M   50% F**

OTHER DEMOGRAPHICS
Highest education, income
Highest % divorced, living alone
Concentrated in public sector jobs

Autonomous Rebels

STRONGEST VALUES	WEAKEST VALUES
Rejection of Authority	Fear of Violence
Equality of the Sexes	Joy of Consumption
Equal Relationship w/ Youth	Need for Status Recognition
Pursuit of Happiness to Detriment of Duty	Importance of National Superiority

Acknowledgments

This psychosocial analysis of my fellow Baby Boomers, and my sixth literary contribution to Canadian civilization, would not have been possible without the collaboration of my insightful and delightful post-Boomer colleague Amy Langstaff. This book, probably more than any other Amy and I have collaborated on, helped us reflect on our own generations, those that came before us, and the ones coming after us. Along the way, I think we have probably come to better understand ourselves and the people we know and love. Thank you, Amy, for being wise beyond your years and remaining my dear and always calm and cool friend.

As with our previous offerings, Amy and I have been aided and guided by the Environics team of research professionals led by Barry Watson. David MacDonald has once again offered many useful insights, especially those related to Boomers and their money. Doug Norris, chief demographer at Environics Analytics and former director general of Social and Demographic Statistics at Statistics Canada, has been an immense help in this project, as in so many others. Computer analysis was undertaken by Jillian Barber and fact-checking by Marion Adams, each of whom ensured we remained inside our advertised margin of error.

Finally, I would like to thank my literary agent, Bruce Westwood, the best there is, and my friends at Penguin Books: editors Diane Turbide and Helen Reeves, and the many copy and production editors who make us look and sound good.

And, of course, there are my fellow Boomers, their parents, and their kids who answered our questions. I hope you will appreciate our insights and forgive our occasional teasing.

Notes

INTRODUCTION

1. *Giving Birth in Canada: A Regional Profile* (Ottawa: Canadian Institute for Health Information, 2004), http://secure.cihi.ca/cihiweb/products/GBC2004_regional_e.pdf; *Recent Social Trends in Canada, 1960–2000*, Ed. Lance W. Roberts et al. (Montreal and Kingston: McGill Queen's University Press, 2005).

2. Our random sample of Canadians will include more recent immigrants, but not in sufficient numbers to offer a robust analysis of their values and attitudes. One in five Canadians is foreign-born, and no discussion of our society is complete without an acknowledgment of the tremendous diversity of our population. But in this book I'll focus mainly on those born in Canada from 1946 to 1965 and those who were born elsewhere and grew up in Canada alongside that cohort. About 2.5 million people immigrated to Canada during the Baby Boom. Many came as adults, but those who arrived as children would have shared some formative experiences with their Canadian-born age peers. They also would have had some different experiences from their Canadian-born schoolmates (although the large proportion who arrived from the United Kingdom would have had a somewhat easier landing than others).

3. Similarly, the Boomers are more alike than the generations that follow: with affluence, increasingly liberal social norms, multiculturalism, and metastatic media, social niches (or what we call "social values tribes") are proliferating.

4. Statistics Canada, *Historical Statistics of Canada*, Section W: Education, Part 3: Post-Secondary Education (series W307-532), Cat. no. 11-516-XWE, www.statcan.gc.ca/bsolc/olc-cel/olc-cel?catno=11-516-X&lang=eng.

5. Human Resources and Skills Development Canada, "Indicators of Well-Being in Canada. Learning—Educational Attainment." HRSDC calculations based on Statistics Canada, *Labour Force Historical Review* (Ottawa: Statistics Canada, 2007), Cat. no. 71F0004XCB, www4.hrsdc.gc.ca/.3ndic.1t.4r@-eng.jsp?iid=29.

6. William Bruneau, "A Canadian Journey: Post-Secondary Education Since 1945," *Education Canada* (Fall 2004), vol. 44, no. 4, pp. 25–27.

ONE: WHAT'S YOUR TRIBE?

1. The Boomers have stayed constant, but the same isn't true of the Generation X tribes I identified in *Sex in the Snow*. Several years after that book was published, we tested the validity of the five young tribes we'd identified for a new book, *Better Happy Than Rich?* We found that the tribes still existed—respondents to our surveys continued to express values that conformed to those five values profiles—but a significant portion of the sample now didn't seem to fit with them. During the late 1990s and early 2000s, a sixth Gen X tribe had come into being: a cautious, stability-oriented group that we named the Security-Seeking Ascetics.

2. If as you read the book you need a quick refresher on a tribe's personality, refer to Appendix C for a one-page snapshot of each segment.

3. Roderic Beaujot and Zenaida Ravanera, "Family Change and Implications for Family Solidarity and Social Cohesion," *Canadian Studies in Population* (2008), vol. 35.1, pp. 73–101.

TWO: THE UNCLEAR FAMILY

1. Anne-Marie Ambert, "Divorce: Facts, Causes, and Conse-quences," *Contemporary Family Trends* series (Ottawa: Vanier Insti-tute of the Family, September 2005), www.vifamily.ca/library/cft/divorce_05.html.

2. Anne-Marie Ambert, "Cohabitation and Marriage: How Are They Related?" *Contemporary Family Trends* series (Ottawa: Vanier Insti-tute of the Family, September 2005), www.vifamily.ca/library/cft/cohabitation.html#Marriage.

3. In our research 48 percent of Boomers are on their first marriage; 9 percent report being "remarried" (whether they're on their second spouse or, like Joan Crawford, on their fifth, we didn't ask); and 11 percent are living with a common-law partner. The other 32 percent are free agents: single, divorced, or widowed.

4. It would indeed be a member of the opposite sex: the Disengaged Darwinists are the only Boomer tribe in which the proportion who acknowledge being gay or lesbian is statistically insignificant (1 percent). The other three tribes are in the 3 to 4 percent range.

5. Statistics Canada, Health Statistics Division, *Births 2007* (Ottawa: Minister of Industry, 2009), Cat. no. 84F0210X, www.statcan.gc.ca/pub/84f0210x/2007000/part-partie1-eng.htm.

6. Katie Roiphe, "The Naked and the Conflicted," *The New York Times* (January 3, 2010), BR1.

THREE: BODY, MIND, AND SPIRIT

1. Kaare Christensen, "Aging Populations: The Challenges Ahead," *The Lancet* (October 3, 2009), vol. 374, no. 9696, pp. 1196–1208.

2. Jean Barman, "Child Labour," *The Canadian Encyclopedia*, www.thecanadianencyclopedia.com/index.cfm?PgNm=TCE&Params=A1ARTA0001577.

3. Hayley Mick, "Fit at 50," and "Woulda, Coulda, Shoulda—Did," *The Globe and Mail* (October 8, 2009), L1.

4. Pauline W. Chen, "Do You Know What Your Doctor Is Talking About?" *The New York Times* (April 2, 2009).

FOUR: OLD DOGS AND NEW TRICKS

1. Brad Stone, "The Children of Cyberspace: Old Fogies by Their 20s," *The New York Times* (January 10, 2010), WK5.

2. Cara Williams, "The Evolution of Communication," *Canadian Social Trends* (Spring 2001), Cat. no. 11-008.

3. Ibid.

4. S. Lebergott, *Pursuing Happiness: American Consumers in the Twentieth Century* (Princeton, NJ: Princeton University Press, 1993).

5. Ted Nordhaus and Michael Shellenberger, *Break Through: From the Death of Environmentalism to the Politics of Possibility* (New York, NY: Houghton Mifflin, 2007), p. 28.

FIVE: THEY STILL HAVE A DREAM OR TWO

1. Reginald Bibby, "The Future Families Project: A Survey of Canadian Hopes and Dreams" (Ottawa: Vanier Institute of the Family, 2004), www.vifamily.ca/library/future/2.html.

2. Marshall McLuhan, Quentin Fiore, and Jerome Agel, *The Medium Is the Massage: An Inventory of Effects* (New York: Bantam, 1967).

SIX: THE LIFE STAGE FORMERLY KNOWN AS RETIREMENT

1. Jack Mintz, "Summary Report on Retirement Income Adequacy Research" (December 18, 2009), www.fin.gc.ca/activty/pubs/pension/riar-narr-eng.asp.

2. Organisation for Economic Co-operation and Development, "Pensions at a Glance 2009—Retirement Income Systems in OECD Countries," Paris, 2009.

3. "Work Till You Drop," *The Economist* (June 25, 2009).

4. Lia Miller, "The Myth of the Deficient Older Employee," *The New York Times Magazine* (December 13, 2009).

5. Michael Winerip, "Generation B: They Feel Your Losses," *The New York Times* (April 19, 2009).

6. Dane Stangler, "The Coming Entrepreneurship Boom," The Ewing Marion Kauffman Foundation (June 2009).

7. Many answers were in French; some I have translated.

SEVEN: RELIGION, NO RELIGION, NO MEANING

1. Warren Clark and Grant Schellenberg, "Who's Religious?" *Canadian Social Trends* (Summer 2006), Cat. no. 11-008-XWE.

2. Janice Gross Stein, "Living Better Multiculturally," *Literary Review of Canada* (September 2006), vol. 14, no. 7, pp. 3–5.

3. When presented with the statement "I consider myself to be a member of a religious faith," these women indicate that they "totally agree."

4. Stacy Meichtry and Amy Merrick, "Vatican in Bold Bid to Attract Anglicans," *The Wall Street Journal* (October 11, 2009), A1.

EIGHT: THE LONG GOODBYE

1. Joe Queenan, *Balsamic Dreams: A Short but Self-Important History of the Baby Boomer Generation* (New York: Henry Holt, 2001), p. 97.

2. Queenan, p. 96.

3. Quebec Festival of Sacred Music online archive, www.festival musiquesacree.ca/eng/2008/grand-messe.htm.

4. Craig Bicknell, "Abra Cadaver: A Fight for Bodies," *Wired* (October 19, 1999).

5. Ruth Davis Konigsberg, "Resomation," *The New York Times Magazine* (December 13, 2009).

6. Margaret Somerville, "Finding Meaning in Dying," *The Globe and Mail* (January 12, 2010).

NINE: WHAT HAVE WE WROUGHT?

1. Bear in mind that using our birth-year cut-off of 1965, some of these *Wunderkinder* are in their early forties—well out of puberty.

2. David Eaves and Taylor Owen, "Progressivism's End," *Literary Review of Canada* (September 1, 2008), vol. 16, no. 7.

3. Statistics Canada, "Canada's Ethnocultural Mosaic, Census Year 2006," Cat. no. 97-562-X.

4. Unless otherwise noted, "post-Boomers" in this chapter refers to everyone born between 1965 and 1993. (Our samples include Canadians aged fifteen and older, and the most recent survey wave discussed in this book was conducted in 2008.) This huge category encompasses more than one generation and obscures a lot of diversity—both demographic and psychographic—but it does give us a high-level picture of the age cohort that's following the generation featured in this book.

5. Statistics Canada, "A Portrait of Couples in Mixed Unions," Anne Milan, Helene Maheux, and Tina Chui, April 20, 2010, Cat. no. 11-008.

6. Robert Hough, "Lighten Up," *Toronto Life* (September 2009).

7. Chris Hoofnagle et al., "How Different Are Young Adults from Older Adults When It Comes to Information Privacy Attitudes and Policies?" SSRN eLibrary (2010), http://ssrn.com/paper= 1589864.

8. Heather West, "Is Online Privacy a Generational Issue?" *Wired* (October 1, 2009).

9. Sue Gardner, speaking at the 2009 Dalton Camp Lecture in Journalism held at St. Thomas University, Fredericton, New Brunswick, on November 18, 2009.

Index